In the Devil's Shadow

In the Devil's Shadow

UN Special Operations during
the Korean War

Michael E. Haas

Naval Institute Press
Annapolis, Maryland

Naval Institute Press
291 Wood Road
Annapolis, MD 21402

Library of Congress Cataloging-in-Publication Data

Haas, Michael E., 1944–
    In the devil's shadow : UN special operations during the
Korean War / Michael E. Haas.
        p.   cm. — (Naval Institute special warfare series)
    Includes bibliographical references and index.
    ISBN 1-55750-344-3 (alk. paper)
    1. Korean War, 1950–1953. 2. United Nations—Armed
Forces—Korea.   3. United   States—Armed   Forces—Korea.
4. Special forces (Military science)—United States.   I. Title.
II. Series.
DS918.8.H33   2000
951.904'24—dc21   99–42004

Printed in the United States of America on acid-free paper ∞
07 06 05 04 03 02 01 00   9 8 7 6 5 4 3 2
First printing

*In tribute to the courage and sacrifice of
the UN special operations men and women who
went into the dark mountains of North Korea—
and never returned*

Contents

Preface

Attempting to capture the history of United Nations special operations during the Korean War is an exercise in humility, in some respects the historian's worst nightmare. As the U.S. Army wrangled with the CIA for "ownership" of the strategic unconventional warfare mission, the air force supported both the army and the CIA, even as it unleashed its own behind-the-lines campaign by air, land, and sea. Against this confused backdrop, the U.S. Navy, operating on a more independent basis, teamed up at different times with British Commandos and British Commonwealth warships to fight its own war against the enemy's rear sanctuaries. This kaleidoscope of uncoordinated activity, the clandestine nature of United Nations operations behind enemy lines, and the need for deceptive cover stories all seem to combine at times and places to mislead the unwary researcher.

For reasons I hope the reader will appreciate, I have intentionally avoided the trap of attempting to record every operation, air mission, or organizational chart I encountered in my years of research. Such a huge collection of dry material would serve no useful purpose, except perhaps as a cure for insomnia. Instead I have chosen to untangle this complex, interrelated drama in a series of four monographs, each in a format intended to clarify the separate army, air force, navy, and CIA special operations activities during the war.

The relative commitment of forces made by each service obviously influenced in turn the relative size of each of the monographs that follow. Acknowledging in advance the limitations of this approach, I confess I have found no better way to present a thoroughly readable account of a thoroughly tangled story of valor and betrayal. Hidden from public for the last half-century, it is a story whose time is long overdue.

Where this book fails in the eyes of those who were there, I offer my sincere apologies in advance. This is particularly true for the Koreans who took the brunt of the death and torture suffered in this "war behind the curtain." So few returned from their missions, and fewer still have chosen to write about their deeds. Where this book succeeds in acknowledging those long overdue the recognition they deserve, I offer it in gratitude for their contributions to our country and, especially, the Profession of Arms found in all countries.

Acknowledgments

It was not a pleasant journey. Too much death, betrayal, and heartache mar the path through the curtain of secrecy that still surrounds the surreal world of Cold War special operations. Nevertheless, it was an introduction to some of the most remarkable people imaginable.

I can think of no more remarkable person I encountered during my journey than my friend and mentor, Ed Evanhoe. This Korean War veteran's incomparable knowledge of this shadowy world was indispensable in guiding me through the "wilderness of mirrors" that still exists, decades after the war, for the sole purpose of deceiving anyone attempting to write this story.

I also owe a special debt of gratitude to Meg Jones, friend, agent, and creator of the title for this book. Her knowledge of military history would provide an excellent education for many of today's senior officers in the armed services. I will always be grateful to my editor Karin Kaufman, whose superb technical skills and patience reminded me that all books published ultimately come from a team effort. Should all writers be so lucky as to have an editor of her caliber.

A must-include in this list of "the usual suspects" to whom I am in debt is an amazing group that always bears close watching: sailors. British field marshal Bernard Montgomery once observed, "Soldiers must learn to endure many burdens. Sailors are one of those burdens." Perhaps so, but for this book I am profoundly grateful to a handful of sailors without whose help the part U.S. Navy special operations played in the conflict could never have been adequately described. Korean War veterans Alan Ray, skipper of the USS *Horace A. Bass,* and Hilary Mahin, boat officer of the same ship, were both invaluable and unstinting in their help. So too were UDT frogman James Short and SEAL Larry Bailey.

I must also single out for praise U.S. Air Force "sailors" Bud Tretter and Jim Jarvis, whose exploits deep behind enemy lines provided insights and detail into secret U.S. operations in North Korea and Manchuria that have yet to be acknowledged by our government. Few people realize the extent to which the air force fought the war on the land and sea as well as in the air.

As with many so many other authors seeking to acknowledge Cold War special operations, I ran into a series of frustrating roadblocks from bureaucrats seemingly committed to stonewalling presidential Executive Order 12958. This document, guiding the declassification of national security information, should have opened a considerable amount of formerly classified information on the half-century-old Korean War. Alas, its effect on these bureaucrats has been minimal, particularly with the Central Intelligence Agency. In this regard, the misleading statements and unethical conduct demonstrated by CIA classification review employees "Chris" and "Lee" proved particularly helpful in fueling my tenacity to provide a documented account of CIA activities in Korea. More helpful still in persuading the CIA to stop its prolonged stonewalling was the impressive intervention on my behalf by Mark H. Lynch, a senior partner in the Washington, D.C.–based law firm of Covington & Burling.

On a brighter note, I remain particularly grateful to artists Steve Garst and Wayne Thompson, that incredible bandit-chief and indestructible Air Commando "Heinie" Aderholt, Lawrence Barrett, Carl Bernhardt, Associated Press reporter Bob Burns, Bob Brewer (deceased), Ray Dawson, Bill Fagiola, Bob Gorton, Joseph C. Goulden, Edward Joseph, M. Kebodeaux, Bob Kingston, Ben Malcom, Herb Mason Jr., Charlie Norton, John Plaster, Bob Sullivan, and Clyde Sincere.

I apologize to those I have somehow overlooked. This book was written with the troubling knowledge that some incredibly brave men and women, whose names still remain unknown to me, suffered the greatest sacrifice possible during these dangerous missions. I can only hope that this book partially satisfies the long-overdue need to publicly acknowledge their sacrifices and accomplishments.

Chronology

1949

January
General MacArthur recommends to the Joint Chiefs of Staff that the United States remove all combat forces from South Korea as soon as possible and not commit troops should North Korea invade.

June
The last U.S. combat troops leave South Korea.

1950

12 January
Secretary of State Dean Acheson omits South Korea from the United States' "defensive perimeter" in Asia during a speech in Washington, D.C., before the National Press Club.

May
Over MacArthur's strong objections, the CIA establishes its initial presence in Japan, a minuscule intelligence-gathering team based in Tokyo.

2 May
Senator Tom Connally of Texas, chairman of the Senate Foreign Relations Committee, publicly concedes that South Korea would be abandoned by the United States if invaded by North Korea. He reaffirms Acheson's position that South Korea is not essential to America's defensive Asian strategy.

25 June
North Korea invades South Korea.

30 June
President Truman stuns both the North Koreans and his own Department of Defense with his decision to commit ground troops in defense of South Korea.

July
Again over MacArthur's strong objections, the CIA sends Hans Tofte to Japan to begin organizing the agency's guerrilla war against North Korea.

August
U.S. and South Korean armies are driven into a final defensive stand inside the Pusan perimeter, near the southern tip of South Korea.

5 August
U.S. Navy attempts first amphibious sabotage mission of the war; two frogmen sent ashore at night from the fast transport *Diachenko.* The mission fails when the two would-be saboteurs are detected.

8 August
U.S. Pacific Fleet's only special operations submarine, the USS *Perch,* arrives in Japan to begin training with hastily assembled, ad hoc raider teams.

14 August
U.S. Navy conducts first successful amphibious sabotage mission of the war, when the Special Operations Group—a hastily assembled UDT–marine reconnaissance team—is launched from the fast transport USS *Horace A. Bass.*

15 September
General MacArthur directs amphibious landings at Inchon.

October
Operation Aviary agents, parachuted earlier into multiple sites along the North Korean–Chinese border, report large numbers of incoming Chinese soldiers to General MacArthur's headquarters. The reports are ignored.

1–2 October
The *Perch* with British Commandos conducts the first successful submarine-launched sabotage mission against the North Korean railway system.

6 October
The *Bass* and British Commandos combine for the first time to attack North Korean rail lines.

7 October
President Truman accepts the resignation of the director, CIA, Rear Adm. R. H. Hillenkoetter, sacked earlier for the CIA's alleged "intelligence failure" to warn of the North Korean attack.

November
An estimated three hundred thousand Chinese People's Liberation Army "volunteers" in North Korea launch their "surprise" attack, routing UN forces southward.

1951

8 January
Anticommunist North Korean refugees, gathered on islands off North Korea's western coastline, make their first request for arms and support from the Eighth U.S. Army.

15 January
Eighth Army establishes the Attrition Section to organize, equip, and train the island refugees into a partisan combat force.

19 January
U.S. Navy UDT suffers its largest single-mission casualties of the war, when two frogmen are killed and two others wounded during a night beach-reconnaissance mission.

15 February
Attrition Section activates a partisan headquarters on the island of Paengnyong-do, 125 miles behind enemy lines, to support future raids against the North Korean mainland.

5 March
Fifth Air Force establishes Special Activities Unit Number 1, a hybrid intelligence–special operations force, performing behind-the-lines missions ranging from airfield surveillance to airborne-ranger type assaults on high priority targets.

13 March
Launched at night from a U.S. Navy destroyer, Brig. Gen. Crawford Sams of the U.S. Army, physician and MacArthur's surgeon general, is escorted by a CIA guerrilla team behind enemy lines south of Wonsan. In the area, Sams finds conclusive evidence discrediting communist propaganda claims of UN germ warfare.

15 March
Operation Virginia I. Eighth Army's Liaison Group parachutes a sabotage team comprising U.S. Army Rangers and Korean guerrillas into North Korea. The poorly planned and executed mission fails, with heavy casualties.

11 April
President Truman relieves MacArthur of command, replacing him with Gen. Mathew Ridgway.

May
A startled Ridgway discovers and immediately stops a proposed operation, well into the planning stage by Far East Command Liaison Group officers, to kidnap or assassinate the senior Soviet general serving with the North Korean People's Army Headquarters.

18 June
Operation Spitfire. The Liaison Group parachutes an American-British-Korean guerrilla team into North Korea. The mission fails, with heavy casualties. For the remainder of the war, the military sends only Korean and Chinese nationals on deep penetration, parachute missions into Communist-held territory.

2 July
CIA headquarters establishes the Joint Advisory Commission— Korea (JACK), the overall cover name for its operational and intelligence activities on the Korean peninsula.

10 July
Cease-fire negotiations between UN and Communist powers begin at Kaesong, South Korea.

29 October
Responding to intelligence from JACK guerrillas, U.S. Navy fighters attack a secret meeting of high-level Communist Party officials gathered at Kapsan, North Korea. An estimated 144 party officials are killed.

December
Royal Marine Commandos are withdrawn from Korean combat.

10 December
U.S. Far East Command (FEC) activates "Covert, Clandestine, and Reconnaissance Activities—Korea" as the executive agency to control all military-CIA unconventional warfare activities behind enemy lines. Over bitter CIA objections, FEC's Intelligence Directorate appoints itself to run the new organization.

1952

12 May
Gen. Mark Clark replaces Ridgway and soon directs an intensive recruiting campaign to expand the partisan units.

November

JACK concludes that its operations "had been too thoroughly penetrated by communists, and would have to be abandoned, including all the personnel of its Special Mission Groups."

29 November

CIA operatives John Downey and Richard Fecteau are captured after their aircraft is shot down in Manchuria during a night agent-extraction attempt using the "All-American" system.

1953

12 January

The commander of a U.S. Air Force special operations wing, along with the crew of a B-29 bomber, are shot down with a combination of air-ground tactics rarely used during the war by the Communists. The odd circumstances of the shootdown suggest a major security leak within the American command.

24 January

Operation Green Dragon. Ninety-seven Korean partisans are parachuted into North Korea in the largest such operation of the war. The group is reinforced on 15 May with an additional fifty-seven partisans. The entire group is killed or captured during the ensuing weeks.

May

UN headquarters orders the evacuation of all island-based partisans from their positions above the thirty-eighth parallel, as part of the armistice negotiations.

27 July

Armistice negotiations are concluded at Panmunjom, South Korea.

Postwar

The CIA concludes that a "large majority" of the intelligence collected during 1952–53 was fabricated or otherwise controlled by the Chinese and North Korean security services.

List of Abbreviations

APD	U.S. Navy high-speed transport
ASSP	U.S. Navy submarine, troop transport
CAT	Civil Air Transport
CIA	Central Intelligence Agency
CCF	Chinese Communist Forces
CIC	Counter-Intelligence Corps
CinCFECom	Commander in chief, U.S. Far East Command
CCRAK	Classified: Covert, Clandestine, and Related Activities—Korea; unclassified: Combined Command, Reconnaissance Activities—Korea
ComNavFE	Commander, Naval Forces, Far East
DoD	Department of Defense
E&E	Escape and evasion
EUSAK	Eighth U.S. Army—Korea
FEAF	U.S. Far East Air Forces
FEC U.S.	Far East Command
FEC-G2	U.S. Far East Command Intelligence Directorate
FEC/LG	Far East Command Liaison Group
FEC/LD (K)	Far East Command Liaison Detachment (Korea)
GHQ	General Headquarters
JACK	Joint Advisory Commission—Korea

JCS	Joint Chiefs of Staff
KLO	Korean Labor Organization
KMAG	Korean Military Advisory Group
L&L	Loudspeaker and Leaflet
LCPR	Landing craft, personnel—ramped
LCPV	Landing craft, personnel—vehicle
LVT	Landing vehicle—tracked
MLR	Main line of resistance
MSR	Main supply route
NAVFE	U.S. Naval Forces, Far East
NKPA	North Korean People's Army
OPC	Office of Policy Coordination (CIA)
OSO	Office of Special Operations (CIA)
OSS	Office of Strategic Services
PLA	People's Liberation Army (China)
POW	Prisoner(s) of war
PSYOP	Psychological Operations
PsyWar	Psychological warfare
RB&L	Radio Broadcasting and Leaflet
ROK	Republic of Korea
ROKA	Republic of Korea Army
SAM	Special air mission(s)
SMG	Special Missions Group (CIA)
SOG	Special Operations Group
TLO	Tactical Liaison Office
UN	United Nations
UNPFK	United Nations Partisan Forces—Korea
UNPIK	United Nations Partisan Infantry—Korea
UDT	U.S. Navy underwater demolition team(s)
UW	Unconventional warfare
VUNC	Voice of the UN Command

In the Devil's Shadow

Introduction

If the best minds in the world had set out to find us the worst possible location in the world to fight this damnable war, politically and militarily the unanimous choice would have been Korea!

Dean Acheson

There was considerable merit to Secretary Acheson's gloomy assessment of the Korean War, though it totally ignores the much-debated role the secretary may have inadvertently played in setting the stage for the North Korean attack. The debate centers on a speech made by Acheson on 12 January 1950 before the National Press Club in Washington, D.C., in which he described the limits of America's military interests in the Far East in the following terms: "This [U.S.] defensive perimeter runs along the Aleutians to Japan and then goes to the Ryukyus. We hold important defensive positions in the Ryukyu Islands (including Okinawa) and these we will continue to hold. . . . The defensive perimeter runs from the Ryukyus to the Philippine Islands."[1]

The fledgling Republic of Korea (ROK)—already destabilized by months of communist subversion from the north—lay conspicuously outside the protection of the defensive perimeter as defined by the secretary just six months before the outbreak of war. Regardless of what Acheson may have meant to say, his comments were interpreted by many at the time as a political signal that the United States would not commit military forces to defend the ROK in the event of a communist attack. But whether or not the North Koreans interpreted the secretary's "signal" as a tacit admission of America's limited interest in Korea, the physical and political realities found on the troubled Korean peninsula certainly did not encourage substantial U.S. involvement.

The Korean peninsula is essentially one huge chunk of granite rock. Deeply gouged as if by some invisible jackhammer, the granite forms a five-hundred-mile long peninsula filled with sharp-edged mountains so wild in appearance that early European arrivals described the geography as "a sea in a heavy gale."[2] Alternately baking and soaking in the summer's hot monsoon season, the barren rock later freezes in bitter winter storms sweeping southward from Manchuria's frozen wastelands. The rice paddies that fill the narrow valleys are fertilized by the most commonly available fertilizer—human feces.

The seas pounding Korea's fifty-four hundred miles of coastline are equally difficult and dangerous for the population. On the peninsula's western shores, the Yellow Sea rises and falls twice every day with tides that reach the height of a three-story building. On Korea's eastern shores, the Sea of Japan freezes coastal waters to block ice every winter, terminating all use of the few safe harbors available. And every year at least one killer typhoon roars across this stricken land.

On top of nature's woes, Korea endures one final geographic curse that has brought to its proud people a never-ending cycle of violence: the long peninsula provides a near-complete land bridge from the Asian mainland to the Japanese islands. Mongol and Chinese armies intent on ending Japan's dominance of the region have used the "Korea Bridge" as an invasion route for centuries. So too have Japanese armies intent on stopping these threatening invaders. This was still the case during World War II, when the presence of a Japanese occupation army in Korea provided the pretext for a Soviet power ploy that would have consequences not even the Communists could have foreseen in 1945.

The Soviet Union declared war against Japan in August 1945, just two days before the Japanese government formally sued the Western Allies for peace. Although the Soviet's opportunistic declaration had no military value, it did allow Soviet premier Joseph Stalin to send his armies into both Japanese-occupied Manchuria and Korea with no audible complaint from his surprised Western Allies. Caught off guard, the United States hastily proposed a joint U.S.-Soviet trusteeship of Korea that provided for the surrender of Japanese forces north of the thirty-eighth parallel to the Soviets, while the Americans would accept a similar surrender in the south.[3] To the surprise of American diplomats, the Soviets quickly accepted the American proposal.

The U.S. proposal to use the thirty-eighth parallel for a political division of Korea totally ignored terrain, major transportation routes, indigenous political institutions, and economic resources. These factors were not considered important to Washington at the time, as the United States viewed the Soviet occupation in northern Korea as it did the Soviet occupation of Eastern Europe—a temporary measure until free elections could be arranged. But by 1948 the prospect of free elections in the Soviet-occupied northern half of Korea still matched that found in Soviet-occupied Eastern Europe—exactly nil.

Seeing no end to Soviet intransigence, the United States initiated free elections (under United Nations oversight) in the southern half of the country that May.[4] Three months later the U.S.-occupied zone became the Republic of Korea.[5] Three weeks later the Soviets created the People's Democratic Republic of Korea[6] from their zone to the north.[7] From this period forward U.S. and Soviet involvement on the peninsula took radically different courses.

The Soviet Union officially announced the complete withdrawal of its troops from North Korea on Christmas Day 1948.[8] Unofficially, the Communists left behind thousands of Soviet advisors and the commitment to build a fully modern, mobile, and heavily armed North Korean army and air force. The Soviets did their job well, for by the outbreak of war eighteen months later, the North Korean People's Army (NKPA) counted an estimated 135,000 strong, organized into ten regular infantry divisions supported by a full complement of armor, artillery, and combat-support units.[9] This Soviet effort stood in stark contrast to the parallel effort offered by the United States to its erstwhile ally in South Korea.

Anxious for different reasons (e.g., budget considerations) to complete a military withdrawal of its own from the Korean peninsula during this same period, the Truman administration turned a blind eye to the Soviet buildup in the North. Not until July 1949, less than twelve months before full-scale war broke out, did the U.S. Army belatedly activate the Korean Military Advisory Group (KMAG; pronounced "kay-mag") "to advise the government of the Republic of Korea in the continued development in the security forces of that government."[10] A low-priority American unit consisting of approximately five hundred officers and men, it did not warrant even a modest comparison with the Soviet effort in North Korea.[11] In contrast to its fully equipped and mobile antagonist to the north, the South Korean security forces were little more than a national constabulary force; ninety-eight thousand strong but armed only with light weapons and a few pieces of obsolescent artillery.[12]

Operating under the administrative control of the U.S. ambassador in Seoul—not MacArthur's Far East Command (FEC) headquarters in

Tokyo or even the Pentagon—the KMAG bypassed the entire military command structure to report the military situation in Korea to State Department civilians. Gen. J. Lawton Collins, who served as the army's chief of staff throughout the Korean War, subsequently described how this odd arrangement misled the Pentagon as to the dangerous imbalance of power developing on the peninsula in the late 1940s: "The State Department and the JCS [Joint Chiefs of Staff] . . . had to depend for their estimates of the ROK army's defensive capabilities on the . . . faulty estimates of [KMAG commander] Brigadier General Roberts. The fact that neither the ambassador nor General Roberts reported to General MacArthur probably accounts for the failure of MacArthur's headquarters to pick up the differences in their estimates of the relative capacities of [the North and South Korean armies]."[13]

Given the worldwide Cold War tensions in 1950 and the known Communist political agitation in South Korea, this pat explanation for the Pentagon's lack of knowledge on events in Korea sounds suspiciously self-serving.[14] Nonetheless, the "intelligence failure" remains a moot point. In his postwar book *War in Peacetime: The History and Lessons of Korea,* Collins notes, "Any controversy over charges of intelligence failure is almost academic: The United States had no plans to counter such an invasion, even had it forecast it to the very day. Its only planned reaction was to be the evacuation of U.S. nationals from Korea."[15]

Despite these limitations in manpower, equipment, and effective U.S. Army support, however, KMAG did prove capable of blocking North Korean attempts to topple the South Korean government through a campaign of guerrilla attacks in the countryside and political agitation in the cities.[16] Thus frustrated and armed with newfound promises of support from Russia and China, the North Koreans brought down their heavy hammer on 25 June 1950. In the early morning darkness approximately 90,000 of its 135,000 soldiers massed on the border, then assaulted across the thirty-eighth parallel behind a barrage of heavy artillery to rout the unprepared South Koreans.[17]

The political shock waves from their attack traveled far beyond the peninsula to change life in faraway America for the rest of the Cold War, a very long and dangerous forty years. The "police action," as Truman called it, dashed American hopes that the atomic bomb would deter future wars. Instead, it started a buildup of conventional forces and nuclear weapons that dominated the United States' way of looking at the world for the next half-century. In the summer of 1950, however, the serious, long-term implications for U.S. society were strictly a backburner issue in Washington. The immediate problem was how to respond to the North Korean attack with a military force operationally and organizationally crippled from years of neglect.

During the first several months of the war, both Communist and United Nations[18] forces took tremendous military risks in their separate attempts to bring the war to a speedy conclusion. And at different times both sides nearly succeeded. It was much like two boxers abandoning all defense to go for a knockout blow to their opponent's head. Neither side could know how long the bout would last, or that a third boxer would soon enter the ring.

In round one—the first two months of the war—the North Korean army came within a heartbeat of driving American and South Korean forces from their final defensive positions on the peninsula, the Pusan perimeter. Facing military disaster, General of the Army Douglas A. MacArthur, commander in chief, U.S. Far East Command (CinCFEC), counterattacked that September with his audacious amphibious assault into Inchon Harbor on South Korea's western coast. MacArthur's move cut the NKPA's overextended supply lines just as the Pusan defenders launched their breakout attack northward. Unfortunately for the allies, his subsequent decision (preapproved in ambiguous terms by the JCS) to send troops far north of the thirty-eighth parallel in pursuit of the retreating enemy prompted a massive Chinese entry into the war.

In November 1950 some thirty divisions of the Chinese People's Volunteer Army—an estimated three hundred thousand soldiers—drove the allied troops out of North Korea in a retreat through a freezing hell of minus-thirty-degree temperatures, snowstorms, and heartbreaking, mountainous terrain.[19] Those who couldn't retreat froze to death where they fell. David H. Hackworth, squad leader at that time, describes the ordeal in the raw terms of infantry combat: "It was a frigid, brutal, soul-destroying time; I knew then how the Wehrmacht must have felt during World War II, or how Napoleon's Army must have suffered years and years before that, when each made their horrible winter retreat from Russia. In the infantry, many men lost their will to live[,] . . . just quit—sometimes with the Chinese within sight. You'd say, 'Come on buddy, get up. Let's go! You're going to be captured!' And he'd say, 'I don't care. I can't go another step.'"[20] Only by the narrowest of margins did U.S. air power avert what came within a heartbeat of becoming the worst military defeat in American history. Round one was over.

Round two consumed the remaining two years of the war. On the ground it involved trench warfare the likes of which had not been seen since World War I. All the horror, disease, cold-weather injuries, and massive artillery duels that marked that war were repeated in Korea. Far above the frontal infantry attacks that bled assault regiments white,

U.S. Air Force, Navy, and Marine Corps fighters achieved a hard-earned mastery of the air. The first jet aces of the three-year-old air force became national heroes in the press, and the media continued to cover the war closely, at least the war they were allowed to see.

This story is about the war the media wasn't allowed to see. The secret war in which the deaths of the unlucky were more often than not simply guessed at on the basis of the one fact known to headquarters: they were never again seen alive after infiltrating behind enemy lines.

> We have been here before.
>
> *U.S. Army general Carl W. Stiner, commander in chief,*
> *U.S. Special Operation Command*

The simple five-word judgment ran across one of the many 35-mm slides presented by the general during a classified briefing given to a select audience of special operations commanders in 1993. The general was referring to the tragic cycle in American military history in which the morale and combat capability of our military forces are brought to their lowest ebb just before these unfortunates are ordered into combat. And at no time in America's turbulent history can a better example of this cycle be found than in the sorry spectacle presented by the U.S. military as it limped out of years of neglect to fight the Korean War. Reduced to near shambles by five years of ill-considered and unrelenting demobilization, America itself had succeeded by the summer of 1950 in accomplishing what the combined might of the Japanese, German, and Italian war machines could not during World War II.

In public, President Harry S. Truman touted his determination to balance the budget as his primary rationale for this radical and unilateral disarmament. But as his private papers would later reveal, the president's public agenda was spurred on in considerable part by his much more personal convictions that held the professional military in considerable disdain, if not outright contempt.[21] Whatever the complexity of the president's motivations, the tangible fallout from his budget-cutting decisions was unmistakable even to the casual observer of military affairs.

Truman's zeal for military budget cutting drove the army's manpower down from 6 million to 530,000, and, in the words of army chief of staff Gen. Omar N. Bradley, into "a shockingly deplorable state [of combat readiness]."[22] Nor was this "shockingly deplorable state" simply a matter of inadequate numbers. At the outset of the Korean War, 43 percent of army enlisted soldiers in the U.S. Far East Command were rated in Class 4 or 5, the lowest ratings on the U.S. Army General Classification Test.[23] In General Bradley's view, the United States of America had at that time "only one division—the 82d Airborne—that could be remotely described as combat ready."[24] Even worse for a fledgling superpower, the abysmal situation carried over to the newly created air force and the navy, America's power projection forces.

In response to the air force's recommendation for a minimum 70 air groups (just under 7,000 aircraft total), Truman fought the number down to 38. Only after the airmen demonstrated their usefulness during the politically explosive Berlin Airlift in 1948, and then only grudgingly, did he allow an increase to 48 groups.[25] This situation had improved only marginally when North Korea launched the first large-scale bloodletting of the Cold War two years later. For its part, the navy took more than a 90 percent cut in its active ship force levels, coming down from 6,768 in August 1945 to 634 in June 1950; its aircraft carrier strength down from 99 to 15; the destroyer force bottoming out at 137 from 377.[26]

If the North Korean attack surprised President Truman, his decision to order this enfeebled military into combat in northern Asia stunned the Department of Defense (DoD). Nonetheless, the Pentagon responded quickly to the emergency, pulling World War II–era equipment, ships, and aircraft out of mothball storage. Simultaneously, the DoD began augmenting its active-duty manning with an expanded military draft and a recall of many combat-experienced World War II veterans. In contrast to this frantic augmentation of the conventional force structure however, no such response was possible for the military's unconventional warfare structure. Augmentation here was not possible for the simple reason that the military services had no unconventional warfare units to augment or even reactivate from the world war.

This last statement frequently evokes protests from historians familiar with the colorful exploits of World War II–era elite units such as the U.S.-Canadian 1st Special Service Force, the U.S. Army's Ranger battalions, and "Merrill's Marauders." But as Special Forces veteran and army historian Col. Alfred H. Paddock Jr. notes in his authoritative book, *U.S. Army Special Warfare: Its Origins,*

> None of these units by definition was an unconventional warfare organization. According to the *Dictionary of U.S. Military Terms,* unconventional warfare "includes the three interrelated fields of guerrilla warfare, escape & evasion, and subversion . . . conducted . . . by predominantly indigenous personnel usually supported and directed by personnel from outside the country." The 1st Special Service Force, Ranger battalions, and "Merrill's Marauders" were primarily long-range penetration organizations that specialized in reconnaissance, raiding, and commando operations.[27]

Conspicuously absent from this list of potential "candidates" is the Office of Strategic Services (OSS) and its unconventional warfare operations in Asia and Europe during the war. Often overlooked however is that the OSS, the sole agency authorized by President Franklin D. Roosevelt to carry out strategic unconventional warfare during the war, was a civilian organization.[28] From its inception on 13 June 1942, both the OSS and its colorful commander, World War I hero and Medal of Honor recipient Maj. Gen. William J. "Wild Bill" Donovan, operated beyond the jurisdiction of any single military service or civilian agency.[29]

Donovan, for example, nominally served under the direction of the Joint Chiefs of Staff as "director of strategic services," but his real power lay in his role as the "coordinator of information," through which he reported only to the president.[30] This controversial independence carried to the field as well, for although more than half[31] the personnel assigned to the OSS were military, these were the field operators, not the organization's senior leadership.[32] Following Truman's directive to disband the OSS on 1 October 1945, its personnel were transferred back to their parent organizations with little if any effort made to record their hard-earned unconventional warfare expertise. As Paddock concludes, "For all practical purposes, any formal U.S. capability for guerrilla warfare disappeared."[33]

The resulting absence of this capability created a national, politico-military deficiency that interested virtually no bureaucracy of importance in Washington during the five years that followed the end of World War II. One notable exception was a seemingly brash claim made by the newly designated successor to the OSS, an organization established in 1947 and whose very name would become one of the icons of the Cold War: the Central Intelligence Agency (CIA, or "the Agency").[34] Empowered during the first year of its existence with National Security Council Directives 4/A and 10/2, authorizing it to conduct national-level "covert psychological operations" and "paramilitary activities," the CIA promptly staked its claim to the national, unconventional warfare mission.[35]

Less than two years later this claim would spark a massive turf battle between the army and CIA, as both struggled to gain bureaucratic control of the unconventional war fought behind communist lines on the Korean peninsula. Of course, none of this bureaucratic wrangling in Washington and Japan was of any interest to the North Korean People's Army on the morning 25 June 1950. Even if it had somehow learned how safe its rear areas were from the threat of U.S.-led guerrillas, all of the NKPA's energies that morning were totally focused on the task of executing a massive, multicorps shock attack across the demilitarized zone into South Korea.

The stories that follow recount the valor and heartbreak experienced by an audacious collection of men and women who fought desperately behind communist lines in an ill-fated attempt to expel communism from the Korean peninsula. Included in the drama are U.S. Army Rangers, British Royal Marine Commandos, U.S. Navy frogmen and submariners, U.S. Air Force airmen and sailors, Korean partisans, and CIA operatives. The stories also recount the dark side of the drama, the squandered bravery and lives lost as the U.S. military scrambled to regain the unconventional warfare capability it discarded so readily at the end of World War II. This drama was as real as anything, as real as death itself.

And as the war progressed, death haunted these behind-the-line operations to such an extreme that it frequently blurred the life-and-death distinction between "high risk" and "suicide" missions. By the second year of the war the death rate for Korean partisans parachuted into North Korea had reached such proportions that one well-documented postwar study concluded, "These decisions [by American officers] to use partisans against enemy supply routes in airborne operations appears to have been futile and callous."[36]

The Koreans weren't the only ones to have suffered from this moral betrayal. Interviewed during the course of this book were American "agent handlers" for these partisans who still carry with them to this day a guilt that permeates every discussion of their wartime activities. And then there was the incredible "Mister" Nichols, the former motorpool sergeant who masterminded what arguably became the most effective UN special operations unit of the war.

One air force general who made extensive use of Nichols's far-flung operations during this period called him "a one man war." Like the fictional cop in the Hollywood film *Dirty Harry,* Nichols was the one everyone needed but no one wanted to know. Whatever his reputation, he later confessed the extent of its personal cost to him: "I had to be the one to give the actual orders when I knew someone was going to be killed. . . . [My bosses] wanted the answers, and in some cases didn't want to be told how I got them. They knew it meant lives. . . . At times I hate to call myself a man."[37] While few combat veterans emerged physically or mentally unscarred from their experiences in Korea, some, like Nichols, were emotionally consumed in its flames.

U.S. Army Unconventional Warfare | 1

If the army's capability to conduct overt psychological warfare was meager in June 1950, its unconventional warfare capability was non-existent. It was not supposed to have such a capability in peacetime; National Security Council Directive 10/2 gave the responsibility for paramilitary activities to the Central Intelligence Agency in June 1948.

Col. Alfred H. Paddock Jr., U.S. Army

The senior officer in the U.S. Army in 1950 was not a man known to defer to others on the strategy of war-fighting. Even had he been, to whom would he have deferred? The phenomenal military career of seventy-year-old Medal of Honor recipient and five-star General of the Army Douglas Arthur MacArthur included a history of achievements in war and peace unsurpassed by any other military figure in American history. And among the best known of the general's views on warfighting, was his staunch prohibition against unconventional warfare forces operating independently in "his" theater of operations.

Rigidly enforced during MacArthur's highly acclaimed islandfighting campaigns throughout the Pacific during World War II,[1] the general's prohibition against unconventional warfare was still in force five years later as he formulated his strategy for fighting the new war in Korea. For as history shows, few leaders with responsibilities similar to MacArthur's have ever cheerfully surrendered control of organizations possessing the potential to seriously impact their crusades. And in the summer of 1950, MacArthur, as both commander in chief, U.S. Far East Command and supreme commander, Allied Powers (Japan), was beginning a crusade the likes of which neither he nor the United States had ever before undertaken.

In this crusade, however, MacArthur's unprecedented authority would be challenged as never before by the last-minute and most-unwelcomed arrival in his theater of operations of precisely the kind of independent organization he so detested. To many observers in both Washington and Japan at the time, MacArthur's resistance to the arrival in Japan of the Central Intelligence Agency seemed petty and archaic at the very least. Nevertheless, FEC's famous commander in chief had his reasons, and they were not as peevish as many judged.

MacArthur may not have known that President Harry S. Truman nominated a personal friend as the CIA's first director, nor that this nominee's qualifications to manage a national-level intelligence organization were based largely on his executive experience with the Piggly Wiggly grocery store chain.[2] But the politically astute general was surely aware that the second director was the nephew of a powerful senator, and that this director's replacement was publicly sacked for the Agency's controversial failure to warn of the North Korean attack. Thus came and went three CIA directors in the first three years of the Agency's existence, taking with them much of the fledgling organizations's hope for attaining credibility in Washington or anywhere else.

Although MacArthur was only one of the many important people left unimpressed with the new CIA, it was to this near-mythical general that Truman and the Joint Chiefs of Staff anxiously turned as chaos exploded in Korea. Only weeks earlier MacArthur's low opinion of the Agency had turned to outright hostility as "immense pressures from Washington" finally overrode his longstanding objections to a CIA presence in Japan. Predictably, this shotgun marriage went sour from the start, as MacArthur's displeasure was further fueled by the Agency's defiant "we're here from Washington—whether you like it or not" attitude.

To no one's surprise the FEC-CIA bureaucratic infighting began immediately, creating consequences that would linger long after MacArthur's dismissal in April 1951. So strong was the ill will between the CIA and FEC that the grudging and belated merger of their respective unconventional warfare efforts in December 1951 took place long after the United States had abandoned military victory in the field as a war-ending option.

In arguing that CIA operations within the Far East Command's jurisdiction were unnecessary, MacArthur justified his position at least in part with the presence of the Korean Labor Organization (KLO), an organization established two full years earlier to gather information on North Korean activities.[3] Operating from the South Korean capital of Seoul, the small KLO was a front for intelligence-gathering operations that reported directly to FEC's Intelligence Directorate. Too small to really be effective, it nonetheless became at war's outbreak the channel through which FEC began conducting its first operations behind enemy lines. For despite losing his battle to keep the CIA out of his theater, MacArthur continued to successfully resist the powerful National Security Council's directives to place unconventional warfare operations within the Agency's jurisdiction. He did so with a MacArthuresque tactic so bald that it worked for the remaining tenure of his command—he essentially ignored the CIA.

The imperial aloofness of the decision was vintage MacArthur, and as the general correctly judged, no one in Washington's command structure had the nerve to challenge this insubordination. Although since his departure in 1935 for the Philippines MacArthur had not returned to the United States,[4] the former West Point Superintendent, former army chief of staff, and World War II hero was keenly aware of his fame with the American public. No doubt the general's personal confidence was also bolstered by the fact that in FEC he had exactly the powerful army machine necessary to support his ambitions.

As would be expected in any land war, the army presence dominates joint-service military operations in terms of both total manpower and the preponderance of senior military rank. This was certainly true of the army presence within FEC's supposedly joint-service staff even before the war. For despite a Joint Chiefs directive sent nearly three years earlier requiring unified commanders to establish a "joint staff with appropriate members from the various components of the services [e.g., air force, navy] in key positions of responsibility," MacArthur's headquarters in 1950 was still colored a distinctly U.S. Army green.[5] So green in fact that "army" and "FEC" become virtually interchangeable terms when describing the subsequent development of the command's unconventional warfare campaign on the Korean peninsula.[6]

MacArthur's determination to effectively delete the CIA from his war planning was all the more remarkable considering that neither the FEC staff nor any of its army, navy, or air force components possessed alternative unconventional warfare forces. As no one on MacArthur's staff was eager to belabor their commander (or possibly their own careers) with this deficiency, the pragmatic subordinates promptly began to create such forces from scratch. Beginning at the top, the staff first created within its own Intelligence Directorate (FEC-G2) the deceptively named Liaison Group (LG).[7] Hastily thrown together and continually evolving throughout the war in a bewildering series of organizational changes, the Liaison Group was in fact the genesis from which sprang all of the command's subsequent unconventional warfare organizations during the remainder of the war.

The LG's staff planners began their work in the worst of all possible circumstances. Urgent demands for intelligence on the enemy's movements rained down upon them with an intensity and speed that matched that of the North Korean People's Army slashing southward down the Korean peninsula. Adding to the planner's woes were their own questions about the new staff function. What exactly could an unconventional warfare campaign accomplish in North Korea? What human and material resources were available? And most important, could years of neglecting this specialized form of warfare be corrected in time to make a difference? In the grim summer of 1950 few were really sure there would even be an American army left on the peninsula before the LG could begin its operations.

Working frantically around the clock, the LG responded in short order with a proposal to launch simultaneous tactical and strategic intelligence collection missions behind enemy lines. Quickly approved, the proposal led to the immediate expansion of the KLO for recruiting and training Koreans to conduct these separate but complementary missions.[8] All of these hazardous penetration missions were to be carried out solely by Korean nationals, as the presence of Caucasians in North Korean–controlled territory would obviously draw unwanted attention. Recruiting Koreans for such highly dangerous work proved easier than the LG expected, for as veteran LG officer Lt. Col. H. F. Walterhouse later observed, the Koreans proved susceptible to at least one and usually more of the following inducements: "Generally there are just five principal causes which stimulate desire in individuals to undertake such perilous missions. They are profit, patriotism, revenge, excitement, and coercion."[9]

Walterhouse concluded his report with the judgment that in the case of KLO agents it was probably a combination of several of these factors, not the least being the "inherent element of brigandage" found in a large part of the Korean population.[10] But it was also during this initial recruiting program that LG officers encountered an obscure group motivated by yet another cause, a group with priceless skills for exactly the kind of behind-the-lines work FEC had in mind.

This group's talent for subterfuge emerged from one of the most consistent aspects of the foreign domination that had stifled Korean freedom throughout the centuries: the foreigner's merciless persecution of the land's indigenous religions. Over the years this persecution created in turn a number of underground religious sects that developed (no doubt at great cost in blood) the art of secret communication and movement. And as the LG soon learned, at least one of these sects, the Cho'ondagyo, numbered in the thousands. After becoming aware of this secretive group, LG operative 1st Lt. Robert B. Brewer quickly secured their active support. And within weeks of their recruitment, the Cho'ondagyo's outstanding ability to return from enemy-controlled territory with vital intelligence became an early hallmark of LG success behind enemy lines.[11]

Whatever their individual motivations or religious background, the agents selected by LG came from every walk of civilian life, both genders, and every age group. And as the recruiters soon discovered, once committed to the mission the Koreans were tenacious in the extreme. A special report prepared by the U.S. Army's 442d Counter-Intelligence Corps (CIC) Detachment in June 1951 describes the remarkable performance of one KLO agent assigned to its sector: "One man, in late middle age . . . lived in a trench ten feet long and four feet deep for three months without seeing the light of day. He broadcast information collected by local partisans to a plane flying overhead every third night. He stayed at his post . . . although almost prostrate from fever and shaken repeatedly by friendly aerial and artillery bombardment."[12]

Referring to the 442d report in a later study, Brewer went a step further in describing the dangers of KLO operations: "His [the radio operator] was not an isolated case; the female agents endured similar privations and torture for the UN cause. Several [of the women] became expert parachutists, and others developed professional acumen in gleaning information from Chinese colonels."[13] If privations and torture were two common threads uniting the first Liaison Group agents, a third such thread was their exclusively South Korean origin. This situation later changed to such an extent that by early 1951, the overwhelming majority of partisans,[14] saboteurs, and spies fighting against North Korea were actually North Korean themselves. But in the fall of 1950, worrying about what the following year might bring was not a luxury available to LG operatives. They were already busy launching the first KLO agents directly into harm's way.

Line-Crossers

> The best [TLO] infiltrators turned out to be children and women with babies. They were stopped and questioned less frequently, they could move more easily around the battlefield than men could, and troops on both sides seemed to have an aversion to shooting children and nursing mothers walking through their lines.

As the war progressed, the KLO agents assigned by the Liaison Group to tactical intelligence missions were designated Tactical Liaison Office

(TLO) agents. More commonly they were referred to simply as "line-crossers," people who crossed on foot back and forth across the forbidding "no-man's-land" that separated Communist and allied front-line positions. To help control its rapidly growing operations, FEC-LG limited TLO intelligence-gathering operations to a twenty-mile-deep band of territory behind enemy lines; deeper operations were reserved for KLO missions.[15] It sounded simple enough on paper, but there were few things "simple" about such operations, and the risks to the agents were appalling.

To make timely use of the tactical information retrieved from their returning TLO agents, the Liaison Group officers operating in Korea worked in close concert with the senior U.S. military command in Korea, the Eighth U.S. Army. In practice, this came down to assigning TLO teams[16] to each front-line U.S. Army and Marine Corps infantry division. Unlike the Americans, however, the South Korean army chose not to use the line-crossers. Viewing them as little more than draft dodgers, its troops would fire on them occasionally, even when the soldiers knew the Koreans were TLO agents on a mission.[17] Regardless of these setbacks, the TLO program soon grew and established standard operating procedures for its dangerous, front-line activities.

Following the arrival of the American TLO officer and his Korean agents at a front-line division headquarters, the officer received a briefing describing the division's tactical intelligence requirement. Initial mission planning involved evaluating the feasibility of the proposed mission as well as coordinating the team's departure and return procedures through the division's forward-most positions. The officer in turn briefed the Korean agents designated to carry out the mission, speaking through the all-important Korean interpreter assigned to each team.

Escorting his Korean charges to their exit point through the front lines at night was an essential task for the TLO, at least in part to protect them from U.S. infantrymen not happy to see any Korean in their trenches. From this point on, however, the TLO could do little but watch and worry as the mission began: "The general procedure . . . was to send the agents along with an infantry patrol and leave them behind when the patrol returned to friendly lines. Use of a prearranged pickup point was dropped after several patrols ran into enemy ambushes. Several agents [lost] their lives when trigger-happy infantrymen shot without challenging [the agents attempting to cross back into friendly lines on their own]."[18]

For those agents lucky enough to return in one piece through the groups of ill-tempered and trigger-happy infantrymen on both sides of the front lines, their first stop was at the division's CIC team. Time was obviously of the essence for the front-line division seeking tactical information on enemy positions and movement to its front, and the returning agents could be easily sidetracked through no fault of their own: "Close liaison with division CIC was mandatory because returning agents normally were evacuated through prisoner of war channels to the division cage. CIC personnel were the first persons notified . . . when the civilians professed to be a TLO or KLO agent."[19]

During the first year of the war the front lines were so fluid that the inevitable flow of refugees seeking to escape the combat also served as useful camouflage for TLO agents dressed incognito as refugees. But by mid-1951 the front lines had stabilized and this once-useful civilian cover was largely gone. From this time forward, the agents had little recourse but to camouflage themselves with the uniforms and weapons of the NKPA for their missions.[20] Thus dressed in enemy uniforms and speaking at best only pidgin English to tired and scared GIs armed to the teeth, many more of these brave agents were killed during their attempts to return through "friendly" lines at night. As one U.S. 3d Infantry Division TLO officer succinctly put it, "A suitable method of retrieving agents from across the front lines never was found."[21]

What was found, however, was an alternative to using young male agents, who on top of everything else always ran the risk of being drafted at gunpoint straight into the first army patrol (South or North Korean) they encountered. One American veteran of this period later concluded that "the best [TLO] infiltrators turned out to be children and women with babies. They were stopped and questioned less frequently, they could move more easily around the battlefield than men could, and troops on both sides seemed to have an aversion to shooting children and nursing mothers walking through their lines."[22]

As alluded to earlier, the TLO operations were most successful when the front lines were in a state of flux. In September and October 1950, for example, TLO agents supporting the allied surge northward from the west coast landings at Inchon proved very effective in reporting on pockets of bypassed enemy troops, hidden weapons caches, and North Korean strong points holding up the advance.[23] But as successful as the line-crosser program proved on numerous occasions, the inherent dangers continued to dog its effectiveness throughout the war. This became especially true from the summer of 1951 forward, when the front lines assumed the basic positions they would retain for the rest of the war (and to this very day).

Even had the TLO program proved more successful, however, its short-range penetrations into enemy territory by agents on foot would still not have answered FEC's demands for strategic intelligence on enemy activity much farther behind the front lines. Those demands were first answered when the LG pulled yet another rabbit out of the proverbial magician's hat with its continued expansion of the Korean Labor Office.

Rabbits

Everyone was frantic. Where have they [Chinese] gone? We were retreating then. . . . The 2d (U.S. Army) Division had been beaten up and was paper-thin. One of them [female agent] came out. She had slept with a lieutenant colonel, Chinese army, and had their whole Order of Battle. . . . Three or four Chinese divisions had side-slipped about 80 miles and were posed head-on against the 2d Division. That report saved the day. . . . The Marines moved up behind the 2d Division . . . and kicked the shit out of them.

The Liaison Group's agent handlers often referred to their KLO charges as "rabbits" when circumstances forced the Americans to discuss agent-related activities over telephone or teletype lines.[24] Before the advent of modern-day encrypted telephone security systems, it was a modest but still useful security precaution. Such elementary precautions protected not only the agents themselves but also the U.S. airmen and sailors who inserted these agents into their target areas in North Korea and China.

In many ways the KLO "rabbits" were indeed similar to the well-known magician's rabbit: appearing from nowhere with no clue as to how they arrived. As the war progressed, however, these incredibly brave rabbits would share another, this time tragic comparison with the magician's act. Time and again they would appear deep behind enemy lines only to disappear without a trace, frequently without a single radio call back to the LG's secret headquarters in South Korea. Nearly a half-century after the signing of the Korean Armistice, the fate of these agents remains unknown.

As the KLO planners turned to their task, deep penetration missions into Communist-held territory, they quickly discovered that Korea's rugged geography limited them to only two feasible penetration options. Against Communist positions deep in the mountainous interior, parachute insertion under the cover of darkness was the only practical tactic. For targets located along the peninsula's extended coastline, infiltration by small, indigenous sailboats or motorized junks offered the best chance of avoiding detection. Neither tactic was easy, but both were relatively simple, and these two methods varied little throughout the remainder of the war.

As with the TLO program, early KLO efforts got off to a rocky start due to the lack of manpower, equipment, training facilities, and, most of all, unconventional warfare experience within FEC or the Eighth Army. For the Korean agents sent forth, this lack of support and expertise quickly proved deadly: "The first two parachute drops were organized and sent off without the faintest trace of preparations, and the result was just as negative. The over-water efforts initially had better luck, but because of the lack of equipment—specifically powerboats—operations temporarily had to cease."[25]

Despite the complete failure experienced with these first parachute-insertion operations, the cessation of waterborne infiltration due to the lack of boats quickly forced the Liaison Group back to airborne operations as its sole remaining option. This in turn led to the establishment of a primitive, parachutist-training facility near the port city of Pusan in August 1950, even as UN forces were making their last-ditch stand around the city.[26] With the sole mission of supporting KLO requirements, the facility soon began training hundreds of Korean volunteers for a highly secret program that would, before the war ended a long three years later, claim the lives of almost every "graduate" actually sent north on a mission. Given its airborne emphasis, it was appropriately called Operation Aviary.[27]

Neither the time available nor the facilities at Pusan permitted an attempt to train the agents as fully qualified paratroopers. To the contrary, the parachute-insertion phase of the overall mission was intentionally deemphasized for psychological reasons when it was discovered that many of the civilian volunteers mistakenly viewed the frightening night jump as the most difficult phase of their much more dangerous mission.[28] In deemphasizing the parachute-insertion phase the American-run school cut its "curriculum" for the agent-parachutists to an absolute bare bones minimum. In the months that followed, each class of approximately twenty agents received two hours of "orientation" by a Korean instructor before Brewer put them through six additional hours of training intended to include all of the following: "Proper door habit, body position, parachute manipulation during descent, how to land, water landing, tree landing, and how to ball and chain a parachute for burial. Field work to be conducted . . . included jumping from a jeep at 20 mph, compass orientation at night, and assembly techniques."[29]

The first Aviary missions followed on the heels of MacArthur's daring amphibious invasion of Inchon Harbor in September 1950. The North Korean army had vanished in northward retreat, but was it a disciplined withdrawal or a rout? What roads were their major units

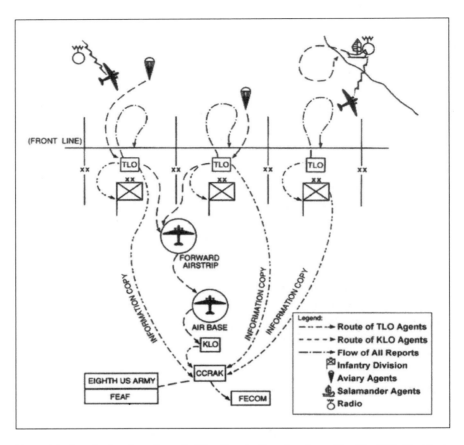

By 1952, the air, land, and sea infiltration tactics developed by the U.S. Far East Command's Liaison Group had evolved together into a very complex operation. The long-range air and sea infiltration operations (Aviary, Salamander) sent Korean agents from the Far East Command's Korean Labor Organization (KLO), while short-range "line-crosser" operations were conducted on foot by Tactical Liaison Office (TLO) agents assigned to front-line U.S. Army and Marine Corps divisions. *Stevens et al., "Intelligence Information by Partisans,"* 29

taking? Where were the enemy's armor and artillery, its infantry reserves? MacArthur well knew that failure to answer these questions had lured more than one seemingly victorious army to its destruction as it chased after an apparently defeated foe. He expected answers to such questions, and the Liaison Group soon got the mission to provide them. With little choice but to move quickly beyond its first two failed insertions, Aviary was tasked yet again, and this time the results proved dramatically different.

In receiving at least some parachute training before being sent on their operational night jump into North Korea, these Korean agent trainees were more fortunate than many of their comrades. Still, the survival rate of those sent on such missions was appalling. *Courtesy of Bob Brewer*

On the night of 26 September 1950, two U.S. Air Force C-47, twin-engine transports carrying nine Pusan-trained KLO parachutists flew northward from South Taegu Airfield in southern Korea.[30] Five agents were dropped into one drop zone; the remaining four into another. Between the two of them the drop zones placed the agents within observation range of the seven major evacuation routes taken by the retreating North Korean army, and all agents were observed landing safely. Days later, eight of the nine agents successfully reported back to their KLO case officers after returning on foot through friendly lines. While judged a technical success, this first mission quickly revealed two major problems inherent with early Aviary tactics.

The first problem to surface was the inordinate time it took the rabbits to return on foot through enemy territory. Inserted without radios, their dangerously acquired field reports were outdated by the time they were personally delivered to the Americans. This delay-in-reporting problem was partially resolved by equipping the agents with World War II–era SCR-694 radio transceivers. Thus equipped, the agents successfully communicated with the air force C-47s orbiting overhead within line-of-sight communications range of the radios. But even equipping the agents with these transceivers offered only a limited solution as the radio proved bulky to carry and difficult to operate for the hastily trained agents.

The second problem had much in common with that encountered by the short-range TLO agents. To reenter friendly territory, the agents had first to allow themselves to be captured and sent to prisoner-of-war (POW) camps for interrogation. Aside from the obvious dangers of being shot by front-line soldiers from either side, the agents could usually count on facing hostile suspicion from UN troops even after having identified themselves with the current code word. And as with the tactical agent program, some KLO agents were killed attempting to cross no-man's-land while others were co-opted as scouts or laborers for use by front-line units. Still others simply vanished forever into the vast POW camp populations.

With or without radios, the promising successes of the early Aviary missions spurred KLO expansion to the point where agents were soon being parachuted into enemy territory as rapidly as they could be recruited and readied. Inevitably, the already marginal training and mission-preparation program suffered still further, as did the agents who were sent straight into enemy territory following their graduation from the Pusan facility. Though the records of these agent losses have long since disappeared from U.S. Army files, if indeed they ever existed, the number of poorly trained Koreans lost on such missions likely reached into the several hundreds at a minimum.

As UN forces chased the remnants of the North Korean army toward that country's border with China that fall and victory seemed at most only weeks away, FEC headquarters succumbed to a euphoria that its troops would indeed "be home by Christmas," as MacArthur had predicted on 24 November. One soldier most definitely not partaking in the premature party, however, was First Lieutenant Brewer, who read with increasingly alarm the reports coming from his agents stationed in the hills overlooking the North Korean–Chinese border:

> By mid-October I had deployed dozens of parachute agents along the border, and immediately significant reports began to come in. By late-October I was making a fuss in every G-2 office from Eighth Army to FEC, about the large Chinese forces crossing into Korea. . . . [By this time] Aviary agents had reported a Chinese Order of Battle exceeding 60,000. Finally, Willoughby did an unprecedented thing. On 31 October 1950 he ordered me to send him my principal agent from the Kangge-Mampojin border area for an in-depth interview. The agent gave a rather complete picture of the Chinese units that had crossed the Mampojin Bridge into Korea during the month of October, including heavy weapons and hospital units, indicating that Chinese intentions were something more than mere border protection.[31]

Following Willoughby's interview of the Korean agent, the apparently appreciative general sent ten scarce SCR-300 infantry radio transceivers to Brewer. Newly arrived to Korea, the lightweight and simple-to-operate radios proved ideal for communications between the agents and the SCR-300–equipped air force aircraft flying overhead. Communications were enhanced still further by the simple technique of trailing a long coaxial cable behind an in-flight C-47, using the cable as a giant radio antenna. But as welcomed as the -300s were, the insufficient numbers in which they eventually arrived diminished the operational impact of their belated issue to KLO. As events were soon to prove, this lack of modern communication equipment led to some extraordinary improvisation in the field.

No better example of this improvisation can be found than that which took place in December 1950, as shattered and exhausted UN formations retreated southward in disarray before the massive onslaught of the Chinese People's Liberation Army (PLA). With contact broken between the attacking Chinese and the retreating allies, anxious UN military commanders were suddenly in the dark as to where the PLA could be massing for its next attack. To find an immediate answer, Eighth Army commander Lt. Gen. Walton Walker tasked Operation Aviary officers to "blanket the waist of Korea north of [Eighth Army] lines."[32] As Brewer recalls the mission, "Walker explained he could stop the Chinese attack only if he knew in advance where the main blow was coming. He was not worried about the North Koreans. I had a problem. I didn't want to send in radio teams on such short notice, and we couldn't meet the deadline with overland or maritime . . . methods. So I borrowed an old Indian trick and had my agents send smoke signals!"[33]

For this special mission, the air force C-47s dedicated to support the effort had the undersides of their wings painted with broad black and white stripes, reminiscent of those used to identify allied aircraft during World War II's famous D-day invasion of Europe. The aircrews then proceeded to drop twelve two-agent teams across the narrow neck of the Korean peninsula, ten to twenty miles in front of UN outposts. Equipped not with modern radios but with variously colored smoke grenades, the agents went to ground to watch for the enemy and await the presence overhead of the specially marked aircraft. Every day at noon a C-47 flew low-level over the path of dropped agents to observe their smoke signals.

If the agents had seen Chinese in numbers over battalion strength, they signaled with red smoke; yellow indicated North Koreans; green signified little or no enemy presence.[34] Despite deteriorating weather that soon led to a solid, low overcast, the aircrews observed

25 percent of the total signals possible.[35] It was crude but effective intelligence, especially when virtually nothing else was available to FEC. The mission accomplished the agents were left, as usual, on their own for the dangerous walk back to friendly lines. Brewer subsequently reported, "The mission was far more successful than I dared hope, and we secured all but two of the [male and female] agents after the operation."[36]

The "smoke jumps mission," as it was called, would clearly have benefited from the use of radios had they been available in sufficient numbers, but many particularly sensitive KLO missions were so dangerous that carrying a radio was not an option even when such equipment was available. Such special missions were frequently reserved for one small group of carefully selected rabbits, recruited from the most unlikely of sources. This group consisted of attractive young women recruited for the KLO by Madam Francesca Donner Rhee, the Austrian wife of South Korea's President Syngman Rhee. A well-known matron of the arts in prewar Seoul, Madam Rhee recruited from within the small circle of theater actresses with whom she was familiar.

The courage of these young women was legendary among the air force's special air missions (SAM) crews, especially those few briefed on the personal nature of their mission. One officer in particular, former SAM commander Brig. Gen. Harry C. "Heinie" Aderholt, remembers these female rabbits: "The agents were furnished by the Koreans. We had hundreds of them. Madam Rhee furnished all the women. They had all the movie stars and everybody, the best-looking girls. We put them out over enemy territory during the winter of '50–'51 when the outside air temperature was forty to fifty degrees below zero. They would go out in cotton-padded shoes and suit. They wouldn't weigh enough to get to the ground, you would think."[37]

But get to they ground they did. Each individual agent then followed her mission plan by associating herself intimately with a high-ranking North Korean or Chinese officer found in the vicinity of the drop. Remaining in his quarters with him long enough to learn units, locations, planned offensives, and so on, she then attempted to disappear into the confusion common to front-line combat areas. If shrewd and lucky enough to survive the "relationship" and the always-dangerous crossing through friendly lines, she then used the prearranged code word from a POW camp. If her luck still held, she was then released to her KLO agent handler for immediate debriefing. Incredibly, some of these actress-agents actually survived their missions to render critical and timely intelligence information.

Some of the most dangerous espionage missions of the war were undertaken by South Korean female agents—many of them former theater actresses— parachuted into enemy territory to seek out senior Communist officers. The emotional and physical strain of these extremely high-risk missions is evident on the faces of these two exhausted women as they sit through their postmission debriefing. *Courtesy of Bob Brewer*

In his postretirement U.S. Air Force Oral History interview, Aderholt recalls one mission in particular in which one rabbit warned of an impending and totally unexpected Communist attack. Her warning came just in time to allow U.S. forces to reinforce a weak sector and deal a punishing defeat on the attackers: "Everyone was frantic. Where have they [Chinese] gone? We were retreating then. . . . The 2d (U.S. Army) Division had been beaten up and was paper-thin. One of them [female agent] came out. She had slept with a lieutenant colonel, Chinese army, and had their whole Order of Battle. . . . Three or four Chinese divisions had side-slipped about 80 miles and were posed head-on against the 2d Division. That report saved the day. . . . The Marines moved up behind the 2d Division . . . and kicked the shit out of them!"[38]

As their successes continued, the imaginative Aviary officers began planning in 1951 for even more daring missions. One such mission in particular was so audacious that it was stopped personally by

MacArthur's newly arrived replacement, Gen. Mathew B. Ridgway. This mission called for nothing less than the kidnapping of the senior Soviet general in North Korea, and as Brewer notes, the mission planning had reached an advanced stage before Ridgway became aware of the politically explosive plan:

> In May 1951 . . . my best North Korean operatives and I were set to kidnap and extract (by helicopter) the senior Soviet advisor to the North Korean People's Army Headquarters. . . . Operation Aviary "owned" the Korean staff at the Russians' living quarters, and we "owned" the 4,000-foot mountain behind the Russian's bungalow.
>
> My plan won approvals from the commanders of the Eighth Army, the Far East Air Forces, and the U.S. Navy Far East, but General Ridgway . . . vetoed it. He wrote across the front page of the plan "This is an excellent plan. I can tell it was written by an experienced airborne officer, but I must *disapprove!* Ridgway."[39]

The courage of Aviary's Korean and Chinese agents was unquestionable. But there was a darker side to Aviary and other American-sponsored operations that depended on indigenous personnel for critical, unconventional warfare missions. This dark side was particularly dangerous because it surfaced without warning and from the least expected direction. And it could, as it did on at least one tragic occasion, cost the lives of the SAM crews that risked their own lives to deliver the agents deep into Communist territory. This particular dark side was found with the treachery that accompanied the presence of double agents inserted by the North Korean and Chinese armies into the KLO program.

Along with the never-ending urgency to recruit agents and partisans for the steadily growing Liaison Group operations, it was inevitable that some double agents would slip through the screening process to find themselves in a position to hurt their enemy. And hurt their enemy they did in the dead of winter, February 1952, during a night insertion mission near the Yalu River, which forms the border between North Korea and China. Author and Korean War partisan advisor Ed Evanhoe described the mission for *Behind the Lines* magazine: "Taking off from Seoul City Airfield during the night of 18–19 February, the C-46 Air Commando transport headed east for the first of its multiple drops, saving the most dangerous for last. Flying through the night sky under a near-full moon the first drops were completed successfully and the plane flew west to a DZ [drop zone] near the Yalu River border with Manchuria . . . and into disaster."[40]

Arriving over the unmarked drop zone, the twin-engine transport slowed to paradrop speed, and the first of two Chinese agents

Paratrooper and Liaison Group officer Bob Brewer (left), seen here with three of his agents, was, by May 1951, well into the planning stage of an operation intended to kidnap or assassinate the senior Soviet general in North Korea. On learning of the proposed operation, General Ridgway, the newly arrived commander-in-chief, Far East Command, abruptly terminated the project. *Courtesy of Bob Brewer*

parachuted out into the night. But the second agent hesitated just before jumping, just long enough to lob a live grenade into the forward cabin section. The agent was safely out the door under an opening parachute when the grenade exploded, instantly killing or disabling the four remaining Chinese agents and one of their American agent handlers. With the C-46 Air Commando on fire and coming apart in midair, the instructor navigator, Capt. Lawrence E. Burger, sacrificed his life by staying at the controls as the remaining crew parachuted to safety.

With their burning aircraft lighting up the night sky as it fell to earth, locating the surviving crewmembers was an easy task for the enemy troops in the immediate area. The next day, the Chinese took the navigator, Capt. Guy O. King, back to the crash site, where he saw six blanket-wrapped bodies. According to the Chinese interpreter, the bodies were those of two Americans and four Asians recovered from the wreckage. But were they?[41] The full story of the treachery did not emerge until after the repatriation of the captured aircrew at the end of

Communist security services accorded a high priority to their infiltration of UN military and CIA special operations forces. The results could be devastating when this happened, as in February 1952, when a Chinese double agent, about to jump from the door of the infiltration aircraft, hesitated just long enough to lob a grenade into the forward section of the C-46 Air Commando. *Painting by Steve Garst*

the war, and even to this day the survivors' stories leave questions unanswered.

Unlike Captain Burger's crew, most mission failures were "evidenced" by little more than a lack of evidence or explanation. The aircrew, agents, or partisans simply disappeared without a trace, leaving FEC officers with only the hope that their operatives died instantly rather than face capture and brutal interrogation. Fortunately for the SAM crews, this kind of in-flight treachery would prove to be, like shark attacks, as rare as it was horrifying.

While attending the U.S. Army's Armor School in 1952, then–captain Brewer summarized his experiences with the Korean Labor Organization program: "The KLO-Aviary programs succeeded in the face of many obstacles, not the least being the lack of experience in the intelligence operatives."[42] Brewer's report doesn't define the standards he used to evaluate KLO performance, but it does contain many professional and personal observations that clearly come from a man with a troubled conscience. Like many of the Americans working the KLO programs, Brewer could well guess how few of "his" agents returned from these hastily prepared missions.

One of the most startling and revealing statements made by Brewer, for example, concern his experiences as the training officer at the Pusan parachutist-training course. Despite the seemingly high priority given KLO operations by FEC's Intelligence Directorate, the Pusan school was so poorly supported that Brewer had to fight simply to provide the agents with standard-issue paratrooper (as opposed to cargo) parachutes.[43] In a September 1950 letter from Brewer to the Joint Special Operations Center (a subsection of FEC's Liaison Group) he campaigns for personnel parachutes with a salesman's pragmatism: "The consideration of use of troop-type parachutes in preference to other [cargo] types is important because it involves the chances of success. . . . Disregarding all humanitarian reasons for the moment, an agent who lands and breaks a leg . . . compromises the whole mission and alerts hostile forces to this type of entry by our agents."[44]

Although the parachute problem appears to have been largely resolved at a future date, the issue of inadequate mission preparation for the agents jeopardized KLO operations from the very beginning of the war. As Brewer notes, "My explanation of the failure of previous parachute operations would be that the men were *completely lost* after a landing and psychologically incapable of rectifying the situation. . . . I would ask for 48 hours notice in order to prepare my notes, construct an improvised sand table, and find out . . . about enemy forces likely to be encountered. I would then brief the agents 12 to 24 hours before takeoff time."[45]

From the few U.S. government references available on KLO operations, it appears Operation Aviary did indeed have a measure of success, though at a terrific cost—borne by the courageous Koreans, civilians mostly, who undertook these missions with the barest of preparations. To supplement these airborne operations, the Liaison Group turned to seaborne insertion, as noted earlier the only viable alternative to Operation Aviary for long-range insertion into North Korea.

The early development of Operation Salamander, as these seaborne operations were so appropriately dubbed by KLO, is even more obscure than that of Operation Aviary. Admiral Sohn, commander in chief of the South Korean navy, is reported to have loaned a single fishing boat to the KLO for agent reconnaissance work during the desperate fighting around Pusan during July–September 1950.[46]

But Salamander, like Aviary, got its real beginning after the Inchon landings that September. And for once, the Korean geography proved more friend than enemy to the LG's planners.

The Korean peninsula offers thousands of miles of rugged and nearly indefensible coastline for infiltrators seeking to observe the many key road and rail lines running through the relatively flat coastal areas.[47] Better yet from an unconventional warfare viewpoint, hundreds of small, uninhabited islands off North Korea's western coastline lie within easy distance of the mainland. Often forested and far too many in number for the Communists to control, they made particularly good launching platforms for KLO agents sent inland for their reconnaissance and sabotage missions.

Throughout the war, the presence of the aforementioned islands made North Korea's west coast the KLO's most "profitable" sector of operations. Supported by a minimum of U.S. Army and Air Force personnel, KLO agents consistently picked their way through minefields both at sea and ashore to penetrate North Korean coastal defenses. So favorable to agent survival rates was seaborne insertion that one postwar study spanning August 1950 to June 1951 concludes that "the rate of [Salamander agent] returns never dropped below 90 percent and the number and value of [Salamander] reports easily equaled those of Operation Aviary."[48] This relative comparison with Aviary underscored the essential point that the two operations worked most effectively when working in tandem, much like a football team that achieves optimum offensive performance when it combines its running and passing game effectively. But unlike the football metaphor there were other factors beyond the control of KLO's team.

On a number of occasions, the scarcity of human and material resources within KLO became a vital consideration when coordinating air-sea operations. For example, some Aviary agents were routed to the coastline for extraction by Salamander teams, while at other times agents from both operations radioed their separate mission reports to the same aircraft orbiting overhead with a tape recorder–equipped SCR-300 radio.[49] But while KLO-internal coordination was usually effective, U.S. Air Force–Army coordination in support of KLO was just one more factor beyond their team's control. And when air force–army coordination in support of LG operations did fail, the errors could prove deadly. Particularly painful was the reality that those who paid the price for the failure were often not the ones who made the fatal error.

One such failure occurred in May 1952, when a seaborne U.S. Air Force intelligence unit operating off the west coast islands reported a fishing junk picking up armed men from the North Korean shoreline. Believing it had spotted North Korean army soldiers, the air force team called for an immediate and ultimately effective airstrike on the unknown junk. Only after the boat was sunk with three wounded and two dead did the air force discover the junk was the command and control vessel for another, American-sponsored partisan force operating nearby.[50] Beyond the human tragedy, the loss of the boat itself was no small thing to an already underfunded operation.

The major insertion problem encountered by Salamander teams was the scarcity of the all-important boats necessary for their mission, the best of which for obvious reasons were the indigenous fishing vessels already present in the area. This lack of boats remained a problem throughout the war, although some sail-equipped fishing boats were subsequently modified with diesel engines to obtain speed when time was critical. U.S. Navy harbor patrol boats as well as U.S. Air Force crash rescue boats were later introduced, enabling agents and partisans to be inserted and retrieved to and from the mainland in the course of a single night.[51]

For two primary reasons, Operation Salamander did not get off to the bloody start experienced by Aviary agents. First, the presence of UN-controlled island bases near the North Korean mainland provided the seaborne KLO agents with a fairly close refuge if quick escape became necessary. Second, coastal patrol elements of British Commonwealth warships proved extremely effective in accomplishing their assigned mission to protect these offshore island sanctuaries, themselves indispensable to FEC's unconventional warfare campaign.

Though still a small mom-and-pop-level effort during the first six months of the war, the Liaison Group achieved some notable successes. Its agents had discretely penetrated North Korea by air, land, and sea, made useful reports, and for the most part returned alive. One obvious factor in these successes was the heart and soul commitment made, under the most difficult of circumstances, by the handful of American soldiers and airmen assigned to resurrect overnight an unconventional warfare capability within FEC. But beyond their undeniable contribution, these field successes were achieved primarily by the near-suicidal courage of their Korean agents. Venturing forth as spies with only the poorest of equipment and training provided by the Americans, they performed well beyond any standard that could possibly have been expected from those who sent them.

And in the winter of 1950, "those who sent them" were suddenly confronted with a new, unforeseen battlefield development, the consequences of which dramatically altered FEC's unconventional warfare strategy for the remaining two and a half years of the war. But if this battlefield development surprised the Americans, the pressures that created it had in fact been building for years before the war even began.

Seeds of Failure

> The loosely organized bands of desperate refugees were heading for the only havens within both their reach and that of the allied navies that already controlled the seas surrounding North Korea. South Korean Navy reports continued to reach Eighth Army, consistently describing the refugees as desperate, hungry, poorly armed . . . and mad as hell.

UN soldiers fighting their way into North Korea for the first time in the fall of 1950 were surprised to encounter entire communities of fervent anti-Communists in many of the areas they passed through. This was the first confirmation in the West that such groups still existed despite years of Communist oppression in the North. Numbering in the thousands, these anti-Communists were now surfacing after years of persecution to openly identify themselves and cheer on their liberators. But only weeks after having irretrievably and publicly committed themselves to the UN cause, these anti-Communists were stunned to watch the Chinese army furiously chasing their would-be liberators back out of North Korea.

Unavoidably left behind in their liberator's wake, the now-exposed anti-Communists could choose only between hiding in the local mountains to await the next UN offensive or fleeing for their lives. Tens of thousands chose the latter course and, in doing so, provided the American army with still another surprise. This surprise came only four days after the advancing Communists recaptured Seoul for the second time in the war. On 8 January 1951 the commander of South Korea's Naval Task Force 95.7 startled Eighth Army headquarters with the first news that thousands of the anti-Communists left behind were making a fighting retreat to North Korea's western shoreline.[52] "The loosely organized bands of desperate refugees were heading for the only havens within both their reach and that of the allied navies that already controlled the seas surrounding North Korea. South Korean Navy reports continued to reach Eighth Army, consistently describing the refugees as desperate, hungry, poorly armed . . . and mad as hell."[53]

To Eighth Army headquarters, the reports offered a potentially dramatic change to both the strategic and tactical military situation on the peninsula. To the American command, the angry refugees' request for weapons and ammunition created the tantalizing prospect of supporting the planned spring offensive back north with widespread partisan warfare in Communist rear areas. Overnight, the UN's potential for unconventional warfare escalated dramatically from the mom-and-pop-level management of a few hundred Liaison Group agents to full-scale partisan warfare. It was a totally unexpected bonus, and the Eighth Army moved promptly to seize the opportunity.

A quick search through its headquarters staff for an officer to exploit this bonus led the Eighth Army to Col. John H. McGee, a 1932 West Point graduate with a very unusual combat record. During World War II McGee had brazenly escaped Japanese imprisonment by diving from a Japanese prisoner-of-war ship sailing near the Philippine Island of Luzon. Following his daring escape, the determined (and still trapped) officer spent the next four months fighting with Filipino guerrillas before being extracted by a U.S. Navy submarine.[54] If his experience in unconventional warfare was limited, it still proved more credible than that of virtually any other officer in Korea at the time.

As with the handful of other army officers with unconventional warfare experience gained during World War II, McGee soon learned that his hard-earned knowledge was of little interest to postwar generals desperately trying to keep entire divisions away from Truman's budget-cutting axe. However, in the Eighth Army at least, that disinterest evaporated overnight with its receipt of reports from the South Korean navy. Soon to become the major American figure in the UN's partisan war behind Communist lines, McGee moved swiftly to organize what were now "his" refugees. Within the days that followed, the colonel's staff organized the first small shipments of desperately needed weapons, ammunition, food, and clothing to the islands.

As the relief effort moved into high gear during the second week in January, McGee directed his around-the-clock pace toward a different goal. Within a few short days, he developed a war plan for his vision of a partisan force that was, as he was about to discover, more sophisticated than either the Eighth Army or FEC staffs could appreciate. Few denied that speed was essential to organize, train, and equip the partisans on the islands if they were to be made ready for Eighth Army's expected spring offensive. However, the U.S. Army as an institution had experienced little in the way of unconventional warfare since the American Indian Wars of the late 1800s. And in the winter of 1950, this corporate lack of unconventional warfare experience led to a series of ill-considered decisions that largely squandered the partisan potential from the very start.

Following the rationale that training and equipping the partisans would be of little use to the overall UN effort if the U.S. Army didn't first establish an organization to support the partisans, McGee worked feverishly to develop a plan for just such an organization. In particular, he understood that the geography of the Korean peninsula made air and naval support critical to unconventional warfare operations behind enemy lines. McGee also knew that in the entire Far East, there was only one organization with the authority to ensure that this vital air and naval support would be provided to the partisans when and where needed.

Only FEC, a joint-service command with subordinate air and naval components, had the bureaucratic clout to order component support to the partisans. In contrast, the all–U.S. Army command in Korea could only *request* such support from FEC. This seemingly slight difference in terminology was (and remains) no small thing in the military system. This proved especially so in the midst of a war in which army, navy, and air force commanders in the Far East found themselves competing furiously for the limited resources available. Fully aware of these bureaucratic realities and their importance to his plans, the enthusiastic McGee set out in mid-January from Korea for FEC headquarters in Tokyo. McGee's ambitious plan called for nothing less than the establishment of the Attrition Warfare Headquarters, a combined[55] partisan command that bypassed the lower levels of bureaucracy to report directly to FEC's powerful Operations Directorate.

A combined command aligned under the Operations Directorate would not only provide the partisans with the required air and naval support but also ensure that the partisans received the same priority for supplies, weapons, and equipment as did regular American combat units. Furthermore, the alignment of the Attrition Warfare Headquarters under the Operations Directorate would clarify the status of the partisans as a combat force, not simply another intelligence-gathering organization responding to directions from FEC's Intelligence Directorate.[56]

It took FEC's staff less than twenty-four hours to reject Colonel McGee's plans. On 15 January 1951, the reviewing officials responded to his proposal by authorizing the Eighth Army (not FEC) to establish the much smaller and operationally limited Attrition Section within the Miscellaneous Division to which McGee was already assigned.[57] Though under the operational control of Eighth Army's Operations Directorate, the Attrition Section would take its "guidance" from FEC's Intelligence Directorate.[58] By establishing this staff element (the Attrition Section) as an alternative to McGee's proposal for a combined command subordinated to FEC-Operations, the staff planners committed at least three critical errors.

First, the decision to activate a staff element rather than a command meant that the Attrition Section could only recommend to conventional field commanders how the thousands of armed partisans under

Eighth Army jurisdiction might best be employed. Second, the decision to manage this combat force as a headquarters staff function removed any possibility that the partisans would receive the priority needed for ready access to the all-important air and naval support that FEC provided only to its subordinate commands. Also lost in the process was the priority necessary to receive logistical support equal to that received by FEC's established commands. Third and most confusing to understand, the staff officers chose FEC's Intelligence Directorate to control a partisan combat force organizationally aligned under Eighth Army's Operations Directorate.

Written records of FEC's rationale for its feeble response are sparse. But factors likely influencing their decisions include the army's lack of unconventional warfare experience and the general belief that another UN offensive was so imminent as to make the Eighth Army the only command capable of responding to partisan requirements in the near term. But was it? Curiously absent from virtually all records of this period is the seemingly obvious question: Where was the CIA, the only organization then authorized to carry out the very kind of partisan warfare suddenly assumed by the Eighth Army?

A partial answer to this question has already been given in terms of MacArthur's attitude toward the CIA and his determination to keep it at arm's length whenever and wherever possible. Thus in January 1951, FEC simply bypassed the Agency with little or no objection from Washington. Another explanation is found in the CIA's response to MacArthur's tactics. Essentially the Agency simply mirrored the general's bureaucratic moves during this period, keeping FEC at arm's length from its own programs, especially its partisan army that was already engaged in combat on the peninsula. As described in greater detail later in this book, this duplication (and misplaced competition) of effort would have serious long-term consequences on the overall partisan program—consequences from which only the Communists would benefit.

Despite these seemingly endless FEC-CIA quarrels and the disappointing setbacks to his proposal, there nevertheless remained in the Eighth Army at least one colonel very determined to make the most of FEC's grudging support. Disappointed but driven to prove the operational validity of his original vision, McGee continued at his furious pace. And in less than ninety days this drive led to the establishment of no less than three unconventional warfare organizations: "William Able Base (later renamed Leopard Base), headquartered at Paengnyong-do but occupying numerous islands along the Korean west coast as far north as the Yalu River estuary; Baker Section, a training and staging base for airborne/special operations, located

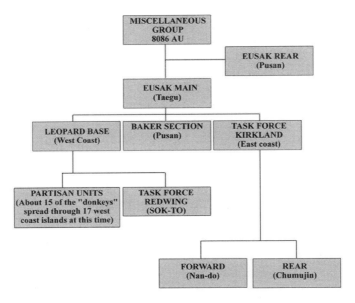

By July 1951 the Eighth Army's Miscellaneous Group staff had put in place the structure for a partisan army that was filled with as much potential as it was problems, the most pressing of the latter being the lack of support coming from the Eighth Army itself. *Cleaver et al., UN Partisan Warfare in Korea, 40*

near Pusan; and later in April, Task Force Kirkland, operating on islands off the east coast, near Wonsan."[59]

Yet another unit designated to conduct sabotage, commando-type operations, and intelligence-gathering missions during this period was Task Force Redwing, an American-led South Korean Marine Corps company, also operating from Leopard Base on Paengnyong-do.[60] But despite the pace at which the zealous McGee was moving to activate these units in the spring of 1951, other events beyond his control were beginning to unfold; events that would soon affect the partisans' future in ways neither the colonel nor anyone else could foresee.

In March 1951 another UN offensive led to the recapture of Seoul and another movement of allied troops northward again toward the thirty-eighth parallel. The following month President Truman publicly sacked MacArthur, replacing him with World War II paratroop commander Gen. Mathew B. Ridgway. In Korea, Lt. Gen. James A. Van Fleet arrived to assume command of the Eighth Army, and in a matter of weeks the two new commanders were working closely to revise the original organizational status of their respective unconventional warfare organizations.

Van Fleet moved first, apparently motivated by an Eighth Army standard operating procedure that prohibited staff functions from conducting field operations. The commander dissolved the Attrition Section on 5 May 1951, reactivating the unit the same day as the Miscellaneous Group, 8086 Army Unit (AU).[61] The unconventional warfare mission remained the same, but as a numbered U.S. Army unit the Miscellaneous Group rated a much-needed U.S. Army Table of Distribution and Equipment that formally authorized for the first time both equipment and U.S. personnel to train and support the partisans.[62] Following Van Fleet's lead, Ridgway moved to align the FEC staff functions supporting the Eighth Army's partisan war with a series of unit redesignations, "all of which had no immediate effect on the partisan effort."[63]

Although Eighth Army and FEC changes marginally improved logistical support for the partisans, the unit redesignations were motivated primarily by Van Fleet and Ridgway's determination to fit the irregular partisan force into a regular U.S. Army organization; that is, the partisan potential was a secondary issue. Nevertheless, all changes were complete by July 1951, the month McGee rotated back to the United States. The remarkable colonel had moved bureaucratic mountains to turn approximately seven thousand ill-clad and hungry North Korean refugees into a partisan force within a very short six months. Despite these unit redesignations, however, the still-cumbersome Eighth Army supply pipeline to the islands succeeded in providing weapons to only four thousand of the revenge-minded partisans.[64]

McGee was replaced by his executive officer, Lt. Col. Samuel Koster, and another officer with guerrilla warfare experience in the Philippines, Lt. Col. Jay Vanderpool, took over supervision of the partisan war effort. Vanderpool had been on loan to the CIA before the war, and in fact had been sent by the Agency to Korea to resolve discrepancies between FEC and CIA estimates regarding the size of the prewar North Korean People's Army.[65] And although FEC's estimates later proved to be far more accurate, the experience added to Vanderpool's credentials as an excellent field replacement for McGee.[66] And as one of his subordinates would later describe Vanderpool, "He was an artillery officer by training but a guerrilla at heart."[67]

Despite the appearance of progress incumbent with these new organizational alignments, little if any operational improvements were actually realized in either FEC or Eighth Army's unconventional warfare campaign. The alignments did, however, set the stage six months later for the jurisdictional confrontation that would poison FEC-CIA relations for the remainder of the war. For in early December 1951,

FEC-Intelligence dictated yet another series of sweeping organizational changes that finally ignited the long-smoldering feud over which American organization would control the overall unconventional warfare campaign behind Communist lines.

"Mobs for Jobs"

> The basic order establishing CCRAK . . . almost completely ignored the Seoul Agreement and threw out almost all of the points insisted upon by CIA in Washington. The tactics adopted by officers of G2 Section, GHQ, therefore, seemed to be to win command and control over CIA, then to present a *fait accompli* to the Air Force and Navy.

As 1951 progressed, so did the proliferation of UN reconnaissance agents, spies, partisans, saboteurs, frogmen, and airmen, operating in North Korea. As briefly noted earlier, both FEC and the CIA were fighting their own separate wars in the enemy's rear area, and doing so with a minimum of cooperation and coordination. But it wasn't just the "military vs. the civilians." Even within FEC the situation was spiraling out of control as a bizarre collection of bureaucratic "bandit chiefs" pursued their individual wars against the Communists' rear area sanctuaries. It was the kind of internal disorder from which only the Communists were benefiting as the war progressed.

In FEC, the addition of the partisan warfare mission had never relieved the Liaison Group of its original commitment to the still-active KLO program. On the seas surrounding North Korea, the U.S. Navy raided coastal targets by both submarine and surface ships carrying a combination of U.S. Marine Corps Reconnaissance Force specialists, Underwater Demolition Team swimmers, British Commandos, and CIA partisans. For its part the U.S. Air Force roamed much of the same territory by air, land, and sea under the leadership of "Mister" Nichols, a former motorpool sergeant with very close personal ties to the president of South Korea. And of course all this activity took place in addition to whatever covert programs the South Korean government pursued, with and without the knowledge of the Americans.

To quote a British Special Forces expression heard during World War II, the UN unconventional warfare campaign had degenerated by late 1951 into a "mobs for jobs" world in which competing bureaucracies offered at best only a token nod toward the "strategic" unconventional warfare campaign. The fundamental problem of course was that no strategic unconventional warfare campaign had ever been developed, despite eighteen months of combat, thousands of UN casualties, and the departure of MacArthur and his clique. Clearly the time was long overdue to sort out once and for all what singular organization,

FEC or the CIA, would be given the authority to develop a strategic campaign and control all UN forces operating in North Korea.

A belated but promising start in this direction was achieved in Washington during the summer of 1951, just as the first UN-Communist negotiations to end the war were beginning in Korea. Perhaps thinking the war would soon be over, CIA director Walter Bedell Smith reached agreement with senior Department of the Army officers that all unconventional warfare activities on the peninsula would be subordinated to the FEC commander (Ridgway) "while actual combat continued in Korea."[68] Still new to the Cold War art of negotiating with Communists, Smith (and many others) could not envision hostilities continuing two full years after negotiations had begun.

What army and CIA officials in Washington left undetermined was the critical issue regarding the manner in which Ridgway would exercise the new authority vested in him with their agreements. Would he appoint FEC-Intelligence or the CIA to function as the senior executive agent for all unconventional warfare operations in Korea? To gather input for this hotly debated and divisive issue, General Ridgway directed FEC-Intelligence to host a series of high-level conferences, held in Seoul on 21–22 October 1951, with senior representatives from the Eighth Army, Far East Air Forces (FEAF), Seventh Fleet, and, of course, the CIA.[69]

The tense meetings concluded with the CIA representatives clearly believing they had at long last won their bureaucratic battle with FEC's "Intelligence Mafia." Based on the merits of their case and with open support from the navy and in particular the air force commanders, the civilians confidently awaited Ridgway's decision to name the CIA as FEC's executive agency for all unconventional warfare in North Korea. The CIA's historical records describe the general outcome of the Seoul meetings as seen through the eyes of the Agency representatives who were there: "CIA officers felt that General Ridgway [FEC], Gen Van Fleet [Eighth Army], Gen Everest [Fifth Air Force], and Admiral Martin [Seventh Fleet] were of the same opinion [supporting the CIA's position]; while, on the other hand, the [Intelligence] officers of G2 Eighth Army and G2 GHQ [FEC] were of a different opinion."[70]

Five weeks later the confident CIA representatives were stunned to learn of Ridgway's decision. Without further discussion or advance notice to the CIA, air force, or navy, FEC-Intelligence published an order establishing an entirely new, U.S. Army–controlled organization to run all unconventional warfare operations. Designated Covert, Clandestine, and Related Activities—Korea (CCRAK; pronounced *sea*-crack), it would report directly to the CIA's longtime nemesis,

FEC-Intelligence. If the decision itself was poorly received in many quarters, the manner in which it was accomplished created such bad blood within the CIA that for the remainder of the war it seriously tainted FEC-CIA relations: "The basic order establishing CCRAK, dated 28 November 1951, almost completely ignored the Seoul Agreement and threw out almost all of the points insisted upon by CIA in Washington. The tactics adopted by officers of G2 Section, GHQ, therefore, seemed to be to win command and control over CIA, then to present a *fait accompli* to the Air Force and Navy."[71]

Not only would the CIA *not* become the executive agency for all unconventional warfare activities, but by its very organizational setup CCRAK itself was fatally flawed in its capability to meet the one goal upon which everyone agreed: achieving effective control of the independent "mobs" running unconventional warfare activities in North Korea. Duplicating the errors that crippled McGee's "Attrition Headquarters" the previous January, FEC assigned CCRACK the responsibility to control these activities without delegating the all-important command authority to effectively exercise this responsibility. In a bureaucratic blaze of "reorganizing for optimum efficiency," FEC had achieved little more than changing the face of the central problem. However, this time FEC was not dealing with a single Eighth Army colonel it could control.

The powerful bureaucracy which bore FEC the most ill was of course the CIA, which since July 1951 had fielded sizable partisan forces in Korea under the cover name of the Joint Advisory Commission—Korea (JACK).[72] Effective with CCRAK's activation on 10 December 1951, JACK's operations became officially subordinated to CCRAK control; or so FEC obviously thought. In reality the picture was considerably different: "CCRAK had no explicit command authority over JACK. JACK was expected but not required to coordinate CIA operations. FEC appointed the CCRAK commander, and the Documents Research Division [CIA liaison office to FEC staff] appointed the deputy commander."[73]

Beyond the predictable turf jealousies, the heart of the CIA's resentment was based on its fundamental conclusion that FEC's army intelligence officers had no real understanding of, or even real talent for, the nature of behind-the-lines work: "It became clear to CIA officers in this theater that the appreciation of Army negotiators of the mission, tradecraft, security devices, and potentialities of CIA was far different from the appreciation held by CIA officers. Army negotiators . . . felt that CIA should now become just another extension of the G2 Section in Korea[,] . . . a collection agency for tactical information . . . whose unconventional warfare program should be guerrillas used in close support of Eighth Army."[74]

No doubt CIA headquarters in Washington suffered the full howl from outraged JACK officers. In the end, however, the Agency's senior leaders chose not to challenge the FEC decision. Perhaps thinking of its larger, worldwide responsibilities and the political cost of a major brawl with the Pentagon, CIA headquarters in Washington chose not to challenge Ridgway's decision. Still smarting from the outcome, however, CIA officers in Korea quickly noted CCRAK's lack of command authority to actually control Agency operations on the peninsula.

At the end of this bruising and confusing turf battle FEC appeared on paper at least to have accomplished two major realignments. It gained military oversight of most CIA operations in North Korea, and in a parallel move it assumed control of the partisan forces from Eighth Army headquarters. With its organization charts thus tidied up, Far East Command staff officers turned their attention to the subject of CCRAK itself.

Perhaps to tease his CIA colleagues, Col. Washington M. Ives of the army, CCRAK's first director, began his tour "by placing a sign in ten-inch letters in front of his office in Seoul announcing the new COVERT, CLANDESTINE, AND RELATED ACTIVITIES—KOREA organization.[75] The revealing unit title was not the best of cover stories for a supposedly secret organization, but fortunately relations between the new CCRAK leader and local CIA operatives were for the moment at least better than those between their respective superiors: "Astounded CIA staffers in Korea appreciating the humor of the situation, helped their old friend the former . . . [U.S. partisan] commander, now the new Commander CCRAK, to improvise the euphemistic title 'Combined Command Reconnaissance Activities—Korea.'"[76]

But whatever brief moment of humor may have sparked at CCRAK headquarters in early December, long-term bitterness still ran deep within Agency officers in Korea. Though both CCRAK and JACK headquarters were located in Seoul, CCRAK took over the former First Methodist Church and JACK took offices some distance away in the Traymore Hotel.[77] Oddly enough, the fact that some JACK staffers were former or even active-duty army officers on detached duty to the Agency seemed to have little effect on reducing this military-civilian rancor. JACK's first director under CCRAK, for example, Maj. John K. Singlaub, recalls the general CIA attitude he encountered in the Traymore Hotel upon his arrival for assignment in January 1952: "I quickly discovered that our archival for personnel, funding, air support, and above all, mission authorization was a hodgepodge intelligence operation managed by FEC called Combined Command for Reconnaissance Activities, Korea (CCRAK)."[78]

Other than its intended impact on Agency operations, the most significant change wrought by CCRAK's activation was that for the first time in the war, FEC would assume direct control (from the Eighth Army) of the partisan force. Unfortunately, the partisans' combat potential remained hobbled by FEC's continued insistence that this thousands-strong combat force still be "managed" by its Intelligence Directorate rather than commanded in the field. During all of these organizational adjustments the North Korean partisans remained blissfully unaware of what these changes signified to them. But as one of their American advisors at the time observed, "This [change from Eighth Army Operations to FEC Intelligence Directorate] was a clear signal to everyone involved . . . that the partisans were no longer considered a viable [combat] resource. Their primary mission no longer was to prepare for a counteroffensive. It was to collect intelligence and do what they could to force the North Korean Army and the Chinese to hasten the peace process."[79]

The "clear signal" that the partisans were considered more of an intelligence-gathering force than a combat capability lasted barely six months before a new FEC commander reversed his predecessor's signal. Replacing Ridgway in May 1952, Gen. Mark Clark soon tasked CCRAK to begin an intensive partisan recruiting campaign, the goal of which was nothing less than doubling the partisan force to twenty thousand by March 1953, then doubling it still again by July of the same year.[80] The latter goal was never achieved, as the war came to a close in the summer of 1953, but figures for that April showed a wartime-high strength of 21,385 partisans on the UN's roster.[81]

As the records show, both Clark and CCRAK were intent on using this greatly expanded partisan movement as a combat, not intelligence-gathering, force.[82] This perception of the partisans as fighters is clearly conveyed in operational plans prepared by CCRAK in 1952 in which the partisans would be expected "to attack on order with all combat effectiveness" should large-scale conventional warfare break out the following year.[83]

Perhaps rethinking the issue of command and control for a partisan force of the proposed size, Clark subsequently transferred control of the partisans from the Intelligence Directorate to CCRAK.[84] These changes, made in December 1952, created the partisan organization that remained essentially in place for the remainder of the war. Whatever the motivation for these late-war changes, however, the decisions came years after the opportunity to exploit the full partisan potential had been lost. Colonel McGee's vision in the winter of 1950–51 for a combat-effective partisan force supporting U.S. goals had been dependent on three mutually supporting organizational criteria, only one of which was belatedly achieved.

The first criteria required that the partisan combat force be commanded as a field force, not managed by headquarters staff officers. This was never achieved. The second criteria required that this proposed field command operate as a combat force, taking its orders through an operations (not intelligence) directorate as did conventional combat commands. This too was never achieved. The third mandated that this operational control be exercised at the highest possible (i.e., FEC) level. Such control did begin in December 1951, but FEC's failure to establish the first two criteria effectively negated the advantages accrued with the transfer of the partisans from Eighth Army to FEC control.

The most authoritative postwar study of the partisan effort, conducted by a Johns Hopkins University team on government contract, concludes in part, "Although Army doctrine concerning guerrilla warfare was not explicit with respect to what to do in a limited war situation[,] . . . applicable doctrine existed on such matters as provision of incentives, status of partisans, and organizational arrangements, but it was apparently ignored or neglected."[85]

Despite these crippling organizational problems the North Korean partisans in the field fought their personal war against the Communists from beginning to end with courage born of their desperate desire to return to their homeland. Early in the war, they proudly came to call themselves "Donkeys," and like their namesake, they proved as stubborn and hard as the ground they fought and died over.

Donkeys

> The D-4 leader called on his [five-man] suicide squad to advance upon it. . . . When they reached the wire . . . four of them opened fire. The fifth man crawled under the wire and moved up to the pillbox[,] . . . pulled the pins on two grenades and holding one in each hand, the man walked right into the position. This knocked out the position.

The majority of the anti-Communist refugees fleeing North Korea in the winter of 1950–51 came from Hwanghae Province, more than six thousand square miles of fertile agricultural land often described as the breadbasket of North Korea. Before the war, this economically and politically important province was estimated to contain a population numbering nearly two million people. But what should have been an equally fertile recruiting ground for North Korea's Communists after the departure of the Japanese in 1945 turned out instead to be one of their biggest frustrations. For as one postwar study report concluded in a masterpiece of understatement, "During the period 1945 to 1950 there is evidence that the communists, both native and imported, failed to enlist the sympathies of important segments of the population of the area."[86]

Included in these "important segments" were the thousands who publicly rallied around the UN forces surging northward through Hwanghae Province in the fall of 1950. And as noted earlier, it was these same groups that found themselves fighting and fleeing for their lives during the following weeks as the Chinese drove southward through Hwanghae that winter. The refugees' violent exodus to the west coast came to an end in January 1951, as the Communists sealed off the coastal exit routes following a series of skirmishes with the poorly armed refugees. The Communists' internal security forces immediately turned inward to eliminate the trapped remnants of the rebellion in Hwanghae. But even as they did, thousands of refugees had already found safe haven under the umbrella of naval gunfire provided by the allied navies protecting the offshore islands to which they had escaped.

Moreover, the largest of these islands teeming with refugees, Paengnyong-do, would soon become the major anti-Communist bastion anywhere north of the thirty-eighth parallel. As has since proven the case in other anti-Communist movements, a fair number of those among the refugees were from the educated class, in this case leaders in their communities in Hwanghae. And once on the islands these businessmen, teachers, mayors, and police officials quickly emerged as leaders in the fledgling partisan movement. Interestingly, most of these leaders rarely involved themselves directly in combat on the mainland, a fact viewed without resentment by most of their followers. Leaving combat leadership to trusted subordinates, these officials functioned more as politicians concerned with developing political support on the mainland, recruiting future partisans, and tending to the needs of the fighters and their families living on the islands.[87]

Once in power, such leaders had, literally, life and death control over the fate of their groups. To balance this power, those leaders failing to measure up to the group's expectations were usually demoted back into the ranks for their shortcomings, though the punishment on a few occasions proved much more severe. In January 1952, for example, Chang Sok Lin, the leader of one such group, was assassinated by his followers after "he started at length to have a love of material and money."[88]

Partisans boarding junks for a raid against Communist positions along North Korea's western coastline. Sail-powered junks were obviously—and dangerously—dependent on favorable winds to make their getaway from the coastline following such raids. *Courtesy of Charlie Norton*

If the complex political motivations of the partisan leaders presented the American advisors with difficult challenges, at least the refugees from Hwanghae Province presented a surprisingly homogeneous front. Almost every subgroup from the province was comprised of people from the same town or county. Women were estimated to represent only 6 to 8 percent of the partisan groups and did not participate in a direct combatant role.[89] In addition to their traditional family roles, wives, mothers, and sisters of the partisans often worked as nurses and sometimes radio operators in the base camp areas.[90] In contrast to these relatively homogeneous groups, however, the makeup of the refugee populations encountered on the islands much farther north was considerably more complex.

Few Americans traveled to the northernmost islands near the North Korea–China border. But UN and church groups delivered relief supplies to the refugees on these islands, without UN military protection and, surprisingly, without much interference from the North Koreans. And counted among the first of these relief agency groups to arrive in the winter of 1950–51 was Sergeant Manbahadur, a Nepalese Ghurka[91] medic fluent in both the Japanese and Chinese languages. Manbahadur recalls the disparity of the refugees he encountered that winter:

"The groups we met were considerably different from each other. Most spoke Chinese, not Korean. Some were well educated Christians, while others were simply political dissidents. . . . Still others were criminals avoided by all the other groups. The criminals made the best fighters after we trained them to use the British and Japanese World War II weapons we gave them. There were some South Korean Navy people there too, though I never knew what they were doing."[92]

For their part, the Americans to the south were even less prepared for the cultural shock that came with their arrival to the islands. It was during their first visits to these camps that the American advisors on Paengnyong-do heard, to their surprise and curiosity, the Koreans referring to themselves with both pride and humor as Donkeys. One version of the tale suggests that the name came about as the Koreans received their first American field radios, which required an individual to sit in an awkward position while hand cranking the generator set. To the partisans, the position reminded them of a man astride a donkey. Another version is that the partisans adopted the virtues of the donkey—endurance, strength, but also meanness—as those which best typified their fighting spirit. In either case, the term stuck and the nickname soon became the official title of most fighting groups.[93] Some groups also took other names, such as White Tigers, a title that reflected both their high regard for courage as well as the spirituality and immortality symbolized in Korean lore by the tiger.[94]

Paengnyong-do was less than an hour from Seoul by air transport, but by any other standard it was a long way from help should the Communists make a concerted effort to overrun its limited defenses. For while the island was 125 miles from the main UN positions, it was only 15 miles from the North Korean mainland. The one "airfield" on Paengnyong-do was available only at low tide, as it was nothing more than a good length of hard-packed beach sand capable of supporting the weight of the resupply transport that routinely flew to the base. Former partisan advisor to the Donkey 4 unit, 1st Lt. Ben S. Malcom, describes life on the bleak island in *White Tigers: My Secret War in North Korea:* "Paengnyong-do was barren, rock-strewn, and wind-blasted. The northwest winds sweeping down from Manchuria and across the Yellow Sea had wiped the landscape clean of virtually all vegetation. At times the wind was so vicious it ripped up tents and toppled hastily constructed buildings."[95]

Though these crudely built facilities on Paengnyong-do served as the main partisan headquarters and supply base, the Donkey leaders kept their units (including families) on a number of other islands closer still to the dangerous mainland. It was on these islands that

The desperate plight of the island-based refugees was reflected in part by the U.S. Army practice of issuing relatively heavy U.S.-made weapons, like this M1 Garand rifle, to every male old enough to carry them. *Courtesy of Charlie Norton*

they trained with their new weapons while eagerly awaiting word from their advisors that the next UN offensive, the one that would take them back to Hwanghae, had begun. And with the same enthusiasm, the swift-moving McGee took less than two weeks after his assignment to the partisan effort to produce an aggressive plan for employing the partisans in the field once the UN's "big push" began.

Though badly disappointed in FEC's refusal to accept his recommendation for a Combined Attrition Warfare Headquarters, McGee nevertheless prepared within a matter of days a proposal for Operational Plan Able.[96] His plan envisioned three separate operational partisan elements, two of which would complete an accelerated (two to three week) training program on their island sanctuaries before beginning operations in North Korea in support of Eighth Army's upcoming offensive.[97] Also coordinated with the spring offensive would be the actions of the third partisan element, a special unit inserted by parachute for special sabotage missions.

The first and largest of McGee's Plan Able elements was headquartered at Leopard Base, the name given in March of that year to the partisan headquarters on Paengnyong-do. U.S. support to the plan was especially thin, considering that the Eighth Army initially provided only eleven[98] U.S. Army personnel to run the operations, training, and communications at Leopard Base, or "Bromide-Baker" as it was known by its radio call sign.[99] In addition, approximately one hundred South Korean sailors and marines provided base security on the island.[100] But the primary protection for the island came initially from the U.S. warships patrolling the Yellow Sea around Paengnyong-do and the other partisan-held islands.

This naval shield was further strengthened the same month Leopard Base got its name, following a conference aboard HMS *Belfast* in which British Commonwealth naval units agreed to add their support to the partisans.[101] In repeated instances during the following two years this naval support proved vital to the survival of the island bases and was a major player in the partisan raids on the mainland. Especially noted for outstanding performance and repeatedly praised with unusual emotion in the American advisors' wartime reports were the Commonwealth and Royal Netherlands warships. And as partisan advisor Archie Johnston added with a twist of humor, the ships had more to offer than just firepower: "One day when I went aboard [Her Majesty's Australian Ship] *Condamine* dressed in my usual wool sweater, field trousers, field cap and jump boots, Captain [Lt. Cdr. R. C. Savage] said 'Care for a bath, Johnny?' I replied 'No thanks. I'm in a bit of a hurry.' He then sniffed the air and repeated 'Care for a bath Johnny?' I took the well-placed hint and the welcome bath."[102]

McGee's plan further divided the two island-based partisan elements into "base units" and "mobile units." As called for in Plan Able, the base units trained and staged short-term raids from their island bases while the mobile units operated on the mainland for extended periods of time.[103] Finally the third partisan element, the Pusan-based airborne unit, would provide "special airborne sabotage agents and also liaison officers for coordinating partisan elements with the U.S. Eighth Army's tactical units."[104]

Within a month, McGee's relentless pace began producing results. That February the proposed airborne element, code-named Baker Section, was formed near Pusan, and in March a Donkey unit conducted the first major partisan raid against the mainland.[105] In contrast to these accomplishments, however, McGee's attempts to establish the second partisan element, the east coast partisans, proved a far more difficult nut to crack even for someone with his tenacity. As the energetic colonel quickly came to understand, the east coast situation comprised geographical, bureaucratic, and cultural problems not found with the Hwanghae Province partisans to the west.

The east coast islands eventually selected by McGee's staff for partisan sanctuaries lay even farther behind enemy lines than did Paengnyong-do. But even this problem was eclipsed by the bigger problem regarding the scarcity of suitable islands from which to choose. After discarding most of the few islands available as too small or too close to the mainland, McGee's staff grudgingly selected Nan-do, a fifteen-acre island approximately six miles offshore and ten miles south of the port city of Wonsan. Nan-do served as the forward base for what would soon be dubbed Task Force Kirkland.[106] As with the west coast partisans, the Kirkland force was intended to raid coastal targets and assist downed UN pilots when called upon. Former Kirkland advisor Ed Evanhoe describes Nan-do as if through the eyes of a disappointed realtor: "Nan-do is little more than three hundred yards across east to west at the northern end, its widest part. From the north end it is roughly six hundred yards to the southern end. The only landing is a small bay on the west side . . . filled with large rocks that make it dangerous to land even when the sea is calm."[107]

Another problem quickly loomed for McGee and the new partisan forces, one that traced its roots back to the rationale for creating CCRAK in the first place. As it turned out, someone else was already running partisan and intelligence operations along North Korea's eastern coastline. And that someone else was none other than JACK, the CIA team in Korea that promptly took strong exception upon hearing of McGee's plans for the east coast partisans. In particular they argued that McGee's proposed area of operations for the partisans, the entire coastline of North Korea from the UN front lines all the way north to the border with the Soviet Union, would compromise their ongoing operations in the area.[108]

In response to JACK's adamant protests, the Eighth Army subsequently reduced the Kirkland partisans' area of operations to less than half that of McGee's original plan: the coastline extending southward from Wonsan to the UN's main line of resistance near the thirty-eighth parallel. For the remainder of the war, Kirkland remained south of Wonsan, generally operating within a fifty-mile radius of the port; JACK continued to operate from Wonsan north to the Soviet border.[109] Having little choice but to acquiesce on the issue, McGee put another disappointment behind him and turned to the more immediate issue of finding partisans to fill Kirkland's ranks. He chose not to take the obvious step of transplanting a number of west coast partisans, as much of their operational success came from their cultural homogeneity and familiarity with their main hunting ground, Hwanghae Province. In the end, McGee's search for Kirkland manpower led him to another one of those strange groups that seem to emerge from nowhere in the midst of war.

This particular group, the Miryang Guerrilla Battalion, was a special unit of the South Korean army comprised almost totally of North Korean refugees and defectors already in South Korea when the war broke out.[110] Unbeknownst to McGee when he approached the South Korean army for permission to recruit volunteers from the battalion, their officers already viewed the entire battalion with considerable contempt. Distrust of the battalion's North Korean roots, agitated further by the battalion's failure in a recently concluded operation, had put the unit on the South Korean army's unofficial auction block, and at a very negotiable price. Evanhoe describes the battalion's unusual transfer to the Eighth Army: "When McGee requested permission to recruit two hundred volunteers from the unit, ROK Army Headquarters used his request to quietly transfer the *entire battalion* to Eighth Army. The [transfer] agreement . . . was written in Korean. Not until late June, when the guerrilla commander . . . demanded pay, rations, and supplies for his men, did [Eighth Army] realize the entire Miryang Guerrilla Battalion belonged to them."[111]

C'est la guerre! In this case McGee was handed a bunch of "seconds" that, for the most part, were destined to become a pale imitation of their west coast counterparts. Low morale among the Koreans was a problem from the start, a situation not helped much with the guerrilla discovery that the used U.S. Army fatigues issued to them had the letters "PW" painted on the back of the shirts. The proud Koreans promptly dyed the shirts black to hide the letters, and from this time forward became known as the "black shirt troops." Another U.S. Army miscue contributing to the low Korean morale was the American expectation—based on ignorance of the Korean culture—that Thailand rice and dried cuttlefish would, alone, suffice to feed the guerrillas.[112] It was just one more example of the mistakes perpetrated by U.S. soldiers posted to advisory duty, without adequate preparation for this difficult role.

With the manning problem seemingly resolved for the moment, Kirkland advisor 1st Lt. William S. Harrison, a World War II paratroop veteran, ran the Miryang Guerrillas through a short training program before moving the first group to Nan-do that May. Once on the island, they established a base complete with the all-important helicopter landing pad and communications center, the latter operating with the radio call sign "Monte-Carlo."[113] Less than thirty days later, Kirkland's partisans mounted their first operation on the mainland in support of large-scale attacks by the South Korean I and III Corps.[114] It was a bizarre event even by the crude partisan standards of the time, as Kirkland partisan Pak Chang Oun recalled the raid many years later: "The night was utmost dark and foggy. They [partisans and Communist soldiers] could hardly recognize each other and at last all got mixed up together. They were so close they had to fight hand to hand[,] . . . pistols and swords. . . . At last they [were able to distinguish friend from foe] only by hair. . . . Theirs [Communists] were short cut[,] . . . our's were long cut. . . . [The partisans] had to feel [a stranger's] head before taking some action."[115]

Not surprisingly, the startled North Koreans responded sharply to this new intrusion deep in their rear sector. On 3 August 1951, exactly two months to the day after Kirkland's "inaugural" mission, a North Korean assault force succeeded in overrunning Sol-som Island, the partisan's closest outpost to the mainland. Only half the size of tiny Nan-do, the island was only eight hundred yards from the North Korean mainland.

By that December the small Kirkland force had virtually ceased to exist as a result of both combat losses and desertions.[116] Reconstituted the following March, the force resumed small-scale operations against the mainland before further augmentation led to its redesignation in December 1952 as the 3d Partisan Infantry Regiment. This expansion proved little more than a paper exercise, however, as by the spring of 1953 widespread desertion once again rendered Kirkland ineffective. But these events took place nearly three years into a war that at the beginning seemed so full of possibilities for both the desperate partisans and their idealistic advisors.

Despite the wretched living conditions that prevailed from the start on the islands, and the obvious dangers awaiting the partisans on the mainland, optimism was the order of the day in early 1951 for both the North Koreans and their American advisors. As Malcom recalls, "McGee and the partisan leaders firmly believed they were the vanguard of a new phase of the war, one that would include substantial use of unconventional warfare tactics in support of a major counter-offensive in the spring of 1951."[117]

Thus armed with this personal optimism, McGee continued with mounting anxiety to press his superiors with the same questions his North Korean partisans were pressing on him: when would the spring offensive begin? When could the partisans hope to free their homeland? As spring turned to summer and the first armistice talks began that July, an exasperated officer finally gave McGee the answer he must already have feared in his heart, "Never!"[118] As McGee later wrote, "The answer 'never' to me immediately suggested the calamity of our [North Korean partisans and their families] who had been forsaken by the United States, their Free World leader. A forsaking by a cease-fire that was a sentence of them to death by a subsequent communist methodically conducted extermination[;] . . . a sentence that I was never permitted to defend them."[119]

The UN's implicit decision not to resume the offensive in the spring of 1951 had both immediate and long-term consequences for the partisans. Militarily it was obvious that they would not be returning to the mainland in force anytime soon, if ever. Politically, it left a huge question mark hanging over the fate of this armed, angry, and stateless people. Falsely blaming himself for the plight of the partisans, McGee left Korea as his tour ended that July, an embittered man.

As for the partisans themselves, their morale went into an understandable slump. Though most continued to fight well, only the most optimistic among them still hoped that the winds of war would somehow turn again in their favor. But as history shows, little if anything again turned in favor of the partisans for the remainder of the war. If the partisans' reaction to the "indefinitely postponed" offensive was predictable, that was far more than could be said for the reaction to the same "understanding" by the Eighth Army and FEC staffs.

Faced with the awkward question of what to do with the thousands-strong partisan force it had trained and equipped, one might have expected a thorough American reexamination of the whole partisan issue. But in "UN Partisan Warfare in Korea: 1951–1954," quite likely the most authoritative postwar study on the partisan war in Korea, Johns Hopkins University researchers describe the American response: "None of the evidence canvassed shows a general reappraisal of objectives for the partisan forces in latter 1951 (when the basic change in the character of the war became apparent), either by Eighth Army, which directed the partisans until December 1951, or by the theater agencies [FEC], which assumed responsibility thereafter."[120]

If the Eighth Army (and later FEC) turned away from the awkward question, it may well have been because the partisans had already become a political hot potato. Ostensibly UN combatants, they were in reality little more than wards of the Americans, stateless warriors belonging to neither North nor South Korea, wearing whatever uniforms were available, not even issued serial numbers or identification tags by the U.S. Army. As for the South Korean army and its government, both remained individually and collectively wary of the partisans' political loyalties, accepting their presence only grudgingly and even then only after the cessation of hostilities in the summer of 1953.[121]

Given the failure of the Eighth Army to update its plan for the partisan role after the beginning of armistice talks in the summer of 1951, Vanderpool had little choice but to continue with McGee's original goals. Outlined in four separate but interrelated categories these goals remained:

1. Defend Eighth Army's left flank and divert approximately 150,000 Communist troops away from the Main Line of Resistance;
2. Sabotage enemy supplies, communications, port, road, and railroad facilities;
3. Gather and forward intelligence concerning the enemy order of battle, troop movements, supply routes, gun positions, and military installations;
4. Support the defense of strategic partisan-held islands.[122]

As noted earlier, Vanderpool, like McGee, learned the basics of unconventional warfare while fighting the Japanese in the Philippines. And in bringing his personal experiences to war he certainly proved no less committed to the partisans than did his predecessor. Malcom provides further insight into the character of this man who in July 1951 became the commander of the entire partisan army in all but name: "Vanderpool's ideas were at times innovative, at times ingenious, at times downright diabolical. He sought to make the most of what resources were available to him in spite of the confusion over command and control. He was going to do what he could to make the operation a success."[123]

Vanderpool's enthusiasm and obvious concern for the partisans' welfare did wonders to restore their morale after the summer of 1951, while on a more pragmatic level his energy soon led to an increase in the tempo of partisan attacks against the mainland. From this time forward, until Clark's decision to accelerate recruiting in mid-1952, partisan strength remained fairly stable. One U.S. intelligence summary places partisan strength during the start of this period at just over eight thousand[124] in September 1951, with an additional two thousand service troops and 550 intelligence agents and saboteurs on the rolls.[125] But apparently these were not the only anti-Communist forces on the mainland. During a wartime interview with Donkey 15 leader Mr. Kim Ung Soo, the partisan referred to his unknown allies in the following terms: "There are some other friendly guerrillas operating up there [North Korea]. I . . . know the location of bands of CCF soldiers who are making trouble against the CCF. There are quite a few deserted CCF soldiers. . . . I have sent several letters in Chinese to get contact with them, but in vain."[126]

Many of these deserters appeared to be fighting simply for food, clothing, and sheer survival, as the Donkey 15 leader guessed that only 30 percent of these unknown bands were "active anti-Communists." Whatever their personal motivations, those prepared to join the partisans, including even former enemies, were screened and given a chance to prove their loyalty. Leopard Base commander Maj. Tom Dye described his surprise upon learning just how far the partisans were willing to go in this regard: "Donkey-11 captured a NKA squad leader, [and] signed him up. Headquarters didn't know about him until 30 days later. [When I] asked 'Why keep him?' I got the answer 'He's a good fighter. Had already been on 7 fights, in his own uniform'!"[127]

Those who passed the Donkeys' scrutiny, like this former NKPA soldier, were brought into the fold without further reservation. Those who didn't pass such scrutiny—Dye estimated that one percent of the partisans were infiltrators—were promptly "liquidated."[128] But despite the North Korean army's obvious inside knowledge of the Donkey organizations, the partisans were still able to strike at will during this stage of the war. And strike they did, judging from the Eighth Army statistics on their operations.

From May to November 1951 the partisans claimed to have killed, wounded, or captured more than fourteen thousand of the enemy in 710 separate encounters.[129] Many in the Eighth Army regarded these numbers exaggerated to an unknown extent, but the bigger problem noted was that even if the numbers were accurate, "they were . . . inflicted on an enemy who apparently considered manpower as cheap."[130] Limiting still further the impact on the enemy was that almost all of these casualties occurred near the coast, far from the scene of decisive combat on the peninsula.

Even as early as 1951, the North Korean army was taking most of its casualties from shallow-penetration, commando-type raids launched by the partisans from their island bases. Soon this raiding pattern became virtually the only tactic available to the partisans for the duration of the war. For as the Communists themselves gradually lost their fear of another UN offensive, they began releasing combat units from the main line of resistance to reinforce their rear-area security forces. With increasing frequency, the partisans found themselves engaging not rear-area security units, but heavily armed infantry formations. And given their mutual hatred, the fighting between the two groups was savage.

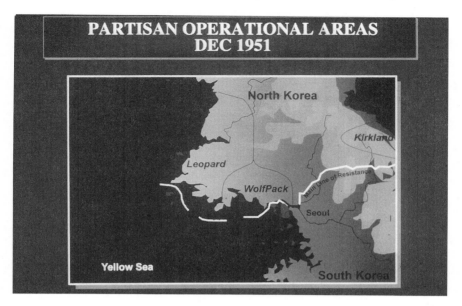

PARTISAN OPERATIONAL AREAS DEC 1951

U.S. Army–directed partisans were most active along the western coast of North Korea, in operational areas designated Leopard and Wolfpack. CIA-directed partisans were concentrated along the eastern coast, though the army also maintained a small partisan force in the Kirkland-designated area. *Courtesy of Wayne Thompson*

Whether fighting under the names White Tigers or Donkeys, the ferocity of the partisans' combat went to a fanaticism seldom found in any army. Many of the Donkey units actually included a designated "suicide squad" comprised of volunteers who proudly fulfilled this role at the cost of their lives.[131] Advisor Malcom witnessed this extreme commitment firsthand while accompanying 120 partisans on a Donkey 4 raiding party to the mainland on 14 July 1952. As Malcom and a group of partisans became pinned down by an enemy machine gun, he watched the Donkey 4 leader react to the crisis: "The D-4 leader called on his [five-man] suicide squad to advance upon it. . . . When they reached the wire . . . four of them opened fire. The fifth man crawled under the wire and moved up to the pillbox[,] . . . pulled the pins on two grenades and holding one in each hand, the man walked right into the position. This knocked out the position."[132]

Perhaps one explanation for extreme behavior that went far beyond simple patriotism can be found in the postwar interviews provided by the partisans themselves. As these American studies confirmed, partisan combat with their Communist adversaries on the mainland was truly a vicious, "no quarter given or asked" affair: "In battle they [the partisans] exerted every effort to bring off their wounded. . . . Capture by the enemy is a fate to be avoided at all costs. Three instances were cited of officers committing suicide rather than be taken. One rescue party found some captured partisans so brutally tortured that it was impossible to remove them. The victims were promptly dispatched along with their tormentors. Sentiment does not override prudence in such a crisis."[133]

Such was the bleak "victory or death" life of the island partisans throughout the war. But as desperate as their combat proved during raids along the coast, the geography over which they fought did offer one small advantage. The proximity and availability of air and in particular naval support usually held an escape route open, should circumstances dictate a fighting withdrawal seaward from the mainland. Even that small advantage, however, was denied those partisans who penetrated by parachute deep into North Korea's wild interior. If such a seemingly small tactical difference on a peninsula seems unworthy of note to some, in North Korea it proved large enough to spell the difference between survival and annihilation for the two separate partisan groups.

Expendables

> Three of the teams were lost immediately. . . . Mustang IV team [operated] for about 6 days before its members were captured or killed. . . . No further word was received [after one radio report]. . . . Teams were lost immediately. . . . Not one member of the above teams is known to have extracted. . . . The Hurricane team, apparently compromised, was lost soon after it was dropped. . . . None of the partisans involved ever returned.

The Baker Section briefly noted earlier was activated to train then insert "special airborne sabotage agents" against carefully selected, high-priority targets. And though it was the training aspect of this mission that consumed most of the unit's time and scarce assets during 1951, Baker did launch two significant airborne insertions into North Korea during that year.[134] That proved unfortunate, for even with the benefit of a half-century of hindsight, the Virginia I and Spitfire missions still appear to be a sorry spectacle of U.S. Army leadership at its worst.

The Eighth Army launched "Virginia I" on 15 March 1951, with four U.S. Army Rangers and twenty Koreans recruited from the South Korean army's officer candidate school.[135] The ranger volunteers were sent to Baker Section only ten days before the mission launch date, then lost the following six days of team preparation time before finally meeting their Korean teammates. To make matters worse, Eighth Army mission planners removed the team leader—the previously introduced 1st Lt. Bob Brewer—only hours before mission launch, belatedly realizing that his capture could lead to the compromise of secret information related to Operation Aviary.[136] Having thus denied the group any chance to develop the team cohesion indispensable for such a high-risk mission, Baker Section then parachuted the leaderless team into an unmarked drop zone, at night and in deep snow.

After being subjected to subzero winds blowing through the aircraft's open exit door for the entire 250-mile flight into North Korea, the Virginia I team finally parachuted into the freezing night, 8 miles south of the correct drop zone. Ranger Martin Watson came down in the middle of a small village, waking in the process all of the dogs and most of its inhabitants, who took due notice of the big Caucasian intruder. After exhaustive slogging for hours through deep snow, the team arrived at its target, a supposedly remote and lightly defended railroad tunnel 30 miles inland from the North Korean coastline. Following a brief reconnaissance, the team discovered that its target was in fact so heavily defended as to make suicidal any attempt at blowing it up.

For the next two weeks, the cold and exhausted team successfully evaded Communist search parties as it moved eastward through the mountains toward its extraction point on the east coast. On 30 March, U.S. Navy helicopters extracted three of the rangers under enemy fire, before North Korean gunners terminated the extraction by downing one of the helicopters. Ranger Watson, helicopter pilot Lt. (jg) John H. Thornton, and five partisans escaped the extraction site in the subsequent confusion, but without the team radio or any other means of arranging a second extraction attempt. The doomed mission was over, though it took another full week before the tragedy came to its final, inevitable conclusion.

Watson and Thornton were captured, interrogated, and brutally tortured before being sent to North Korea's infamous POW camps. Both survived the war, though Watson was among the last Americans released in the final exchange of prisoners (Operation Big Switch), nearly six months after the armistice was signed.[137] Some weeks after the capture of the Americans, two of the five remaining Korean partisans struggled back to friendly lines. That proved to be their undoing, however, as the South Korean army subsequently executed both soldiers upon learning they had been captured, then released after promising to spy for the Communists.[138]

Undeterred by the Virginia I fiasco, McGee's Miscellaneous Division soon turned its attention to planning another, much more ambitious airborne insertion. Unlike the quick "slash and dash" plans for the failed sabotage mission, Operation Spitfire was intended to set up a long-term, partisan base deep in Communist-controlled territory. The projected area of operations for this group formed a huge rectangle from twenty to eighty miles behind the Communists' main line of resistance, nearly five thousand square miles of central North Korea.[139] The unusual makeup of the Spitfire team reflected McGee's hopes of avoiding the mistakes committed in the Virginia I mission.

Selected by McGee to command the operation was Capt. Ellery Anderson, a British officer and former Special Air Services operative with behind-the-lines combat experience in Europe during World War II. Already in the Miscellaneous Division, Anderson had volunteered months earlier to lead missions into North Korea if the opportunity ever arose. McGee also allowed Anderson to bring into the mission a second British officer, a lieutenant who, unknown to McGee, had no special operations experience or even parachute training.[140]

Though short in experience, Lt. Samuel Leo Adams-Acton proved long in motivation and of potentially greater value to McGee, fluent in the Chinese he spoke as a result of his upbringing in China.[141] During this period McGee also succeeded in recruiting for Spitfire a third British soldier and two Americans (including one of the three surviving rangers from the Virginia I operation). Completing the Spitfire team were a total of thirteen Koreans, all selected on the basis of their familiarity with the proposed area of operations and their willingness to undergo parachute training.

To avoid the earlier problem of dropping the main team in the wrong location, a pathfinder team comprised of Anderson, two American sergeants, and two Korean partisans parachuted at night into their designated area on 18 June 1951, a week before to the arrival of the main party.[142] During the parachute landing Anderson injured his back to such extent that he was subsequently evacuated by helicopter four days later. Four days later, another night drop delivered Adams-Acton, the third British soldier, and eleven Koreans.

All jumpers in this second group were injured to varying degrees after being dispatched into trees and rocky terrain some distance from the drop zone marked by the pathfinder team. As the days progressed, the problems with air support continued to bedevil the Spitfire team. Inexperienced aircrews proved incapable of finding the drop zone, even when the team marked the spot with multiple flashlights and established radio contact with the aircraft overhead. This lack of army–air force coordination and properly trained special air missions crews led to a final calamity during a scheduled resupply drop on the night of 5–6 July.

Failing to locate the drop zone that night, the aircrew returned to its airfield at dawn, refueled, and returned immediately to fly a low-altitude search for the team's "secret" location, in broad daylight. After having unwittingly alerted every Communist unit in the area as to the general location of the team, the aircrew dropped the resupply bundles, by accident right on top of the team's hidden base camp some distance from the drop zone.[143] Irretrievably compromised and running for their lives, the Spitfire soldiers lasted only hours before being caught by Communist troops hot on their trail. In the end only half the team managed to walk back to friendly lines. Never heard from again were six Koreans, one American, and one British sergeant.[144] Spitfire had been decimated in less than three weeks without coming close to accomplishing its mission of setting up a partisan base behind enemy lines.

The fallout from the Spitfire calamity extended beyond the mission itself. Returning to Baker Section from his hospitalization in Japan, now-major Anderson encountered a cold reception as doubt was cast upon the true extent of the injuries that resulted in his helicopter extraction from the operational area. When word leaked out that Anderson was about to be appointed the new chief of Baker Section, every American in the unit reportedly asked for reassignment from the section.[145] Whatever the truth, the appointment was shelved and Anderson was later transferred quietly back to the British army.

The determined adventurer Adams-Acton survived his first taste of behind-the-lines warfare and, after recovering from his wounds, was later assigned to a group of west coast partisans operating from islands north of Leopard Base. Only six months later, in December 1951, the lieutenant and two other UN advisors were captured as the Chinese overran their forward island outpost. After eighteen months of imprisonment and torture and less than two weeks before the armistice was finally signed, Adams-Acton and a U.S. Army lieutenant assaulted a prison guard in a futile attempt to escape their camp on 16 July 1953. Though the American survived his recapture and was returned to UN control shortly thereafter in Operation Big Switch, it appears from his report that Adams-Acton was shot to death in a fashion strongly suggesting deliberate execution.[146]

The abortive end of the Virginia I and Spitfire operations generated a fateful discussion within the Miscellaneous Division staff regarding the feasibility of future parachute infiltration operations. From this discussion, two major decisions were reached. First, airborne insertion of sabotage and intelligence-gathering teams would continue despite the experiences to date. Second, no American or British soldiers would accompany the Korean teams sent on these missions. Varying reasons were given for removing UN personnel from future airborne missions.

These reasons included the high-profile presence of Caucasians in an Asian culture, foreign language problems, even the differences in food requirements necessary to sustain American and Korean appetites in the field. Although not without merit, none of these factors played a significant role in the failures of the Virginia I and Spitfire missions. Apparently overlooked in these discussions was the fundamental fact that it was the incredibly poor mission planning by these same officers that doomed the two efforts before any of the above noted factors could have possibly affected the mission's outcome.

Failing to emerge from their discussions, perhaps to save face, was the obvious decision to either cease such operations or insist on the resources and time necessary for adequate mission preparation. What did emerge was the American decision to cut U.S. Army and British losses while continuing to parachute Koreans into North Korea. And this is precisely what happened for the duration of the war. In the following two years, Baker Section alone parachuted more than 350 additional Korean partisans deep behind enemy lines. This number does not include the untold hundreds that appear to have been parachuted into North Korea during the same period by the CIA and the KLO operation. The most exhaustive postwar report on these missions describes the results of these missions with depressingly repetitive phrases: "Three of the teams were lost immediately. . . . Mustang IV team [operated] for about 6 days before its members were captured or killed. . . . No further word was received [after one radio report]. . . . Teams were lost immediately. . . . Not one member of the above teams is known to have extracted. . . . The Hurricane team, apparently compromised, was lost soon after it was dropped. . . . None of the partisans involved ever returned."[147]

The report summarizes this unconscionable, two-year-long continuance of suicide missions with the terse conclusion found in the epitaph: "In most cases there is no information whatsoever as to what happened [after the Korean parachutists landed], although it is possible that some teams were able to operate for a time. . . . These decisions to use partisans against enemy supply routes in airborne operations appears to have been futile and callous."[148]

If any of the senior American officers privy to the classified results of these missions protested orders to continue the slaughter, there is no record of their statements in any government records or personal memoirs uncovered by this author.

As the war drew to a close in the spring of 1953, the partisans became a major "bargaining chip" in the long-running, UN-Communist negotiations. The Communists obviously wanted them disarmed and withdrawn from the islands north of the thirty-eighth parallel before the armistice agreements were signed. For obvious reasons, the UN chose to keep the still-potent partisan force on the islands as an inducement to keep the armistice negotiations on track. And not surprisingly, the South Korean government and army remained extremely wary of accepting thousands of armed and bitter North Koreans as new citizens in their war-torn country. The South Koreans could hardly be faulted for what some might consider a lack of charity toward a wartime ally. The Americans had made little attempt during the war to consult the South Koreans on a partisan force that was in all but name an extension of the U.S. Army in South Korea.

Two months before the armistice agreements were finally signed, the partisans were withdrawn from all but five of the islands (as agreed upon in the armistice negotiations), in Operation Pappy.[149] Thousands of partisans, their families, and tons of equipment were moved in a sealift completed in multiple stages. Tensions ran high as the partisans were gradually disarmed and sent to South Korea as stateless refugees, citizens of no country. Thousands deserted rather than be drafted into the South Korean army, a military plan scheduled for completion by February 1954.

Eventually Eighth Army emptied the remaining five islands, and most of the once-again refugees began their painful integration into South Korean society; most but not all. Many apparently returned to North Korea, either to continue the fight or attempt to blend back into their prewar communities. In the months following the signing of the armistice, a few frantic radio transmissions pleading for weapons and ammunition continued to come from those who chose to continue fighting in the North. But the calls were received by Americans already instructed not to respond to the politically awkward transmissions coming from these surviving "expendables" . . . and eventually the calls died out.

Advisors

> Was this a trap? Was I to be taken ashore and handed over to the North Korean Army or the Chinese? I was in a real dilemma. If this was a trap, my career as a partisan advisor would be short and rather ignominious. But if I refused to go, both [the Donkey leader] and I would lose face: he because I refused to trust him and me because I had shown fear in the face of the enemy.

For the first two years of the war neither FEC nor Eighth Army commanders appear to have made any formal effort to recruit or even identify incoming replacements with previous OSS or unconventional warfare experience. The word "appear" is an important qualifier here, however, as it seems the U.S. Army was unaware that a bureaucratic competitor was snatching these highly experienced soldiers from under its very nose. As Korean War special operations veteran and historian Ed Evanhoe notes, "The CIA had several [U.S. Army] personnel assignment clerks at South Camp Drake's replacement depot [in Japan] in their pocket. These clerks went through the records of personnel coming in from the States, looking for anyone with OSS or unconventional warfare experience, then assigned them to various Agency cover outfits [e.g., JACK]. The personnel people got paid an under-the-table-bounty. It took FEC a long time, until mid-1952, to realize what was going on and put a stop to it. I can only assume the Agency had a similar deal going with Fifth Air Force."[150]

Not surprisingly, such policies—or lack thereof—brought a mixture of the good, the bad, and the ugly into the ranks of partisan advisors. Colonel McGee himself is a case in point.

It's unlikely that the Eighth Army could have selected a better officer than McGee to launch the partisan program. But it's also worth recalling that until his selection, McGee's total unconventional warfare experience had been accrued during his four-month stay, as a POW escapee, with the Filipino guerrillas. And although his understanding of guerrilla warfare basics is evident in the thoroughness with which he prepared Operational Plan Able, it can also be argued that the consecutive failures of the Virginia I and Spitfire operations also show the limitations of his short experience in the Philippines. McGee (as well as JACK's former-OSS veterans of war in Europe), simply overestimated the adaptability of their World War II–era unconventional warfare experience as it applied to Communist-style warfare in North Korea.

The failure of the Far East Command to seek out special operations expertise from within the overall ranks of the U.S. Army, for the only war it was fighting at the time, appears to reflect the low priority its commanders accorded unconventional warfare. In contrast to this viewpoint, however, the CIA was more than happy to recruit combat-experienced special operations expertise when and where it could find it. The case of Maj. Singlaub is an excellent case in point.

Singlaub, an infantry officer, had not only served with the OSS in Asia during World War II, but as an intelligence officer had witnessed the Chinese Communists overrun Manchuria in the late 1940s during the Chinese civil war. Capping this impressive special operations resume, Singlaub was training U.S. Army Ranger companies for deployment to the war zone when, in December 1951, the CIA recruited him for special operations duty in Korea.[151] One might have thought that the army would have howled like a banshee at this talent drain. Instead, it let Singlaub—and presumably others like him—go without complaint, while leaving FEC and the Eighth Army staffs to fill key special operations billets from amongst those who, by the luck of the draw, were assigned to their respective staffs.

With little or no help from the army's personnel system, McGee and Vanderpool were forced to do their own recruiting by word of mouth and personal interviews with individuals whom they rarely knew well. At first a small number of U.S. Army Rangers became available following the dissolution of the superbly trained airborne-Ranger companies in August 1951. But even at its peak strength, this elite force numbered no more than seven hundred in Korea, and nearly one of every nine rangers died in combat on the peninsula.[152]

The most common form of advisor recruiting was as unconventional (and unauthorized) as Vanderpool's "diabolical" mindset. Experiences subsequently related by former advisors Archie Johnston and Ben Malcom, for example, describe how they met the enterprising Vanderpool. Johnston recalls leaning over the rail of the U.S. Navy transport that brought him to Korea when an unknown lieutenant called out to him by name, instructing Johnston to call his "friends" when he reached the Replacement Center in Seoul: "How he knew my name . . . I'll never know. [After briefing Johnston] Van called the Replacement Center and told them Tokyo had approved my transfer to FEC-LD(K)[,] . . . then Van called Tokyo and told them the Replacement Center had approved my transfer. I was now a partisan."[153]

Thrust without preparation into wartime advisory duties with a foreign culture whose language he didn't speak, Johnston had only his instincts to guide him through the cultural norms of the proud and complex Korean partisans. And as Johnston quickly learned, even a casual comment from an advisor could evoke a totally unexpected response from "his" Koreans:

> On a visit to the training area, Lee—the Wolfpack 1 Executive Officer—and I entered the front gate and the sentry failed to salute us. I made an off-hand remark to the effect that how could you expect to have soldiers who could learn to fight if they can't even learn to salute? Lee became furious and called the [partisan] company to fall in. He then made a speech in Korean and two guerrillas held the gate guard's right [saluting] arm over our jeep fender. Lee then broke the man's arm with a rifle butt. "When he gets his arm out of a cast, he'll know how to salute," Lee remarked to me.
>
> Later . . . I said to Lee that [his behavior] seemed a bit extreme to me. Lee was genuinely puzzled and said, "I don't understand you Americans. If we should break an enemy soldier's finger to get information, you cry

"Atrocity!" yet you saw me break the arm of one of my own men and I call it discipline!"[154]

Perhaps Johnston could have stopped the arm-breaking incident. But such an act would have been a fatal blow to any hopes of establishing an effective working relationship with the partisans, as both the partisan leader and the American would have lost considerable "face" if Johnston had taken such action. Even though the Americans were assigned only as advisors to the Donkey units, they were in fact commanding the partisans in all but official U.S. Army records. Johnston soon developed a system of command that he found effective for his unique situation; what he referred to as his "five unwritten rules for combat partisan leadership":

1. Never allow the partisans to question an order from an Advisor.
2. Never ask a Korean to do anything; tell him.
3. Never lie to a Korean.
4. Never get drunk in front of a Korean.
5. Never make a "pass" at a Korean woman.[155]

A sixth point not on Johnston's list, brought to my attention by Sergeant Manbahadur, the Ghurka medic, states, "*Never* praise anything Japanese in front of the Koreans." As Manbahadur recalls, forgetting this cultural hot point once cost an Australian advisor a bad beating from a group of partisans not about to forget their years of suffering under Japanese rule. Initially assigned to a medical support unit within the British Commonwealth Brigade, Manbahadur's subsequent transfer to relief aid activities in the islands involved an assignment in which appearances were very deceiving indeed . . . just as they were meant to be:

> I was transferred to a civilian relief aid organization in Seoul before being put aboard a British frigate heading north to the islands. Only after we were out to sea was I called to a private briefing on my real mission. Under cover of distributing relief supplies to the refugees I was to recruit educated Koreans for intelligence gathering and communications work . . . for an early-warning network to watch North Korean activity up north. I was dressed incognito as a church official and worked mostly with the Christian Koreans. I never heard of the word "advisor" until much later.[156]

Manbahadur was given only the absolute minimum information necessary to perform his singular mission, a standard precaution for undercover agents exposed to the constant threat of capture. Following encoded instructions from "Stanley," an individual who never identified himself beyond his code name, Manbahadur moved from island to island distributing food. And at each island, he also taught selected Koreans how to use both the hand-cranked, generator-powered radios he gave them and the weapons he also provided. Manbahadur's Asian heritage and foreign language abilities were ideal assets for such work in the remote islands. Fortunately for the much less-qualified American advisors to the south, they too were generally treated with respect by the tough partisans; at least those who conducted themselves along the general guidelines described by Johnston.

The partisans' respect was critical, as it was absolutely indispensable to any American that sought to be effective or simply survive his tour on the islands. For if Lee's reaction to Johnston's remark regarding a slack sentry was a startling eye-opener to Johnston, other advisors were also tested by the partisans in unique and varying ways. A much more dangerous test, for example, was the one put to the advisor, 1st Lt. Ben Malcom. At the time the young officer had completed a grand total of eighteen months active duty before being shipped to the U.S. Army replacement depot at South Camp Drake on the outskirts of Tokyo.

Singled out from the other South Camp Drake replacements for reasons never made clear to him, Malcom was interviewed (by Vanderpool) and immediately selected for partisan advisory duty. Though commissioned an infantry officer, Malcom like Johnston possessed no unconventional warfare or language skills that would seem to explain his selection for the interview. It would not have been usual for the times, however, if someone had noted his rural Georgia heritage and the natural flair for military service that has made the notable presence of Southerners such a hallmark of the American army during much of this country's history.

Only days after his brief orientation at Vanderpool's headquarters in February 1952, Malcom suddenly found himself facing a question undoubtedly faced by many of the young partisan advisors throughout the war: Was he willing to trust his life to the good faith of an unknown North Korean, who passed life-or-death commands to those about him in a language the young officer couldn't understand? In Malcom's case it was a Donkey leader inviting the young American to accompany him onto the North Korean mainland to "visit" a supposed partisan sanctuary. As Malcom recalls: "Was this a trap? Was I to be taken ashore and handed over to the North Korean Army or the Chinese? I was in a real dilemma. If this was a trap, my career as a partisan advisor would be short and rather ignominious. But if I refused to go, both [the Donkey leader] and I would lose face: he because I refused to trust him and me because I had shown fear in the face of the enemy."[157]

In the end, Malcom accompanied the Donkey leader into enemy territory and lived to write about his experiences. Even so, the fact that young lieutenant's instincts and courage carried the moment hardly dilutes the point that the U.S. Army was placing such men in dangerous situations for which little if any effort had been made to prepare them. For what the new advisor didn't know when the Donkey leader tested his trust was that the North Korean himself wasn't fully trusted by the more experienced American advisors on Paengnyong-do. And this particular Donkey leader wasn't the only one viewed with suspicion by the Americans. As Malcom's supervisor had long-since discovered to his considerable personal discomfort, Communist infiltrators among the partisans were sending a continuous stream of information back to the mainland: "They [the North Koreans] know our general organization, our names, serial numbers, our strength, and our disposition. One radio, Peiping I think, came out with it once and gave the U.S. officers' names and serial numbers, the date they took command, etc."[158] The Communists also instituted a public policy of announcing bounties worth several thousand U.S. dollars, a lifetime fortune to the destitute Koreans, on the heads of the more prominent advisors. And compounding still further the very real danger to any advisor placing his trust in the wrong Korean was the relative scarcity of other Americans to turn to should he find himself suddenly in dire need of assistance.

During the month Lieutenant Malcom "visited" North Korea for the first (but not last) time, the U.S. Army strength on the islands averaged less than eight advisors per one thousand partisans.[159] This already-inadequate advisor-partisan ratio actually declined during the remainder of 1952, before FEC's successful partisan recruiting drive in early 1953 generated a wartime high of some two hundred partisan advisors.[160] And as many of these Americans were in fact performing supply, communications, and intelligence "house-keeping" functions in Seoul or at Leopard Base, very few advisors indeed were actually collocated with the partisans on the outer islands. Under such circumstances low-ranking enlisted soldiers frequently found themselves commanding entire battalions as if they were senior officers. Obviously the character and enthusiasm of the individual officer or "sergeant" advisor[161] became a key factor in the effectiveness of "his" Donkey unit. Yet another key factor in their effectiveness was, as Malcom noted, the willingness of the American to risk his life by joining "his" partisans in combat on the mainland.

The Eighth Army's "no Americans behind enemy lines" policy that followed the failure of Operation Spitfire appears to have applied only to airborne operations in which the prospects of mission accomplishment or even survival were negligible. In contrast to the suicidal parachute missions, however, the memoirs of the island-based advisors reveal that they were allowed the personal discretion to fight in North Korea largely as they saw fit. And although some Americans undoubtedly declined the opportunity to set foot on the mainland, others committed heart and soul to the success of their Donkey teams. Few better examples of this latter class of advisor can be found than in the combat performance of M. Sgt. Roy E. Meeks, former Ranger and subsequent advisor to Donkey I leader Mr. Chang Jae Hwa. Meeks's gutsy performance in combat was described after one particular battle on the mainland by the Donkey I commander:

> [Meeks] carried the corpse of our medical officer for about 7000 yards [from] deep inland all the way to the beach. He had the corpse on one shoulder and an AR [automatic rifle] on his left shoulder, and four hundred CCF [Communist Chinese Forces] were chasing him. When Meeks [then discovered his officer and the partisan command post section were missing] . . . he took the suicide squad personally, and went deep inland about three kilometers . . . [to search for the command section]. He was completely surrounded by the enemy. He threw hand grenades and fought until he could get out of there.[162]

As there was no shortage of Korean courage on such missions, the presence of American advisors was generally considered to contribute two equally important functions. First, of course, was to demonstrate the advisor's faith in the U.S. training he had personally drilled into the partisans, as well as his confidence in the partisans themselves. Second, and perhaps more important, was the advisor's role in coordinating the all-important air and naval gunfire support necessary to knock out the enemy's superior firepower.

The U.S. Army had every reason to be satisfied with advisors such as Johnston, Malcom, and Meeks. But as noted earlier, their individual performance in such a foreign environment was more a reflection of their personal character than any advisor screening or special training provided them by the army. This situation began to change for the first time in early 1953, when FEC began receiving the first group of unconventional warfare specialists from the recently activated 10th Special Forces Group (10th SFG), based at Fort Bragg, North Carolina. The Special Forces troopers were sorely needed on the islands following FEC's mid-1952 decision to quadruple the size of its partisan force.

From October to December 1952, the UN Partisan Forces—Korea grew from just under nine thousand to more than sixteen thousand en route to the previously noted, final wartime total of more than twenty-one thousand.[163] But though seemingly a step in the right direction at last, the introduction of the Special Forces troopers soon highlighted a number of unexpected problems in the partisan operations.

The primary problem encountered was that the Special Forces training at Fort Bragg (as with McGee's ad hoc experiences in the Philippines) had little relevance to combating Communist warfare in northern Asia. The 10th SFG in particular had oriented its training toward conditions found in Soviet-occupied Europe, along much the same lines as had its World War II–era predecessor, the OSS. Indeed, a few of the 10th SFG soldiers were Eastern European refugees, brought into the U.S. Army and trained for the express purpose of returning to Europe for service in the Special Forces.[164] But as the first Special Forces troopers arrived in Korea, they quickly learned (as had McGee, Vanderpool, and the CIA) that their preparation for partisan war in Europe was woefully inadequate for the harsh realities of Communist warfare in Korea. Other problems soon surfaced, as described in a telling, postwar report: "It was felt [by the Special Forces personnel themselves] that they were improperly utilized. The younger officers and enlisted men evidenced strong resentment after being led to believe they would be assigned to combat jump missions [e.g., Virginia I and Spitfire], combat raids, and amphibious landings behind enemy lines. For the same reasons these people were not particularly adapted to working with partisans in what became a relatively static position."[165]

Not surprisingly, a number of these highly motivated and aggressive Special Forces advisors responded poorly to the lack of meaningful offensive action and the lonely conditions on the barren islands. Exacerbating the problem still further was their assignment in Korea as individual replacements, after the soldiers had trained for months to fight as members of close-knit, twelve-man "A Teams." Three months before the war ended, an Eighth Army Intelligence officer ordered to review the overall partisan force and its advisors subsequently reported widespread abuses in the program. These included black-marketeering, excessive drinking, abusive use of the rest-and-recuperation incentive trips to Japan, and training deficiencies that in at least one case resulted in the unjustifiable deaths of several Korean airborne trainees.[166]

The U.S. Army never established a program to select and train partisan advisors for unconventional warfare in Korea. And as just described, the belated introduction of Special Forces advisors to Korea was not only a case of too little, too late, but brought with it particular problems of its own. If as stated earlier the ranks of the partisan advisors comprised "the good, the bad, and the ugly," it could hardly have been expected to turn out any other way.

PsyWarriors

> The psychological [warfare] situation is far too complex to be handled by poets and gentlemen of the press in Washington. . . . One U.S. medium tank has proved far more effective than all the bag of [psychological warfare] tricks, which merely offend good taste and give nothing concrete where want is great.

Although not every army officer agreed with this World War II–era judgment,[167] it was nonetheless representative of the general military contempt expressed toward the politically controversial practice of psychological warfare (PsyWar), the "planned operations to influence the opinions, emotions, attitudes, and behavior of hostile foreign groups." And the overall popularity of the judgment goes far in explaining why, when the U.S. Army went to war in the summer of 1950, its total, operational PsyWar capability was found in the Tactical Information Detachment, a twenty-man unit based at Fort Riley, Kansas.[168] And like so many other aspects of the army's institutional disdain for unorthodox warfare, this bias against psychological warfare traced its roots to the army's still vivid memories of its conflicts with "Wild Bill" Donovan's OSS during World War II.

In March 1942 a distinctly reluctant JCS made its first and only attempt of the war to develop a national-level, PsyWar program. Moving unenthusiastically and only then after persistent prodding from Assistant Secretary of War John McCloy, the JCS established a Joint Psychological Warfare Committee and appointed a combination of senior military and civilian officials to manage the new program.[169] This effort lasted less than a year, however, as interagency rivalries quickly crippled committee attempts to coordinate anything, including even the baseline requirement of defining the national psychological warfare mission itself. Frustrated, the Joint Chiefs withdrew from the effort nine months later and, grudgingly, handed the task over to the civilians running the already controversial OSS.

Ironically, even those officers holding a low opinion of PsyWar still resented the JCS decision, if for no other reason than they held a still lower opinion of OSS civilians "intruding" in military affairs. Few better expressions of this "we don't want it but we don't want 'them' to have it either" bias can be found than in that quoted at the beginning of this section. To its credit, the U.S. Army went on to develop some very effective, theater-level PsyWar capabilities in both Europe and the Pacific during the war. But the postwar army chose not to institutionalize this particular wartime success, and the dissolution of the OSS in 1945 effectively terminated the PsyWar capability within the U.S. government. Five long and tumultuous years would pass before the Korean War forced the military to reestablish the capability, and once again the army responded only after persistent prodding by senior Department of the Army civilians.[170]

Despite prolonged efforts by Secretaries of the Army Gordon Gray and Frank Pace Jr. (Gray's successor) to establish a military PsyWar capability during the late-1940s, it was not until six months after the outbreak of war that the Department of the Army reluctantly established the Office, Chief of Psychological Warfare. But if the subject of psychological warfare found little support with army generals in Washington during this period, it had by a fortuitous twist already found more support through the foresight of a two-star general in the General Headquarters (GHQ), Far East Command. That foresight was demonstrated three years earlier when the Far East Command's assistant chief of staff for intelligence,[171] Maj. Gen. Charles Willoughby, established FEC's Psychological Warfare Branch.[172]

Although numbering only half-dozen officers when the hostilities began, the small branch proved remarkably responsive to the sudden attack. Within twenty-four hours of the initial assault, its first propaganda leaflets were falling through skies over the Korean peninsula, and within forty-eight hours its first PsyWar broadcasts were emanating from prewar Radio Japan studios in Tokyo.[173] The branch's small staff expanded rapidly to thirty-five full-time personnel within the first six months of the war, before its upgrade to section status and subsequent transfer to FEC's Operations Directorate in 1952. Throughout the remainder of the war, the Psychological Warfare Section functioned as the theater's executive coordinating agency for all UN PsyWar activities, including both tactical and strategic-level field operations.[174]

The first tactical PsyWar unit fielded in Korea was the Tactical Information Detachment expanded and redesignated the 1st Loudspeaker and Leaflet (1st L&L) Company shortly after the war began. Rapidly mobilized and sent from Fort Riley, Kansas, to Korea in the fall of 1950, the company served as the Eighth Army's front-line propaganda unit throughout the war. As a tactical PsyWar unit, its area of leaflet and loudspeaker operations was limited to a forty-mile-deep band of territory immediately behind enemy lines. Propaganda operations beyond the forty-mile limit were designated "strategic" and carried out by the 1st Radio Broadcasting and Leaflet (1st RB&L) Group, organized in the United States and later sent to FEC in July 1951.[175]

In addition to its fixed-base studio operations from Japan, the 1st RB&L Group also supported its subordinate 4th Mobile Radio Broadcasting Company in establishing a system of low-power radio stations throughout South Korea. To help rebuild the postwar economy, this mobile radio equipment remained in South Korea until 1956, leaving behind the Voice of the UN Command (VUNC) radio station that was itself not disbanded until 1971.[176] In addition to these military Psy-War efforts, the U.S. State Department carried out "consolidation propaganda" in those areas under the civil administration of the South Korean government.[177]

Disseminating their messages with a combination of radio, leaflet, and loudspeaker tactics, the U.S. Army "PsyWarriors" reached out to three separate target audiences: North Korean military, South Korean military, and the civilian populations of both countries. For each target very specific propaganda messages had been developed to:

1. Weaken the effectiveness of the North Korean (and later, the Communist Chinese) Peoples Army.
2. Bring the truth about the war to the people of North Korea.
3. Bolster the morale of the South Korean troops and civilian population.[178]

While the radio teams broadcast from fixed-base and mobile radio stations in Japan and Korea, loudspeaker and leaflet messages were delivered from another combination of air and land methods. Each delivery method had specific targets, as for example the Tokyo-based radio broadcasts directed at the one hundred thousand radios estimated to be operating in North Korea. The priority attached to this particular delivery method was such that upon the 1st RB&L's arrival in Japan, it was immediately put to work to expand the fledgling VUNC radio service, only recently put into operation.

Operating from the former Armed Forces Radio Service studio in Tokyo, VUNC broadcasts were delivered on several different frequencies at different times, in Korean and Chinese, from powerful transmitters in various sites throughout Japan. Korean nationals, some of them former employees of the Korean Broadcasting System, helped prepare and then deliver many of the programs. This around-the-clock operation was in full swing when in October 1950 the VUNC staff heard of an unexpected broadcast opportunity that was simply too tempting to ignore.

Earlier that month, advancing UN forces had driven the North Koreans from their capitol city of Pyongyang, capturing in the process Radio Pyongyang, the Communist's major propaganda radio station. Upon discovering that the facilities could be made operational in short order, the VUNC staff promptly set to work to do exactly that. And within three weeks the VUNC staffers were enjoying the decidedly perverse pleasure of broadcasting anti-Communist propaganda six hours a day from the "new" Radio Pyongyang.[179] In the end, however, the pleasure proved short-lived, as the Communist Chinese retook Pyongyang another three weeks later. Unlike the "original owners," however, the VUNC staff marked its departure by stripping the radio station of everything not nailed down, then destroying the remaining equipment before returning to Japan.

The use of radio to broadcast propaganda during (and after) the war had special advantages and disadvantages. On the plus side, radio proved more effective than leaflets when targeting a North Korean army and population noted for their relatively high illiteracy rates. On the negative side, those North Koreans caught listening to VUNC were subject to harsh penalties, and understandably, many chose not to take the risk. Even "friendly" factors such as the lack of a nationally coordinated PsyWar program could detract from VUNC's potential. The lack of coordination between its broadcasts and those transmitted by the Korean section of the New York City–based Voice of America (VOA), for example, came back to bite the Americans on more than one occasion. As author Stephen E. Pease concludes in his informative book *Psywar,* "VUNC had good coordination with its own elements . . . but poor operating relationships with agencies outside the Army. . . . This friction [e.g., between VUNC and VOA] hurt the effectiveness of the propaganda. People receiving mixed messages become confused and the senders' credibility suffers, an unforgivable PSYWAR sin."[180]

The biggest drawback found with VUNC's radio propaganda was the timeliness factor; that is, the medium was not sufficiently flexible to respond to rapidly changing battlefield conditions. This drawback was not deemed critical, however, as the need for a quicker response was satisfied with the leaflet and especially loudspeaker capabilities found in other PsyWar units.

The leaflet operations in particular proved very useful against a North Korean population with little access to individually owned radios and against area targets susceptible to messages affecting their particular region or town. Plan Blast leaflet missions, for example, advised civilian populations to flee well in advance of UN bombers that would soon attack military and industrial targets near their homes.[181] Of course such leaflets also served less humanitarian purposes, notably the disruption of industrial production and the blocking of military road traffic by the fleeing civilians.

Other leaflet missions targeted specific North Korean or Chinese army units known to have suffered extreme casualties in recent battle. Offers of medical aid and food in exchange for surrender often proved effective to wounded and exhausted Communist soldiers, who saw few alternatives for improvement in their situation. Still other leaflets asked front-line Communist soldiers, "Where is your own air force?" For infantry soldiers taking a deadly pounding from UN aircraft obviously free from attack by the North Korean People's Air Force, such leaflets were particularly disheartening. That the soldiers could verify the credibility of such leaflets simply by looking toward the skies further enhanced the leaflets' intentionally demoralizing effect on individual spirits.

Despite their undeniable advantages, leaflet operations were susceptible to abuse on occasion by the "more must be better" American philosophy that frequently emphasized quantity over quality. This was especially true before the appointment in April 1951 of Ridgway as FEC's commander in chief. Noting this "pre-Ridgway" period of the war, one authority on the subject concluded, "The prevalent attitude of army commanders [toward leaflet operations] in Korea had been to simply bury the enemy in paper."[182] And making this tendency much easier to succumb to was the prodigious production rates of the leaflet units. For example the 1st RB&L alone "often produced more than two hundred million propaganda leaflets a week."[183]

Even when field commanders succumbed to the "bury 'em in paper" attitude, however, they could still claim the obvious truth that paper was cheaper than bullets, and a lot cheaper than allied casualties. More important to these commanders was the feedback they were getting from PsyWar teams that the leaflets seemed to be working on the enemy. From interrogations of 435 North Korean POWs captured shortly after the breakout of UN forces from the Pusan perimeter in September 1950, a PsyWar research team from Johns Hopkins University reported, "Fifty-five percent [of the POWs] gave leaflets as an important reason for surrender, while seventy-five percent or more [of the overall group] reported they read and believed [the UN] leaflets. Twenty percent believed they would be shot for reading leaflets[,] . . . sixty percent believed there might be a medium penalty for reading leaflets."[184]

Acknowledging in advance the difficulty of assessing the complex emotions that lead each individual soldier to surrender, the Johns Hopkins researchers concluded with a "reasonable guess" that "of the total of approximately 120,000 prisoners taken by 22 October 1950, the UN leaflet campaign can be credited with the equivalent of decisively effecting the capture of 12,000, plus or minus 6,000 prisoners. The [financial] cost of a PsyWar capture to a conventional kill appears to have a probable ratio of 70:1 in favor of PsyWar."[185]

UN psychological warfare teams emphasized cartoonlike figures in their propaganda leaflets, such as this one showing Soviet premier Joseph Stalin controlling a puppet in the form of North Korean leader Kim Il Sung. *U.S. Air Force*

The principal problem for the enemy soldiers targeted with such leaflets was the harsh penalties imposed on them should they be caught carrying the bits of paper attempting to induce their surrender. Not surprisingly, those soldiers most susceptible to the propaganda took special care in hiding the leaflets, many of which doubled as "safe conduct passes." One former military policeman assigned to the U.S. Army's 24th Infantry Division recalls his encounter with Communist soldiers using such passes: "My duty was to screen refugees going from North Korea to South Korea, and to sort out North Korean and Chinese soldiers from the civilians. I was shown literally hundreds of safe conduct passes. . . . The Chinese soldiers were shot by their officers if they were found with one of these leaflets on them. They sewed them into their uniforms and put them up their rectums to escape detection."[186]

To reach its target audience despite the drawbacks associated with radio and leaflet-delivered propaganda, FEC's Psychological Warfare Section exploited the potential for loudspeaker operations to the fullest. Just as the leaflets were delivered from aircraft and even 105-mm artillery shells,[187] the loudspeakers were mounted on both aircraft and jeeps; the latter assigned to Eighth Army's 1st Loudspeaker and Leaflet Company. But unlike the radio and leaflet programs whose results might not become apparent until weeks or even months after their delivery, the loudspeaker operations could on occasion produce startling results even as they were broadcast.

One such occasion took place during May 1951, when one of the two loudspeaker-equipped C-47s assigned to the Fifth Air Force's Special Air Missions Detachment unexpectedly flew over a single group of eighteen hundred Chinese soldiers near the front lines. Responding immediately, the PsyWar aircraft began dropping its leaflets even as its huge celestial voice boomed, "Life or death—it's your choice" to the group below. Already savaged by UN artillery, the last remnants of the group's declining morale caved in. After dropping their weapons on the spot, the entire group followed instructions from the PsyWar plane circling overhead and marched with its equipment and pack mules to a nearby surrender point.[188]

A similar situation occurred again later in the war, in which three hundred Communist soldiers were persuaded through airborne loudspeakers to surrender. In that instance the PsyWar broadcasters made sure the soldiers below also saw the four F-51 Mustang fighters circling overhead with an even more persuasive message—napalm-filled tanks slung under their wings for immediately delivery should the soldiers not follow the instructions of the PsyWar team.[189] It was truly an offer they couldn't refuse—and they didn't.

One of the most remarkable PsyWar campaigns of the war was undoubtedly Operation Moolah. The program unabashedly broadcast its sole purpose of publicly bribing a Communist MiG-15 fighter pilot, Chinese, Korean, or especially Russian, to defect with the most modern type fighter then in the Soviet inventory. General Clark personally launched the program in April 1953 with a broadcast over VUNC radio. Shortly thereafter a half-million leaflets were dropped over the Sinuiju and Uiju MiG-15 airfields (just inside the Chinese side of its border with North Korea) with the following offer: "The sum of $50,000 US dollars to any pilot who delivers a modern, operational,

Mounted on psychological warfare aircraft, airborne loudspeakers could have an immediate and dramatic impact on battlefield developments. The use of female broadcasters proved especially demoralizing to the North Korean soldiers huddled below, forced to endure the feminine taunting from above with little means of striking back. *U.S. Air Force*

combat-type jet aircraft in flyable condition to South Korea. The first pilot who delivers such a jet aircraft to the free world will receive an additional 50,000 US dollars bonus for his bravery."[190]

Significantly, the Chinese and Korean-language messages also asked that the leaflet be delivered to any Russian pilot known to the holder of the leaflet. For despite public Russian protests to the contrary, American fighter pilots in Korea were convinced that the best of the MiG-15 pilots they were encountering in "MiG Alley" were in fact Soviet pilots. The enemy's response to the radio and leaflet bribery campaign startled the Americans:

> Shortly after the start of Operation Moolah the [VUNC] radio broadcasts in Russian language were jammed. . . . Oddly the Chinese and Korean languages transmissions were not. For eight days there were no MIG sorties at all, an unprecedented stand-down. . . . [When resumed] the quality of the MIG pilots was noticeably poorer. . . . It was obvious that the excellent So-

viet pilots were no longer flying. After Operation Moolah the MIG pilots compiled the worst record of the entire war. UN [F-86 jet] Sabres downed 165 MIGs to only three losses, a fifty-five-to-one ratio![191]

As it turned out, no MiG pilot defected before the armistice ending hostilities was signed four months later. But only a month after the armistice was signed, on 23 September 1953, a North Korean People's Air Force pilot flew his MiG-15 into Kimpo airfield outside Seoul and immediately requested political asylum.[192] Reportedly not having heard of the reward, he appeared publicly at least to have been motivated solely by his hatred of the Chinese and Soviet advisors controlling the destiny of his country.

Operation Moolah also generated a considerable response and debate within the U.S. government. President Dwight D. Eisenhower considered it "unethical," while Clark disagreed on the grounds that the offer was public (and the reward was paid to the North Korean pilot who defected). To satisfy Eisenhower's unease, the CIA "devised a plan whereby [the pilot] would openly reject the reward money in exchange for quietly receiving technical education benefits and other financial considerations equal to the reward."[193] The president's discomfort with the ethical considerations of Operation Moolah no doubt reflected the uneasiness of many others in Washington, still troubled with the concept of psychological warfare in general. Despite the Cold War being already well under way by the time war in Korea broke out, few American politicians or military leaders yet comprehended the extent to which PsyWar would dominate the next forty years of ideological competition between East and West.

Their slowness to comprehend and respond must surely be one of the great ironies of our time. Although America's political leaders struggled with mixed success at best to communicate the benefits of Western values to the world, America's "civilian PsyWar team," its advertising industry, became the world's undisputed leader in communicating many of these values in a different way. If indeed it was economics, not politics, that brought the downfall of communism, then America's Madison Avenue PsyWarriors must surely be entitled their due in this outcome.

U.S. Air Force Special Air Missions | 2

If I were called upon to name the most amazing and unusual man among all those with whom I was associated during my military service, I would not hesitate for a second in picking out Donald Nichols as that individual. . . . I have often referred to him as a one man war.

Gen. Earle E. Partridge, commander, Fifth Air Force, 1948–51

Maj. Gen. Earle E. Partridge first met M. Sgt. Donald Nichols in 1948, soon after the general arrived in Japan to assume command of the Fifth Air Force.[1] And though Partridge received periodic briefings from the Counter-Intelligence Corps sergeant during the subsequent two years leading up to the war, the general later admitted his sparse knowledge of Nichols's activities in Korea during this prewar period. Little wonder, considering that Nichols's world was found in the mean streets and back alleys of prewar Seoul, a long way from the plush offices found at Fifth Air Force headquarters in Tokyo. The war gave Partridge cause to take a deeper look into Nichols's operation in the summer of 1950, and he was astonished at what he found.

For what the gruff, burly Nichols had established on the Korean peninsula during the prewar years was not simply an intelligence organization but the genesis for what would become the most successful special operations unit of the war. It was by any account a bizarre organization to be run by the "wild blue yonder" air force. But then again, neither the newly arrived CIA nor the Far East Command's army intelligence team could compete with the quality of sensitive information generated by Nichols's contacts, deep penetration agents established years earlier throughout Korea. By 1950,

Nichols was a man with access twenty-four hours a day to both General Partridge and South Korean president Syngman Rhee, not to mention a host of shadowy Asian characters whose names will never see print.

Possessing only a sixth grade education but fluent in the Korean language, Nichols was the spymaster whose warnings accurately predicted within days the North Korean invasion of South Korea, only to watch his warnings fall on deaf ears at MacArthur's headquarters. This former motor-pool sergeant was also the combat leader who personally conceived, organized, and led a daring helicopter mission deep into enemy territory to strip parts off a downed MiG-15 fighter, then the most highly sought after intelligence prize of the war.[2] But Nichols's world had a darker side as well, a side visited by Partridge and others time and again when the urgent need for results became too important to question the methods used, when the need was too sensitive to put in writing. For this brand of warfare Nichols coined a new term, something he called "Positive Intelligence."

Nichols himself admits that he created the term Positive Intelligence in prewar Korea, where he was already well on the way to establishing a powerful intelligence apparatus throughout the entire peninsula. In his autobiography *How Many Times Can I Die?* Nichols writes, "By this time (1947/8) our unit was really moving in 'high, very high' South Korean government circles. All doors were open to us. In those days no one in this area knew or even thought about *Positive Intelligence* (PI).[3] We invented it for this area and taught others, as we saw fit, for our own benefit."[4]

"Our unit" was Sub-Detachment K, 607th Counter-Intelligence Corps (CIC), stationed at Kimpo Airfield on the western outskirts of Seoul. After reporting to the sub-detachment in June 1946, Nichols soon began making extensive and effective use of Korean civilians to establish a covert network throughout the entire length of the politically troubled peninsula. Moreover, as President Rhee's trust in Nichols grew, the president took the highly unusual step of placing selected South Korean coast guard and air force personnel under the unquestioned command of the American sergeant. But what really swept Positive Intelligence beyond the scope of previous U.S. counter-intelligence operations, was the historical coming together of "the man and the moment" as Nichols went to war in the summer of 1950. He would emerge three years later a legend in South Korea's most powerful military and intelligence agency circles, an enigma even to the American special operators who worked for him and to this day an unknown to the American public.

Nichols's sub-detachment had become a well-oiled machine by 1950, its effectiveness stemming largely from its deep-penetration, political contacts throughout both South and North Korea. One measure of this effectiveness was demonstrated the month before the war started, when his agents persuaded a North Korean pilot to defect with his Soviet-built IL-10 ground-attack fighter. It was the first aircraft of its kind to fall into U.S. hands, and extensive debriefs of the willing pilot proved extremely valuable to the air force's Air Technical Intelligence experts. The plane itself was promptly dismantled for shipment back to the Zone of the Interior, as the continental U.S. was then known in military parlance.

But before this rare intelligence prize could be shipped back to the United States, Nichols's team and all other Americans in Seoul were forced to flee for their lives when one hundred thousand–plus North Koreans poured over the thirty-eighth parallel like a huge swarm of killer bees. Leaving "a bloody wake of massacred civilians to mark their rapidly advancing line,"[5] the North Korean People's Army forced his team to abandon their hard-earned IL-10 acquisition. Staying behind on his own volition to destroy abandoned equipment and aircraft at Kimpo Airfield, Nichols himself barely escaped at the last minute by clinging to the side of a small boat crossing the Han river just south of Seoul.

The experience was a bitter glass of wine for the man who had repeatedly warned FEC headquarters in Tokyo of the impending North Korean attack. But his warnings had been sent in vain, for as the Fifth Air Force commander later observed, "Nichols's reports were suppressed and disregarded."[6] His last report actually predicted within seventy-two hours the "surprise" attack that subsequently stunned a totally unprepared Truman administration. Not so surprising, it was Nichols's terse report from Seoul on the morning of 25 June 1950 that gave MacArthur's headquarters its first official notification of the North Korean invasion.[7]

After catching up with the retreating American embassy staff south of Seoul, Nichols learned of both his promotion to the rank of warrant officer and his next assignment. Amidst the confusion at the American camp he was recognized by U.S. ambassador John J. Muccio, who immediately asked him to maintain personal contact with the South Korean military service chiefs. Nichols served in this role for the following month before being relieved for appointment as a special representative to the director, Special Investigations, Far East Air Forces, a move designed for no other purpose but to free him for bigger things. And the bigger things came fast, as General Partridge was a man in a hurry that summer.

For his first task Nichols was sent to secure "by any means possible" one of the Russian-built T-34 tanks with which the Russians had equipped the North Korean army. Despite its extensive support to Russia during World War II, the United States had somehow missed getting an example for study of this highly successful weapon. One result of this omission was the very disagreeable surprise experienced by Fifth Air Force pilots as they watched the rugged T-34 withstand their cannon and rocket attacks on the vehicle. Following the general's orders, Nichols promptly borrowed a tank retriever vehicle from a frontline army unit and secured, under enemy fire, an abandoned T-34. A grateful Partridge promptly awarded Nichols's initiative with a Silver Star medal for valor, along with another tasking.

If the general's first request seemed more suitable for one of the army's tank officers than an air force intelligence operative, Partridge's second request seemed more suitable for an infantry officer. The general's problem concerned the Communist guerrillas harassing Fifth Air Force planes operating from Taegu Airfield, a vital resupply base in South Korea. Could Nichols do something about the guerrillas? Partridge asked. Nichols responded by personally leading twenty South Korean soldiers into the hills around the airfield, at night, to attack the guerrillas in close quarters combat. Nichols's surprise attack brought a sharp reduction in guerrilla activity around the important airfield, and yet another request from Partridge. In response to the general's need for information Nichols infiltrated forty-eight South Koreans by parachute behind enemy lines on thirteen different missions, to supply the Fifth Air Force with its most complete target list to date of enemy installations. Later that year he also sent parachutists behind enemy lines to rescue the surviving aircrew from a downed B-29 bomber.

Nichols's parachutists came from a crude jump school set up earlier by him for just such missions.[8] As he later recalled with humor, little did he know at the time that he himself would become one of its graduates. While observing training at the school one day he watched a transport loaded with Korean trainees land for no apparent reason. Upon learning that they had refused to jump he determined to set the example by donning a parachute himself and warning the students of the consequences if they refused to follow him out of the aircraft. After all, he told them, he too had never been to jump school. As Nichols relates in his autobiography, "I really didn't at this time think that it would be necessary for me to jump. However, after we became airborne, I noticed all eyes were on me. When we went over the Drop Zone, old man

Nichols jumped. I was quite elated to see the blossoming of every other chute on the plane spread out above me as I dropped."[9]

By this time Positive Intelligence had obviously evolved into a special strike force of some unknown hybrid. If Fifth Air Force headquarters wasn't sure how "air force blue" it was, General Partridge knew he liked it, and that he had the final "vote" on the issue. Regardless of its unorthodox activities, the time had clearly come to give Nichols's force the organizational support it needed to reach its full operational potential. This support was initiated in March 1951 with a Fifth Air Force headquarters letter that provides a rare insight into that command's wide-open approach to aggressive intelligence collection. The letter tasked Nichols's newly activated Special Activities Unit Number 1 to:

1. Provide intelligence operations of a *positive nature* [emphasis added] designated to meet the objectives of this command.
2. Perform operations (sabotage, demolition and/or guerrilla) necessary to accomplish destruction of specific objectives.
3. Assist allied agencies responsible for providing evasion and escape facilities to downed UN airmen.
4. Coordinate with other allied UN intelligence agencies as required by existing directives.[10]

The Fifth Air Force was soon compelled to delete "guerrilla warfare" from this task list, in deference to the fierce outcries from army and CIA organizations already conducting such operations. That administrative deletion appears to have been offered only out of bureaucratic politeness, however, as the air force "blue suiters" had no intention of surrendering any of their operational prerogatives. For by this time Nichols was providing the Fifth Air Force with "one stop service" for requirements ranging from sensitive HUMINT (the military acronym for *hum*an *int*elligence collection), to airborne-Ranger-type assaults against high-priority targets. On 17 April 1951 Nichols earned the United States's second highest medal for valor by personally leading a dangerous mission against an intelligence target so secret that the citation to his Distinguished Service Cross would only describe it as "information of inestimable value."[11]

Indeed it was: the wreckage of a Soviet-built MiG-15, the most advanced Communist fighter entered in the war and a major threat to all UN aircraft flying over North Korea. To defeat this threat the U.S. Air Force badly needed technical information on the MiG, but despite the high priority assigned this task, no example of the fighter had yet fallen into allied hands. Although the wreckage was too far—some one hundred miles—behind enemy lines to retrieve, technical intelligence experts could still glean considerable information from study of its

Donald Nichols (*lower right,* in a white t-shirt) pulled off one of the major intelligence coups of the war in July 1951 with the retrieval of this battle-damaged MiG-15 fighter from behind enemy lines. *Courtesy of Bill Fagiola*

most important parts. To this end, Nichols and five Korean specialists "proceeded behind enemy lines in an unarmed helicopter . . . despite fragmentation hits scored on the engine and intense anti-aircraft and automatic weapons fire[,] . . . landed in an area only a few miles from a major enemy supply depot[,] . . . photographed the materiel, recorded all inscriptions and technical data, and supervised disman-tlement of vital parts [for loading] aboard the helicopter. Although suf-fering serious damage to the rotor blade, the crippled aircraft flew 80 miles over the Yellow Sea to make an emergency landing on a friendly island."[12] The "friendly island" was Cho-do, just off North Korea's western coast. Itself located some one hundred miles behind enemy lines, the island was one of Nichols's primary operating bases in enemy territory and in fact his point of departure for the final flight into the MiG-15 crash site.[13]

The following July Nichols mounted another, much more complex and ultimately more successful operation to retrieve the wreckage of a downed MiG-15 lying in the coastal mud flats northwest of Pyong-yang. So high was the priority accorded the capture of a MiG fighter that the UN supported Nichols with a combined U.S.–British–South

Korean fleet directed by Rear Adm. A. K. Scott-Moncrieff of the British Royal Navy.[14]

To carry Nichols's specialists to the site and retrieve the aircraft, the U.S. Navy provided a landing ship, utility, the LSU-960, that had been modified for the mission with the installation of a crane capable of pulling parts of the aircraft out of the mud.[15] American and British aircraft were also brought in to provide air cover over the retrieval site. It was another demonstration of Nichols's exceptional organizational abilities and his talent for finding the best people for his purposes. Maj. George T. Gregory, one of Nichols's executive officers during this period, describes the diverse kinds of people the enterprising Nichols brought to his operation: "His [Nichols] men included scholars with advanced degrees, and burly athletic types without higher education, but who could walk all night through enemy forests, ride horses, paddle canoes, parachute from low altitudes, and kill a man with a single karate blow and able to speak three or four foreign languages."[16]

To align Special Activities Unit Number 1 with the U.S. Air Force's established intelligence structure the unit was re-designated the 6004th Air Intelligence Service Squadron (AISS) the month following its activation. The squadron was activated on Headquarters, Far East Air Forces orders, in what appears to have been an effort to ensure top-level control of an extremely sensitive, intelligence/special operations asset. Although the organization of the 6004th would continue to evolve throughout the war, its core structure was comprised of the following three detachments:

> Det One: Collect Air Technical Intelligence and conduct Prisoner of War interrogations.
> Det Two: Collect & disseminate Air Intelligence information. Due to the unusual nature of this work and other circumstances, both the primary and secondary missions have been classified Top Secret by the Commanding General, Fifth Air Force.
> Det Three: Plan, coordinate, and support Evasion and Escape activities for the recovery of UN airmen downed in enemy territory . . . and to assist in the organization and specialized training of personnel necessary to accomplish the basic mission.[17]

Characteristic of the times, not more than a few weeks passed before the Fifth Air Force tasked Detachment 1 with a mission that underscored its commitment to retain it's operational prerogatives regardless of any joint-service sensitivities.

On 1 June 1951 Nichols sent fifteen South Korean air force saboteurs on a parachute infiltration mission to blow up two railroad bridges. Enemy uniforms, equipment, weapons, and identification papers were carried by the teams should they need to bluff their way past enemy challenges. But despite Nichols's attention to detail and planning both missions failed as all the saboteurs were captured by the Chinese, a rare total loss for Nichols.[18] Moving beyond this setback Det 1's mission soon reverted to the more traditional technical intelligence and POW interrogation roles. It was during this transition that Nichols moved over to assume command of Det 2, later acknowledged as the most aggressive U.S. Air Force intelligence unit of the war.

Unlike Det 1's mission, which could usually be accomplished within established military intelligence channels, Det 2's Positive Intelligence mission took it far beyond any channels familiar to the U.S. Air Force. In particular, the detachment's top-secret activities led to its description by one postwar study as "the first covert collection agency of a tactical nature in the history of the U.S. Air Force."[19] Activated in Seoul on 25 July 1951 the detachment began its operations with seven officers (Nichols commanding) and twenty-six airmen.[20] As noted earlier, the latitude of its mission was extremely generous in an operational sense. In a wide-ranging mission summary Nichols was authorized to "direct intelligence operations behind enemy lines with special emphasis on . . . positive intelligence[,] . . . coordinate with allied intelligence agencies[,] . . . gather positive intelligence on the effectiveness of (allied) air operations . . . vital points of the enemy's transportation system . . . revetment hide out areas[,] . . . plan and direct such special operations as may be required to support . . . the Fifth Air Force and Far East Air Forces Intelligence missions."[21]

Most of these missions could be accomplished only by "eyes on target," a reconnaissance tactic requiring the operative to personally observe the target at close range; obviously at great risk to the observer's life. What the summary didn't specify was exactly whose "eyes" were to take such great risks, how they were to conduct surveillance in the target area, and most important to the owner of these eyes on target, how to stay alive in the process. The answer to the "whose eyes" question could be found in the personnel manning statistics for this most unusual U.S. Air Force detachment. By January 1952 only 5.7 percent of the detachment's 665 personnel were American, officers representing a minuscule 1.2 percent of the total.[22] But Det 2 had to deal with one overwhelming operational reality that no number of Americans could remedy. Flatly stated, no Caucasians could hope to survive in the detachment's target areas, and official air force records leave little doubt as to why this was so.

According to one 6004th AISS unit history report, "The main difference between its (Det Two) mission and that of Det One, is that Detachment Number 2 generally works north of the bomb line."[23] By July 1952 twenty-three of Nichols's sub-detachments were "sending a steady stream of radio reports back to Nichols's headquarters from behind enemy lines."[24] By year's end this number grew to thirty-two sub-detachments as Nichols sent still more eyes into North Korea.[25] To support this growing effort (and replace casualties) the detachment grew to a strength of nine hundred Koreans, 178 of which came from the South Korean air force.[26]

Most of the remaining Koreans were recruited from the ranks of the UN partisan forces,[27] which brought with their proven valor in combat something else not as useful for intelligence work.[28] For as their American supervisors soon learned, most of these former partisans were far more interested in fighting than intelligence gathering, an admirable quality anywhere else but in Det 2. Stringent supervision by their Korean sub-detachment commanders proved necessary to keep the problem under control. One problem definitely *not* under control, however, was the rising death toll of these agents in the field. As the Chinese and North Koreans began to comprehend the political reality that UN forces would not attack north of the thirty-eighth parallel again, they began releasing more front-line forces for internal security duty in areas in which the agents had previously operated successfully.

As Nichols's agents soon learned to their bitter cost, routine missions became tough and the tough ones became one-way missions. The agents weren't the only ones to suffer from this new and deadly reality. In his haunting memoirs, Nichols describes the price tag for knowingly sending men to their death, about lonely, dark nights in which he confesses:

> I hate to call myself a man. I had to be the one to give the actual orders when I knew someone was going to be killed. Maybe some of my bosses could have told me how to go about filling some of those requirements; however, I doubt it. They wanted little to do with them. They wanted the answers, and in some cases didn't want to be told how I got them. They knew it meant lives; sometimes many.
>
> It's easy to give an order such as "I want a MiG-15" or "I want some enemy officers, a few enemy tanks to experiment with, some of their tank 85mm tank ammo," etc. However, filling these requirements is another problem, which requires lives.[29]

With nine hundred Koreans in the field conducting Positive Intelligence not found elsewhere in the U.S. Air Force, it was imperative that the detachment set up its own training program for its unique operations. Unfortunately, the pace of field operations and the deaths of some of its most experienced agents delayed this program until the second half of 1952. Once operating, however, the training center comprised three schools run by both American and Korean instructors. The curriculums included:

1. Interrogation: Agent-trainees were taught the fundamentals and techniques for interrogating both prisoners of war and Koreans they would encounter in the target area while operating behind enemy lines.
2. Agent: Trainees learned techniques for accurate intelligence gathering on enemy airfields, aircraft, and radar. Small arms training and guerrilla warfare skills were also included and physical fitness was emphasized.
3. Paratroop: As parachute infiltration was a primary means of entering enemy territory, a jump school was organized to teach the basics.[30]

Both in numerical size and its importance to FEC's joint-service intelligence community, Det 2 was clearly growing beyond what anyone could have anticipated early in the war. This growth had not gone unnoticed by the army and CIA, both of which began in 1952 to voice suggestions as to what organization should control the detachment's growing operations. To fend off such bureaucratic predators Headquarters, Far East Air Forces retained a tight grip on the detachment, while the Fifth Air Force continued to provide general administrative and logistical support for the unit. Actual mission coordination was usually conducted through CCRAK, the Far East Command's clearing house for all unconventional warfare operations in North Korea after December 1951. CCRAK also provided Nichols's agents with mission-specific equipment drawn from its warehouses by special arrangements established through the Fifth Air Force.[31] This latter arrangement further confirmed Det 2's secondary mission, which called on it to support selected unconventional warfare missions beyond the scope of Fifth Air Force requirements.[32]

The air force had no objection to the detachment's commonsense cooperation with CCRAK, but it objected strongly when the army-dominated organization promptly set out to secure operational control of this valuable air force asset. As important as these bureaucratic struggles were at the top levels, they remained of little interest to the agents in the field who remained focused on more important (to them at least) issues. And foremost among these issues was the life-or-death problem of getting to and from the target area without being detected; a problem that continued to grow as the Communists further consolidated their territory. For Nichols and his sub-detachment commanders it was a continual game of trying to outfox the Communists, who of course were playing the same game against their agents.

Infiltration by parachute would continue to be the primary if not the only practical means of long-range penetration into North Korea's mountainous interior. The early-war experiences had proven the effectiveness of radio-parachute teams, and Nichols's agents were frequent users of Fifth Air Force assets dedicated to supporting military (and CIA) operations behind enemy lines. But for all the different air force units flying his teams north of the bomb line, there remained throughout the war virtually only one way back to safety for these agents—the slow and dangerous journey on foot. The one viable exception to this long-range, air infiltration was the previously noted Operation Salamander—agent insertion by sea.

The Korean peninsula offers thousands of miles of remote, rugged coastline for those seeking discreet entry onto the mainland. And the road and rail traffic running through the flat coastal areas adjacent the coastline make ideal targets for both partisans and agents. But though partisan raiders could make good use of the fast, armed gunboats provided by the U.S. Air Force's crash boat crews, stealth and deception remained the keys to mission success—not to mention survival—for Nichols's agents. And to that end the always-creative Nichols found the money to acquire local, shallow-water craft identical to those used by Korean fisherman.

By the close of 1952 Det 2's fleet had grown to "thirty vessels of all descriptions and sizes" to support its combat and resupply missions throughout the partisan-held islands.[33] Nichols also maintained access to much larger vessels to support his island activities, including for the biggest loads one of the U.S. Navy's amphibious assault ships. This support was critical because as it turned out there was a lot of activity on these islands. Located at most only a few miles from the shoreline, forested and far too many in number for the Communists to control at any one time, the islands provided exceptional launching platforms for unconventional warfare operations against the mainland. And the islands offered still something else of particular interest to Fifth Air Force leaders and their combat aircrews.

United Nations pilots flying over North Korea knew that a bale-out from their crippled aircraft over the peninsula's rugged interior meant almost certain capture and torture. To stand any chance of rescue their best if not only hope was to get at least as far as the offshore islands, where partisan forces (including Nichols's teams) operated. The air force designated these islands as "safe havens," a place for the pilots to head if baling out over enemy territory appeared unavoidable. But if the safe haven concept sounded plausible and made for good pilot morale, in practice it rarely justified the pilots' hopes. Despite air force reports crediting partisans or friendly Koreans with helping a number pilots evade capture after being downed in enemy territory, further investigation makes clear that luck, not an effective escape and evasion (E&E) program, account for many of these rescues.[34] One well-publicized rescue in particular underscores the lack of communications that crippled the E&E program throughout the war.

On 1 May 1952 U.S. Air Force colonel Albert W. Schinz, F-86 fighter pilot and deputy commander, 51st Fighter Interceptor Wing, parachuted from his battle-damaged fighter into the sea near one the small islands off North Korea's western coast. Before baling out he contacted Air Rescue with his position and was told to hang on for the night to await pickup the following day. Making it safely to a nearby island and knowing that the Fifth Air Force knew his general location he awaited pickup—for the next thirty-seven days. In his paper "Special Operations in Korea," Col. Rod Paschall, director of the U.S. Army's Military Institute, graphically describes what then happened: "Thirty-seven days later, near starvation and thoroughly disgusted with the US escape and evasion system, Schinz crawled into his hut for another lonely night of waiting, only to be rudely awakened at two a.m. as he found himself staring into a flashlight and a gun barrel. To his further astonishment, he heard 'Whoopee! American colonel!' spoken in English by (CCRAK) partisans who were deployed in the area."[35]

Although relieved to be picked up at last, Schinz's relief turned to anger upon learning that the partisans in these air force–designated "safe havens" were not issued receivers that could pick up distress calls from the survival radios issued to the pilots. In fact Schinz's rescue was purely a matter of luck. The partisans were actually out looking for another pilot they believed had baled out over the area days earlier. Although Schinz was safe his rescue would bring tragedy to the partisans who found him. During Schinz's subsequent debrief at the Pentagon he named the island on which he was rescued by the partisans. Headquarters, U.S. Air Force released the story to *Life* magazine, which published the saga in its 28 July 1952 issue.[36] The Chinese may have read the story too, for shortly thereafter a large raiding party stormed the island, killing all partisans present.[37]

Schinz's misadventures in 1952 confirmed how little progress had been made in the E&E program since a very frustrated Fifth Air Force had designated Det 3 (6004th AISS) as its focal point for such operations a full year earlier. In fact, Det 3's activation was borne of a still earlier air force frustration with the CIA's failure to establish a clandestine E&E program in enemy territory. General Partridge's dissatisfaction in this regard is made clear in a Fifth Air Force paper, "Evasion & Escape Historical Synopsis," summarizing the E&E situation during the first four months of the war.[38] Upon asking his staff when an effective E&E network could be established to assist airmen evading through enemy territory, the unhappy commander was told, "All clandestine activities in connection with Evasion and Escape are delegated to an agency not under the operational control of the Air Force, and that repeated assurances of substantial covert operations within the near future had been received from this agency . . . but as yet no agents had been placed in the field."[39]

By this stage of the war the clandestine E&E mission had already been institutionalized within the CIA's jurisdiction, and Fifth Air Force efforts to reclaim the mission met stiff resistance from the Agency. Though a joint military–CIA meeting held later that year added manpower to the E&E program the Agency maintained its bureaucratic primacy for the mission. Despite everyone in the "E&E game" seeming to want the mission, none of the players seemed able to find the resources needed to give it the day-to-day priority given more high profile, unconventional warfare missions. Overall, the covert E&E program in North Korea continued to represent the low point of military and CIA operations in North Korea, which continued to grow steadily in other areas. And like the other organizations the 6004th AISS continued to grow too.

In proposing yet another expansion for the 6004th in September 1953, one air force report describes Nichols's unit simply but accurately as "the primary collection agency of FEAF."[40] Noting the unit's liaison as an organizational equal with the Documents Research Section (the CIA liaison with FEC), the letter assesses the squadron's bureaucratic position relative to other military intelligence organizations within FEC: "While an exact parallel with CIA's operations and Navy's cannot be drawn, it may be noted that in Korea we now have a detachment operation (Det 2) on an equal basis with a CIA operation of regimental strength and a Navy operation equivalent of a Group."[41] Considering the senior rank of officers normally commanding regimental or group-size operations, the air force's decision to allow the relatively low-ranking Nichols (by now a major) to retain command of its most importance intelligence asset is indeed remarkable.

Although anecdotal sources have their obvious limitations, they do provide rare, personal sketches of enigmatic figures such as Nichols.

Seldom known to wear military rank and rarely a complete uniform of any type, the commander appeared to instill confidence in everyone ranging from field agents to the most senior commanders for whom he worked. Sgt. Ray Dawson of the U.S. Air Force, serving with CCRAK in 1952, recalls the night he went to Nichols's compound in downtown Seoul to discuss operations with him: "The first thing I noticed was the presence of a large number of Air Force security police outside Nichols' building; usually it was just Korean military police. As I entered Nichols' room it was so dark it took a minute for my eyes to adjust to the light coming from one small oil lamp of some sort. When they did adjust I saw the reason for the Air Force security police outside. . . . I was looking at General Partridge and General Doolittle! They, along with Nichols, were all sitting cross-legged on the floor, talking to (a casually dressed) Nichols."[42]

One of the most enduring aspects of special operations units, for better or worse, is the impact a dominant personality exerts on the relatively small organization. Nichols clearly saw the potential not only for Det 2 but also for what could be achieved by integrating his efforts with those of CCRAK, the CIA, and other Fifth Air Force special operations units. Or was it they who benefited by integrating their efforts with his? It was Nichols alone who never rotated out of the combat zone during the war, who provided the continuity and leadership for the successful efforts of so many organizations. Special operations and Positive Intelligence may have been too integrated to separate, but the combined potential was exploited to the fullest by one of the most unique warriors the United States has ever brought to the battlefield.

Nichols retired from the air force in 1962, his health failing from a number of diseases to which he was exposed in Burma, China, and Korea. He died on 2 June 1992, at the age of sixty-nine, in the Veterans Affairs hospital in Tuscaloosa, Alabama. He was inducted into the Air Commando Hall of Fame in 1995, soon after a researcher first declassified and published reports of his wartime exploits.

Special Air Missions

> We saw thousands and thousands of [Chinese] troops, trucks, bumper to bumper! It was a moonlit night, snow on the ground. . . . We flew right down, turned our landing lights on [the trucks], and they still wouldn't fire!

Like the legendary Mongol archer that fought with a quiver full of specialized arrows carried for different types of targets, FEC also fought its unconventional war with some very specialized "arrows." These were the spies, saboteurs, partisans, and psychological warfare teams that sought every opportunity to destroy the enemy's strength and morale. But like all arrows, FEC's weapons were useless without a strong bow to launch them. The amphibious operations described earlier provided one such bow, but the agents and partisans thus launched seldom penetrated far inland. Only the parachute insertion of agents into North Korea's interior could penetrate the curtain of mountains that hid the enemy's main positions and maneuvers so well. And to launch these arrows FEC turned to a group of airmen that soon formed one of the most effective weapons to emerge during the first year of the war.

The Special Air Missions Detachment evolved from Unit 4, a small force thrown together during the first weeks of the war with aircraft assigned to the 21st Troop Carrier Squadron. Deployed from Japan to South Korea to support the earliest agent-insertion missions, Unit 4 moved to Kimpo Airfield on the outskirts of Seoul that fall, only to be forced back south to Taegu Airfield less than ninety days later by the attacking Chinese. Distancing its aircraft from the front-line combat had obvious advantages, but it came at the expense of much longer mission times over enemy territory for the already overextended aircrews. As one U.S. Army officer assigned to liaison duty with Unit 4 observed at the time, "The missions have become much longer since moving our base of operations [back to Taegu Airfield]. In addition, KLO has stepped up the number of flights per month. It is not fair to expect crews to fly all night on tactical [special air] missions and then fly all day on cargo and evacuation runs."[43]

During the first several months of the war the 21st attempted to minimize the exposure of individual airmen to Unit 4's high-risk missions by rotating fresh aircrews into the unit every two weeks. Done in the spirit of fairness, this rotation policy did not, however, extend to overmanning the unit for its dual-mission, day-night activities. It was an exhausting schedule that succeeded far beyond what might otherwise have been expected—a performance credited largely to the many airmen who voluntarily extended their two-week rotations. An early 1951 report describing Unit 4's support concluded that "under Captain Harry C. Aderholt, CO of Unit 4, the crews have developed considerable skill in the special techniques required on these special missions. . . . Flying intelligence missions, which often last five or six hours during the hours of darkness, as well as Combat Cargo Command missions during the day, has exacted the utmost in stamina and endurance from pilots and crews."[44]

Although the dangerous practice of ignoring monthly flying hour limitations continued for the next several months, the unit's return to

A British expression, "mobs for jobs," described the proliferation of special operations units in World War II. The UN effort in Korea was little different. It is entirely possible that all of the different units represented in this seemingly posed photograph could actually be putting their agents aboard the same aircraft for multiple, unrelated missions. *U.S. Air Force*

Taegu in February 1951 did change their operation in a number of other ways. Included in these changes were a new unit designation and another change of airfield, as spelled out in orders establishing the Special Air Missions Detachment at Taegu South Airfield on the twentieth of the same month. Formed largely from disbanded Unit 4 assets, the new SAM would "provide air transportation for US Ambassador Muccio, Republic of Korea President Rhee, Lieutenant General Ridgway (CINCFEC), Eighth Army Staff, other agencies with legitimate lift requests, and to operate psychological missions as requested by Eighth Army."[45]

By day the SAM aircrews continued flying routine cargo runs as well as VIP flights carrying the highest-ranking U.S. and Korean officials traveling throughout Korea. By night the same aircrews switched to special air missions, putting in long hours on dangerous, low-level infiltration flights deep into North Korea. Despite their inevitable exposure to brutal interrogation should they survive being shot down during one of these night missions, no one seems to have questioned the practice of bringing them into such close proximity with the most senior UN officials in Korea only hours before these secret flights.

The new SAM was equipped with one World War II–era B-17 heavy bomber-turned-VIP-transport; one C-47 transport also upgraded to VIP standard; two loudspeaker-equipped "Voice" C-47s for psychological warfare (PsyWar) broadcasts, and three standard-model C-47s transferred from the deactivated Unit 4.[46] The new orders also changed the existing two-week rotation policy by placing all SAM personnel on "indefinite detached service from this [21st Troop Carrier Squadron] unit."[47] Even FEC had proposed changes in mind for the new SAM Detachment.

Noting the threat posed by enemy night fighters to SAM's stepped-up night infiltration missions, Operation Aviary officers suggested modifying its C-47s with self-sealing gas tanks and an olive-drab paint scheme (SAM aircraft flew in air force–standard, flat silver metal finish). Also included in the list of suggested improvements were engine exhaust extensions to reduce the visibility of the low-flying aircraft to ground observation, and improved radar sets and radios.[48] Despite all the talk of improvements, however, the Fifth Air Force in the end found only enough money to equip the C-47s with the new, ground-to-air SCR-300 radios. Thus equipped the Unit 4/SAM aircrews went to war with what they had, supporting in the process Operation Aviary's first successful parachute infiltration of a radio-equipped agent team behind enemy lines.[49]

This "first" was of critical importance to the demoralized UN force that was in full retreat during the winter of 1950–51. Falling back from the surprise intervention of Chinese forces the previous November, it was the second time in less than six months that the U.S. military faced the bloody and humiliating prospect of being run off the Korean peninsula. With contact broken between attacking Chinese and retreating allied forces, FEC commanders found themselves urgently asking, "Where are the Chinese?" The crude "smoke jumps mission" described in chapter 1 might have proven useful a second time, but only if the weather cooperated sufficiently to provide good air-to-ground visibility. But "cooperative" is not a word often associated with Korean winters, and the Aviary-SAM team responded to FEC's request with yet another first of the war.

In the freezing winter darkness of 9 December 1950 a single C-47 parachuted a radio-equipped agent team, code-named "Hotel Victor One," into a desolate track of land in the Chinese army's path of advance. To the immense relief of the Aviary and SAM officers aboard the transport, they were soon rewarded with a strong radio signal com-

Capt. Harry C. "Heinie" Aderholt. "Better to beg for forgiveness than ask for permission": Following its discovery of Aderholt's unauthorized night attacks against enemy truck convoys, using C-47 transports illegally modified to carry F-51 fighter-type napalm-jelly drop tanks, Fifth Air Force headquarters quickly put a halt to the SAM commander's aggressive initiative. *Courtesy of Harry C. Aderholt*

ing from the agents somewhere in the blackness below.[50] How important were the intelligence reports subsequently transmitted from this single team? One knowledgeable postwar study called it "the vital essential element of information [needed on enemy movements by FEC at the time]."[51] But however vital the information may have seemed after the war, the FEC officers listening to Hotel Victor One's reports that winter had a tough time swallowing the answer to the question they had sent forth with the agents.

The radio team's reports of massive Chinese convoys pouring southward across the Yalu River were the last thing FEC wanted to hear, especially after General MacArthur's premature and public prediction that U.S. troops would be home by Christmas of that year. Aviary and SAM officers who had actually seen the convoys watched in dismay as their reports were labeled "erroneous" by headquarters officers unwilling to accept the bad news that China was now in the war. Aderholt himself watched from the cockpit of his C-47 as the stream of trucks carried the Chinese down on the unsuspecting and vulnerable allied armies. As Aderholt recalls in his official U.S. Air

Force memoirs, "We saw thousands and thousands of troops, trucks, bumper to bumper! It was a moonlit night, snow on the ground. . . . We flew right down, turned our landing lights on [the trucks], and they still wouldn't fire. We came back and reported and were told 'Well, the B-26s [medium bombers] will get them!'"[52]

The B-26s didn't get them, and fortunately for Aderholt, Chinese fire didn't get him. Under strict orders not to betray their positions by firing at low-flying aircraft, the Chinese soldiers obeyed even when it became obvious they had been spotted. Incredibly, the Chinese still refused to fire even when on succeeding nights Aderholt and his SAM crews attacked the trucks with one of his personal improvisations—F-51 fighter-type napalm drop tanks slung from beneath the fuselage of C-47 transports. The only stipulation Aderholt placed on his aircrews was that the primary mission (e.g., parachuting agents) was to be completed before they were free to attack targets of opportunity with their very unauthorized "C-47 low-level bombers." Although extremely accurate when used, the practice was immediately terminated by a startled Fifth Air Force headquarters after its staff became aware of Aderholt's unorthodox initiative.[53]

It wasn't so much that the Fifth Air Force was opposed to dropping things from SAM aircraft, it just had its own ideas on what those things should look like. And what headquarters had in mind—beyond agents of course—were the psychological warfare (PsyWar) missions that dropped millions of propaganda and surrender leaflets from the skies over Korea, as well as the powerful air-to-ground loudspeakers that also sought to undermine the enemy's morale. Especially disheartening to Communist soldiers was the sight of a slow-flying and unarmed C-47 flying pass after pass low over their positions with no fear of attack from the North Korean People's Air Force. Female broadcasters were frequently employed for the loudspeaker messages, their feminine voices adding insult to injury to the prideful Koreans below. Field interrogations of defecting soldiers conducted in Korea concluded that voice broadcasts were more effective than surrender leaflets, a conclusion credited in part to the large number (nearly 30 percent) of illiterate soldiers found in the Communists' ranks.[54]

Literate or illiterate, however, the Communists could always be counted upon to provide a hot welcome to any SAM aircraft straying too low on these missions. This was especially true for the leaflet dropping missions, a lesson the Americans would learn the hard way. The initial PsyWar flights flown during the first months of the war dropped their leaflets from two thousand feet, an altitude soon found too high to assure that the leaflets landed in the desired area.[55] Descending to five hundred feet solved the drop accuracy problems and flights continued with standard leaflet loads averaging three to four thousand pounds per mission. Unfortunately for the aircrews, the lower altitude also solved the accuracy problem for the enemy soldiers below, who now had the aircraft within easy range of their machine guns and rifles.

It was during one of these low-level leaflet drop flights in February 1951 that a PsyWar C-47 was so badly damaged from enemy fire that following its subsequent crash landing at a forward airfield it was declared a total write-off.[56] While dropping leaflets near Seoul the aircraft was hit by enemy small arms fire that severed all rudder control cables and caused a runaway propeller that required the right engine be shut down. Barely maintaining aircraft control and staying aloft only on their sole remaining engine, the crew limped back to a friendly airstrip only to discover that extending the landing gear used all of the plane's remaining hydraulic fluid. Racing down the runway with no brakes left to slow it down, the C-47 veered off the runway, in the process sheering the landing gear, tearing both engines from their mounts, and leaving the aircraft with "the wings bent considerable."[57]

A review of the conditions that led to the February crash persuaded the air force to switch to night leaflet drops as the only viable countermeasure to enemy ground fire. But even this change in tactics provided only a partial respite to the SAM's increasingly violent world. A 21st TCS unit history report for March notes cryptically, "Aircraft are receiving battle damage while accomplishing Special Air Missions in Korea. Three airplanes received major damage and five received minor damage during March 1951."[58] And the 21st TCS report for the following month concludes:

> One aircraft from this organization has been missing since the morning of 30 April 1951. This aircraft had four crewmembers and two psychological warfare men aboard. This aircraft departed from K-37 [Taegu Airfield] on a leaflet drop mission in the Kumhwa-Wonsan area behind enemy lines. The aircraft commander was heard giving the distress call "May Day" and an emergency IFF [identification friend or foe transmitter] signal was observed. . . . This is the third crew from this organization (SAM) that has been listed as killed or listed as missing since the start of the Korean war.[59]

"To operate psychological missions as requested by Eighth Army" would prove to be more than a mission statement for the surviving SAM crews as the war progressed. It would also become a fitting memorial for those whose death came on missions so secret that the United States would continue to hide their existence from public scrutiny for decades after hostilities ceased in Korea. And it was certainly no coincidence that this official government policy continued in full force for the much larger unit that replaced the SAM Detachment for the third and final year of the war.

B Flight

> When we gave the green light for the [Korean] parachutists to jump, they simply slid off the wood benches and dropped. In the event they hesitated, we had a toggle switch in the cockpit that dropped the whole lot . . . bomb racks, benches, and parachutists from the aircraft.

The U.S. government allowed a full twenty-four years to elapse after the termination of overt hostilities in Korea before it agreed to declassify the wartime activities of B Flight, 6167th Operations Squadron, Fifth Air Force. Activated in April 1952 to replace the Special Air Missions Detachment, B Flight's highly classified missions were flown with a combination of B-26 medium bombers modified for agent parachute operations, as well as the versatile C-46 and C-47 transports. Based from its inception at Seoul City Airfield, the presence of the new unit's black-painted aircraft was a noticeable addition to a base already so busy with classified flight operations that it was referred to by many as "Spook City."

Even an abbreviated summary of the declassified document describing B Flight's "Combat Doctrine" in Korea helps explain the long-held secrecy surrounding this little-known unit. In replacing the smaller SAM Detachment the highly classified B Flight was created solely for the purpose of expanding the Fifth Air Force's unconventional warfare program to include:

> CLASSIFIED Missions: Transporting and resupplying personnel and units operating behind enemy lines . . . for the purpose of gathering intelligence information and covert activity . . . or for aiding rescue, escape or evasion.
>
> PSYWAR Operations: Missions assigned by psychological warfare section of the Fifth Air Force and/or Eighth Army . . . encompassing leaflet drops and speaker missions.
>
> FIREFLY Operations: Flare drops . . . to aid ground units . . . in night combat . . . and bomber A/C in night attack of enemy.
>
> OTHER Missions: As may be assigned by the Fifth Air Force. This includes personnel snatch with transport A/C.[60]

Such a document could leave little doubt in the minds of the newly assigned airmen as to the risks they were about to undertake, and at this stage of the war the air force was no longer asking for volunteers.

The classified missions were initially flown in all three types of aircraft assigned to the flight. From these early experiences in 1952 the crews soon concluded that the glass-nosed version[61] of the B-26, modified with a platform in the bomb bay to carry parachutists, was the ideal aircraft for agent-insertion missions.[62] This platform modification to the bomb bay added wood benches above the standard bomb racks, on which a maximum of six parachutists could sit while en route to the drop zone. And there was still one other modification—one definitely not briefed to the Koreans. As former B Flight navigator Maj. P. G. Moore recalls, "When we gave the green light for the parachutists to jump, they simply slid off the wood benches and dropped. In the event they hesitated, we had a toggle switch in the cockpit that dropped the whole lot . . . bomb racks, benches, and parachutists from the aircraft."[63]

If the parachutists hesitated, perhaps it was because they had long since noticed that those already sent on previous missions had never been seen or heard from again. Things had changed drastically since the early days of the war when behind-the-lines operations were conducted with an agent survival rate approximating 70 percent. Another thing that had changed since 1951 was that American and British soldiers no longer led these deep-penetration missions into North Korea. Described in greater detail in chapter 1, FEC's use of non-Korean soldiers on airborne partisan operations was terminated the previous year following the unacceptable loss of UN soldiers in the failed Virginia I and Spitfire operations. Despite FEC's decision, however, firsthand accounts by the airmen taking the agents into North Korea and China suggest that American civilians were still infiltrated into these areas when their employer deemed the mission of sufficient importance to warrant the risk.

Major Moore recalls one such mission in 1952 in which his B-26 crew took an unidentified American parachutist into Manchuria.[64] Moore, who honed his navigator skills during World War II while serving in the air force's elite Pathfinder squadrons, used the best maps available for these insertions into China—maps published in 1912 and marked "Japanese General Staff." As Moore recalls, "There was a mountain range north of the North Korean-Chinese border that featured a saddle between two extinct volcanoes. There was a drop zone in the saddle and we went up there with parachutists more than once. Twice I took a blonde-haired American there. He wore an Army uniform without rank, and spoke fluent Chinese. I don't know who he worked for or how he got back."[65]

To minimize the flight time over enemy territory, the B-26 crews normally departed Seoul to the east, flying out over the Sea of Japan.

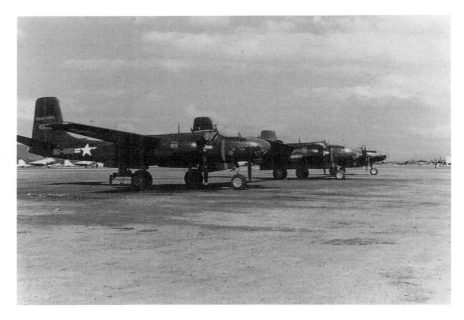

The telltale glass nose distinguishes these B Flight special operations B-26s from the solid-nose ground-attack models of the same bomber. Up to six parachutists could be carried in the modified bomb bay, which also included a special "one way" feature should the agents hesitate to jump when ordered. *Courtesy of P.G. Moore*

With the aid of a navigation beacon aboard one of the U.S. Navy's aircraft carriers stationed in the area, the crew then flew as far north as possible before turning inland over North Korea to search for the small signal fires that marked the partisan drop zones. Sometimes the flight into enemy territory was the easy part, as was the case on the night of 30 March 1953 when Moore earned his second Distinguished Flying Cross, this one for bringing his crew home alive. The language of the citation accompanying the award provides a classic example of a special operations award given for valor, under circumstances never destined for public record. I have added selected explanatory phrases in italics to underscore this uniquely military style of recognition:

> Major Moore was a navigator of an unarmed, unescorted B-26 . . . performing a classified night interdiction mission [*"interdiction" in an unarmed aircraft?*]. . . . This mission penetrated deep into enemy territory in the vicinity of the Yalu River [*no mention of which side of the Yalu River, which separates North Korea from China*]. The target area [*a drop zone for partisan parachutists*] was near enemy operational airfields . . . guarded by

heavy anti-aircraft weapons, radar stations, and searchlights. . . . Moore successfully directed the low-flying [*parachute-dropping altitude*] aircraft around and through mountainous terrain [*and the searchlights which had by then caught the intruder in their beams*] . . . to the water.[66]

Without discounting that always-valuable ally, luck, it appears that Moore's invaluable Pathfinder experience played a major role in bringing the entire crew through their frightening ordeal. But Moore's experience was very much the exception among B Flight's aircrews. Arriving in B Flight for the most part with little if any night low-level flying training or experience, the airmen were subject to an air force assignment system that made it possible for them to rotate back to the United States in as little as six months. Though good for individual morale, this system inevitably placed inexperienced aircrews on special air missions demanding much higher skill levels than they possessed or were capable of learning within the time allotted for their combat tours. And the grossly inadequate three to four days that B Flight allowed for the "indoctrination" of these nonvolunteers did little if anything to reduce the severity of the problem.

This lack of experience was exacerbated still further late in the war by a Fifth Air Force policy that gave credit for two missions to any airman flying a single mission lasting more than five hours over enemy territory. As the chronological length of an individual's combat tour was determined by the number of combat missions flown, the already low experience levels in B Flight sank still further. Inevitably, partisans and supplies were parachuted into the wrong place with tragic results. In its Unit History report for the last six months of 1952 the 6167th Air Base Group notes, "The primary problem of the Group has been the lack of qualified personnel due to constant rotations. Of particular importance is the shortage of navigators."[67]

This acknowledged shortage of experienced SAM crews had surfaced long before 1952, however. In fact it was the air force's embarrassment over the mistakes made by one such inexperienced aircrew in the failure of Operation Spitfire, that motivated its belated decision to activate B Flight in the first place. Unable to locate the Spitfire team's drop zone at night, the C-47 crew returned after daylight to parachute the supplies right on top of the group's "secret" camp, in plain view of every enemy soldier in the immediate area.[68] Although the team immediately fled the area it was ambushed the following morning with the loss of several lives and the obvious abort of its mission.[69]

But if the air force had its aircrew experience problems the problems encountered on the ground behind enemy lines reached such grim proportions that by late 1952, airborne partisan operations had literally become suicide missions. Most of the partisans appear to have been killed or captured within days of their infiltration, if not on the drop zone itself. The results if not the particulars of each failure were known to CCRAK planners, leading one well-documented postwar study on the subject to criticize "these decisions to use partisans against enemy supply routes in airborne operations appears to have been futile and callous."[70] In contrast to this dismal operational and moral record, however, B Flight could point with justifiable pride to the acknowledged success of its PsyWar efforts that by this stage of the war had become relatively sophisticated.

B Flight's leaflet dropping missions were usually flown with its C-46 and C-47 transports, both types flying with the main cargo door removed for hand-thrown leaflet distribution into the airstream. The more humanitarian leaflets might warn civilian populations to flee the area before heavy bombers arrived with their lethal cargo. Most messages, however, were aimed at demoralizing the enemy as a whole or urging individual soldiers to surrender by using the leaflet itself as a safe-conduct pass. Accurate leaflet drops were eventually made from seventy-five hundred feet, a much safer altitude than the dangerously low levels attempted by the 21st TCS earlier in the war. This higher altitude was made possible by the development of a slow-burning fuse that allowed the leaflet "bombs" to drop to the required lower altitude before a small powder charge ignited to blow the bundle open, dispersing thousands of leaflets over the target area.[71]

As in every modern war, attempts to measure the effectiveness of the PsyWar program in Korea proved difficult at best. However, one early-war study done in Korea by a research team from Johns Hopkins University concluded that "the [financial] cost of a PsyWar capture to a conventional kill appears to have a probable ratio of 70:1 in favor of PsyWar."[72] From its field research the Johns Hopkins team learned that Communist soldiers feared air attack far more than artillery, tanks, or infantry.[73] And the aircraft weapons feared most were machine guns, high-explosive bombs, rockets, and napalm in that order.[74] The same Johns Hopkins research (largely POW interrogations) provided an additional insight that led to yet another special mission for B Flight, this one in direct support of U.S. front-line units.

Communist troops had learned early in the war that by moving and attacking at night they could exploit the U.S. Air Force's near total lack of a night ground attack capability. Quickly putting their newfound knowledge to good use, the North Koreans and Chinese became adept at isolating and overwhelming allied units with night, human-wave assaults. The air force's response to this tactic was designated

Firefly, a program that turned night into day by dispensing one-million-candlepower parachute flares from B Flight's aircraft. Tactical coordination in the target area was critical with each mission, for after entering the target area at an altitude of ten thousand feet, the flare ship was dependent upon airborne or ground controllers for directions to its specific drop point. Armed in the aircraft, the high-intensity flares were set to ignite one thousand to fifteen hundred feet below the aircraft. At two thousand feet above the terrain each one of these flares illuminated approximately one square mile of the ground below.[75]

In a war in which the technology for night vision devices was still in its infant stage, these Firefly missions were a tactic that could spell the difference between life and death for the UN soldiers. During a maximum effort on the night of 29 March 1953, for example, B Flight dropped 1,004 flares to highlight wave after wave of Communist infantry assaulting American positions in the notorious "Old Baldy" sector of the front lines.[76] Still other special operations tactics were in their infancy during the war, and B Flight would have a chance to pioneer these as well.

In November 1952 a Fifth Air Force headquarters letter, classified Secret, announced the introduction of a new capability for retrieving downed airmen or agents from enemy-held territory.[77] Officially designated the Personnel Pick-up Ground Station, it was known more simply by the pickup aircrews as "the snatch system." As usual the simpler name said it all, for the system called for an aircraft in flight to do just that: literally snatch an individual from the ground and reel him into the aircraft as it flew from the pickup area. The system was similar to the more-familiar one used by banner-towing aircraft in which a wire is strung horizontally between two vertical poles, with a second wire leading to the object to be snatched from the ground. In practice the operation requires that a tail-hook equipped aircraft swoop within a few feet of the ground, snare the horizontal wire and, climbing immediately for altitude, pull the banner (or downed pilot) up behind it.

In Korea the horizontal "wire" was a nylon rope that would stretch when pulled, thereby avoiding the self-defeating prospect of tearing the downed airman in half as he accelerated from zero to ninety miles per hour almost immediately. Set-up of the system was necessarily simple as time was obviously of the essence once the enemy spotted the low, slow-flying aircraft in its vicinity. After dropping the necessary ground equipment in a fifty-pound bundle to the airman or agent below, the aircraft circled the area until the individual was ready for pickup. It then began a low, slow pass to snag the nylon rope with its hook. Successful field trials proved the technical feasibility of the concept, but all involved in the trials noted the extreme vulnerability of the aircraft to ground fire on the "snatch" pass.

B Flight attempted two pickups of downed personnel in enemy territory during the first half of 1953. The first attempt failed when the airman was captured before the pickup aircraft could reach the scene. The second failed for reasons that remain to this day only partially explained. On 24 May 1953, just three months before the war ended, a C-47 "snatch pickup" was attempted of five B-29 bomber crewmen shot down the previous January.[78] After establishing radio contact with the downed bomber's pilot, 1st Lt. Gilbert L. Ashley, and receiving assurances that the area was free of enemy troops, the B Flight crew dropped the fifty-pound bundle and began circling the area. Upon receiving word from Ashley that the ground equipment was ready the plane's pilot, Maj. David M. Taylor, began his first retrieval approach in the early morning dawn. But as he later recalled, "It just didn't look right to me. . . . That's when I called Ashley [again] on the final seconds of the approach and told him 'If there's anything wrong, now's your chance to tell me.' He came back, 'Everything is fine.' In an instant, machine gun fire ripped into the underside of the C-47. The [vertical poles for the snatch system] down there weren't poles. They were .50 caliber guns. . . . We were so close the bullets were coming straight up from the 'poles.'"[79]

No follow-up rescue of the group was attempted, though Taylor was sent back to the area days later and, to his surprise, again established contact with the downed airmen. Using personal information provided by U.S. intelligence for each member of the bomber crew, he confirmed their individual identities on a tape recorder-equipped radio. Even more surprising to Taylor the group spoke as if nothing unusual had happened during the recent snatch attempt. At the time FEC believed this particular group of airmen to be under the protection of one of the UN partisan teams parachuted into the area the previous January. Obviously the partisans had been captured and compromised, setting the stage for the ambush of Taylor's aircraft. Unknown but quite likely is that Ashley had a gun held to his head as he talked to the B Flight pilot. None of the five aircrew were ever returned and the U.S. government subsequently declared them dead.

Clearly Taylor's crew was lucky to have survived a trap sprung at such close quarters. A similar ambush in China the previous November succeeded in downing the CIA's pickup aircraft, an Air America C-47, on its low-slow pickup run.[80] The two surviving Americans,

Richard Fecteau and John Downey, were convicted of espionage and spent decades in Chinese prisons before diplomats finally secured their release.

B flight would fly and fight to the finish in Korea as its unit history for the last six months of 1953 reports: "During the last twenty-six days of the Korean hostilities, seven hundred, eight-two combat hours were flown with no loss of aircraft. . . . Two hundred, ninety-one combat missions were flown; one hundred, seventeen were classified [i.e., agent insertions], seventy-three were leaflet and one hundred were flare."[81]

It is psychologically difficult for both victor and loser to maintain an aggressive combat spirit in the waning days of a war, when personal sacrifice becomes meaningless and personal survival, the most basic instinct of all, becomes overwhelming. It is more difficult still when the individual's war is fought behind a cloak of secrecy. Without the psychological support of public recognition or the safety of numbers, flying single-ship missions into the black of night becomes the airman's most intimate nightmare. The flyer's imagination runs riot with fearful thoughts of death or capture and torture, the only two alternatives to his successful return. But as the record shows, the B Flight crews flew and fought to the last, performing every task that was expected of them until the bitter end.

The Air Force "Sailors"

> They lived in close quarters for long periods of time . . . went hungry, damn near froze to death, got shot and hit . . . shot at and missed . . . worked hard to keep the boat in repair . . . endured when they were dead tired . . . were scared when "Bed Check Charlie" came over in his bi-plane at night and dropped hand grenades on them . . . were cautious when a MIG would search for their boat hiding in a fog bank.

When the Korean War exploded onto the world scene in the summer of 1950, the three-year-old U.S. Air Force was still very much the new kid on the block in our nation's capital. And to the surprise of only a few the senior residents on this block, the long-entrenched Army and Navy Departments were still stonewalling Joint Chiefs of Staff efforts to determine which of their jealously guarded "roles and missions" would be assumed by the airmen.[82] Although the NKPA brought much of this stonewalling to an abrupt halt that summer, rivalries postponed are not rivalries abandoned. And few roles and missions rivalries were left as wide-open for future argument as was that of unconventional warfare.

This particular rivalry didn't seem to bother the air force, however, as it set off to war that summer with an equally wide-open approach to

war fighting best described by the philosophy "if it isn't expressly prohibited, it must be permitted." And one of the most startling consequences to flow from this philosophical approach is found in the remarkable war record achieved by the U.S. Air Force's 22d Crash
Rescue Boat Squadron (CRBS). By the war's end this most unlikely of
unconventional warfare units would emerge from combat in the frigid
ocean waters surrounding North Korea and China, with a history of
valor beyond anything even its strongest proponents could have envisioned in 1950.

The genesis of what became the 22d CRBS had the most humble of
beginnings in the Korean War, as the last of the crash rescue boats in
the Far East had been put into dry storage for shipment back to U.S.
only three months before war broke out.[83] Worse yet, experienced airmen and officers with marine career specialties had been scattered to
other career fields and bases throughout the Pacific. Suddenly faced
with the very real prospect of airmen in battle-damaged aircraft attempting to escape North Korean airspace for the relative safety of the
open sea, Headquarters, FEAF frantically set about to reassemble its
crash rescue boat capability.[84]

The urgency of the headquarters effort can be gauged in part by the
response it generated, for less than two weeks later the Boat Section,
6160th Air Base Group (ABG) was activated on 7 July at Itazuke Air
Base, Japan, under the command of 1st Lt. Phil Dickey.[85] In no less a
rush the lieutenant promptly moved out to reassemble all former boat
crewmen still in the Pacific theater, as well as whatever boats were
still seaworthy. Dickey had good reason to press hard for sailors and
boats, as his entire command at the activation ceremony consisted of a
grand total of one 114-foot freight/passenger ship (FP-47) and four airmen. The lieutenant found his efforts to acquire seaworthy boats easier than getting the crewmen, and in short order the Boat Section
added a second 104-foot ship, as well as seven 63-foot and eight 85-
foot boats.[86]

It was in getting his crews back together that the lieutenant found
himself coming to the irritable attention of several senior officers,
themselves frantic to get their own undermanned units ready for war.
Fortunately for Dickey supportive phone calls from headquarters soon
straightened out the senior officers, if not their antipathy toward the
young officer. The lieutenant continued his effective word-of-mouth
recruiting campaign throughout the small, crash rescue boat community, an effort that soon brought together a beginning cadre of eighty-
five airmen-sailors. With crew and boats thus barely assembled, the
section immediately received orders dispersing its boats to bases
throughout the Pacific. This crash rescue coverage was less than thin

The Korean War–era U.S. Air Force fought on the sea as well as in the air. Operating deep behind enemy lines, wooden-hulled eighty-five-foot crash rescue boats penetrated both ice-choked seas and coastal defenses to launch partisans, saboteurs, and spies into North Korea and even China. *Graphics: Wayne Thompson; technical consultants: Jim Jarvis and Bud Tretter*

as it was intended to support both the surge in air transport already crossing the Pacific from the United States, and the combat missions flown over Korea. Regardless, the boats were sent to Guam, Okinawa, several ports in Japan, and straight into the line of fire itself in Korea.[87]

Four of the eighty-five-foot boats sent to South Korea were subsequently ordered farther north still, into North Korean waters and as close as possible to the targets being struck daily by allied aircraft. It was a duty station mandated by absolute necessity as during the course of the war the allied air forces lost nearly one combat aircraft per day[88] to combat action over North Korea.[89] Some of the rescues were relatively straightforward, open-ocean pickups of airmen fortunate enough to have baled out of their crippled aircraft over the Yellow Sea or Sea of Japan. But on more than one occasion the boat crews found themselves in a new role, fighting hard to retrieve an airman still trapped on the North Korean coastline.

This was exactly the situation on 8 September 1951, when the crew of the R-1-676 was alerted for a dangerous pickup attempt of a downed fighter pilot, stranded on a sandbar in the mouth of the heavily defended Chinnampo River estuary. The rescue call came in as the eighty-five-footer was refueling at Cho-do,[90] less than five nautical miles west of the downed pilot's location. Pulling away from the island at full power as it sounded general quarters, the boat raced toward the estuary as its crewmen manned their gun stations for the hostile reception awaiting them on the mainland. Heavier fire support would be essential for this pickup attempt, and fortunately the HMNS *Eversten,* a Dutch destroyer cruising in the immediate vicinity, responded to the boat's call for help. Former staff sergeant James

R. Jarvis, second-in-command as mate on the R-1-676, recalls what happened as they approached within easy range of the North Korean gunners:

> After cautiously approaching the sandbars, we started taking fire from the North Korean artillery. We put a raft over with two men [to retrieve the pilot] and returned fire with the four .50 calibers we had. . . . Just then HMNS Eversten lost sight of us and was forced to cease its supporting gun-fire. . . . Our boat was soon bracketed by North Korean coastal artillery. . . . As the raft [with the pilot aboard] returned to the boat . . . a shell burst off the starboard bow, wounding Johnson [the cook] . . . but he recovered and continuing firing the .50 until he passed out. Several of the crew were recommended for decorations ranging from the Silver Star to the Bronze Star, none of which were ever awarded; Johnson at least got the Purple Heart for his wounds.[91]

By stationing themselves so far north to recover allied pilots in distress the boats soon came to be regarded by others, still unknown to the crews, as a precious commodity for yet another purpose. These unknown "others" were found in FEC's unconventional warfare and intelligence communities—operatives who used the islands off North Korea's coastline as bases from which to launch agents and partisans against targets in North Korea and China. But seaborne transportation to support their offshore efforts was always in short supply and fast raiding craft virtually unobtainable; at least until the crash rescue boats arrived. Moving quickly to take advantage of the boats' presence in the islands, the operatives soon secured air force permission to task the eighty-five-foot craft for offensive combat operations.

To assure the needed mission-response time to special operations boat requests (and to control a scarce asset), Headquarters, Fifth Air Force directed its Operations Directorate to assume direct control of Detachment 1, with the 6160th ABG retaining administrative and logistical responsibilities. This unusual arrangement was followed by a headquarters staff review of the extreme dangers and brutal weather conditions that the crews and their boats would be forced to endure in such a hostile environment. But although this review concluded that a thirty-day-long combat tour was the maximum allowable for each crew, operational priorities in the islands frequently pushed this maximum crew endurance limit to a full two months.

Such extensions on human limits took a predictable toll on the crewmen, with more of the airmen-sailors subsequently hospitalized for exposure to the elements than for enemy action. Still others were evacuated with yellow jaundice, the result of inadequate diets on the boats. Regardless of such casualties the wartime reality for the crews

"You don't need guns very often, but when you do, you tend to need them rather badly." The air force sailors mounted seven heavy machine guns on their boats, four of which were found on the bow in the legendary "Quad-fifty" arrangement shown here. *Courtesy of John Hagan*

came down to one hard fact: The mysterious "spook" outfit that controlled their operations behind enemy lines refused to release the boats for any but the most dire of maintenance requirements. And it wasn't long before the crews discovered that the unit controlling their destinies in Korea was none other than Det 2, 6004th Air Intelligence Services Squadron, commanded by the ubiquitous spymaster Donald Nichols.

Their boats had the required size, range, and speed, to support Nichols's far-flung requirements, but something beyond this combination would be needed if the boats were to defend themselves against North Korea's vigilant coastal security forces. Different combinations of firepower were experimented with before the boat crews settled on the reliable .50-caliber Browning heavy machine gun. With the big slugs coming out of the barrel at 2,930 feet per second, the gun had a maximum effective range of nearly one mile. Mounted in pairs, the .50s were twice as devastating, but when mounted in fours they became the legendary "Quad-fifty" of the Korean War. Adapted by the U.S. Army to deal with the human wave assaults of Communist infantry on the peninsula, the Quad-fifties proved equally adaptable to the crash rescue boats once steel support plating was added to the deck to absorb the weapon's massive recoil.

To those knowingly sailing in harms way the Quad-fifties brought the priceless peace of mind that can only come with ownership of a weapon that puts out two thousand rounds per minute toward the object of the gunner's displeasure. Unwilling to scrimp when it came to their survival, the boat crews also mounted single .50s in gun tubs on both port and starboard sides of their boats, as well as a seventh .50 mounted on the aft deck. Monthly unit histories are terse to the point of frustration for historians seeking to shed light on the harm these airmen-sailors encountered on their missions, but clues are provided in official reports such as the following for May 1951: "Evacuated 200 UN guerrillas from behind enemy lines to prevent their capture and execution; June: . . . operating . . . in the Yellow Sea, transported captured Chinese prisoners and friendly guerrillas to rendezvous behind enemy lines; September: Crash boat departed for the Fifth Air Force (ADV) north of 38th parallel. . . . On two occasions vessel fired upon by shore batteries. . . . Cpl Jim Johnson wounded aboard this vessel."[92]

Attempting to sneak past enemy defenses at night with a boatload of blood-thirsty partisans proved nerve-wracking work for the airmen, who never knew when or from what direction enemy fire might search out their thin-hulled boat. Added to these man-made dangers was nature's combination of minus-twenty-degree Fahrenheit temperatures, thick ice, and the Yellow Sea's notorious thirty-foot tidal flow. All these factors made for a very lethal environment that frequently seemed to the crews to be waiting patiently for a tired boat commander to make a mistake, just one. Years after the war one such boat commander summarized the boat crews' ordeal behind enemy lines with the epitaph: "They lived in close quarters for long periods of time . . . went hungry, damn near froze to death, got shot and hit . . . shot at and missed . . . worked hard to keep the boat in repair . . . endured when they were dead tired . . . were scared when 'Bed Check Charlie' came over in his bi-plane at night and dropped hand grenades on them . . . were cautious when a MIG would search for their boat hiding in a fog bank."[93]

In January 1952 an appreciative Nichols personally acknowledged the contributions made by Boat Master[94] Jarvis and his crew on the R-1-667 with the simple words: "These men have been a great asset to this organization and their departure [to Japan] constitutes a considerable loss." Typical of the secret world in which they lived and fought even this brief recognition for missions unspecified came in a letter labeled "Restricted."[95] For their part Communist coastal defense gunners got their chance to acknowledge another boat crew's performance only three months later, when they caught the R-1-667 squarely in their gunsights. The results were noted in a cryptic message found in Detachment 1's unit history report for the month of April 1952: "Received a message from R-1-677 operating in North Korean waters that they were fired upon and hit. . . . Holes in and thru the planking on port side, hot water heater jacket punctured, hole in engine room blower and various holes in galley compartment."[96]

Like the U.S. Navy's famous torpedo boats of World War II, the crash boats' defense was limited to firepower, speed, and the quick thinking of their commanders. Their wooden-hulled boats offered little hope should a serious mistake or simple bad luck catch up with its crew in North Korean waters. Offering less hope still was the fate of any boat crew captured while on one of the most dangerous and tightly held secret missions of the war, the infiltration of saboteurs and spies onto the Manchurian coastline of China.

Not surprisingly, U.S. government records authorizing American infiltration missions into China during the Korean War have either been destroyed or buried so deeply in "plausible denial" cover stories that they will never see the public light of day. What cannot be denied, however, are the memoirs and oral histories of the airmen who willingly flew and sailed into Chinese territory on these high-risk missions. Such histories are remarkable not only for their detail but also because they reveal for the first time that not all the agents inserted were Asian. From the logs of the R-1-667, for example, Jarvis notes that "between 16 November 1951–10 January 1952, several missions to that area, including Port Arthur [China], and the Yalu River [Chinese side]."[97] One of the November missions in particular stands out in Jarvis's memory:

> Our boat was advanced based at Cho-do. . . . An agent, apparently from the 6004th Air Intelligence Squadron, arrived by SA-16 amphibian aircraft [another special operations unit; see following story], and was brought to the boat. He was approximately twenty-five years old with blond hair and blue eyes. He spoke fluent Manchu. He stayed with us for three days. A very amiable fellow, a graduate of Princeton. . . . He said his salary was $25,000 a year. The crew liked him very much . . . then we received the "go."
>
> It was a 97 nautical mile run from Cho-do to the drop point. The trip into the area was timed so that we would arrive at midnight. We lowered a one-man raft off the stern of the boat and the agent climbed into the raft. He was dressed in a Chinese peasant's costume of black pajamas. During his stay with us I questioned him about the wisdom of sending in a blond,

blue-eyed person into China. . . . The answer was that he would be taken as a Manchu, many of whom were blond, blue-eyed with essentially none of the color or facial characteristics of a Chinaman.

He rowed ashore, slashing his raft to let out the air and buried it in the sand. I thought slashing the raft was a pretty stupid idea because he might need it when we were to recover him in three days. The crew was at General Quarters covering him in case of discovery. There was no problem as he scampered between the rocks and disappeared. We returned three days later to retrieve the agent, but we never saw him again. This trip was uneventful, except for the possible loss of the agent.[98]

Was this the same American that B Flight navigator P. G. Moore recalls parachuting into Manchuria? The physical description certainly matches, but I have uncovered no record of this individual in government files. As Jarvis notes, such missions were not atypical for the boat crews and they continued throughout the war. Delbert "Bud" Tretter, a crewman aboard the R-1-664, describes his mission into Chinese waters in March 1953:

Staff Sgt. Robin Lloyd,[99] Master of the R-1-664 and I were called to Mr. Nichols's headquarters. Nichols informed us that we were to pickup five South Korean spooks at Cho-do, then drop them off in the proximity of Antung, the MIG base located north of the Yalu in Manchuria.

By encoded Morse signal Nichols requested we leave Cho-do after dark the following night. None of the 85-foot gray boats were equipped with radar, fathometers, or other navigational aids. Navigation was by dead-reckoning or celestial using a sextant. We ran in the dark, showing no lights and in radio silence. Lloyd was a Brit[,] . . . also a master at navigation, and we had no problem locating the area of insertion. We were anxious to get the hell out of there as there were large, armed motor junks as well as MIGs . . . and we were not supposed to be in Manchuria in the first place. We never saw the spooks again.[100]

By the summer of 1952 Detachment 1's initial cadre of 85 airmen-sailors had grown to 31 officers and 232 airmen, dispersed throughout the air force's crash rescue boat detachments in the Far East.[101] Reflecting this expansion, the unit was reorganized that June as the 22d Crash Rescue Boat Squadron.[102] These events did not, however, necessarily translate into a better headquarters understanding of the rigors endured by the handful of eighty-five-foot boat crews still supporting the secret war in North Korea. Far away from such dangers the squadron's monthly histories, written from warm offices in Japan, dutifully record the need for continued emphasis on personal appearance and uniform requirements. Jarvis recalls the disparity between combat and headquarters mentalities with his return to Japan from one tour of duty in North Korean waters: "We were chastised upon return to Japan after 3 months operating out of Cho-do, that we should not have patched the bullet holes in our boat (-667) with tin can lids because they rusted, and stained the paint! We should not have worn paratrooper coats and leather flying boots to keep warm, after all we weren't in the Army nor were we aircrew. We should have sorted out the spent brass from the .30 caliber and .50 caliber guns into separate barrels before we turned in the brass for new bullets."[103]

Despite these clashes with the squadron staff, the 22d's gray boat crews continued to prove themselves as versatile as the situation demanded.[104] Some missions were straightforward attacks on coastal targets, such as those undertaken with South Korean marine raiding parties. A great deal more subtlety was required for other missions, such as transporting counterfeit North Korean currency to the coast for further disbursement to UN agents working in North Korea. International law provides that the enemy's economy is a legitimate target in war, and unconventional warfare attacks against this target can be far less obvious than the use of conventional weapons. In April 1952, for example, FEC published "Guerrilla Operations Outline, 1952," a document in which it candidly notes, *"North Korean Currency Exchange:* Due to the large requirements for North Korean currency and the limited sources available, commanders will encourage bank robberies and other suitable means of procuring this currency."[105]

Given the practical limits of bank robbing as a procurement system for large amounts of North Korean currency, FEC turned to its commercial quality printing presses to print the required counterfeit money. The more difficult problem, however, was inserting the money into North Korea in sufficient quantities to achieve the desired effect. To this end it was the air force boat crews who were usually selected to carry the large bundles of "funny money" from Cho-do to the North Korean coastline for subsequent pickup by friendly agents. For the boat crews it was just one more strange mission in a decidedly strange war.

The twenty-four-hour-a-day pressure from an unforgiving sea and enemy coastal gunners never relented on the young sergeants commanding the boats. And not all the threats came from the sea or coastline. In October 1952 the crew of R-1-664 intercepted an audacious North Korean junk approaching the harbor at Cho-do, one of the two primary U.S. special operations bases behind enemy lines. Two prisoners were taken from the junk, but immediately thereafter the -664 sustained an hour-long attack by North Korean fighter aircraft apparently alerted by the North Korean crew. The fighters were accurate enough to wound one crewman and inflict minor damage to the boat despite the frantic evasive actions taken by the surprised crew.[106]

The story of the crash rescue boat crews in North Korean waters is a story of airmen taking the war to the enemy in a manner far more dangerous than the primary, coast guard–like duties that were their traditional role. If their style did little to soothe the U.S. Navy's sensitivities to the "roles and missions" debate, their courage, seamanship, and willingness still accounts for one of the most colorful chapters in the history of U.S. Air Force special operations.

Libertas per Veritatem!

Libertas per Veritatem! ("Freedom Through Truth!") The spirited emblem of the 581st Air Resupply & Communications Wing seized the spirit: brilliant red, yellow, and blue colors on a shield topped by that universal symbol of peace, a wreath of olive branches. But then something catches the viewer's eye. Why is the large sword on the shield piercing completely through the heart of this venerated peace symbol?

Never before had the U.S. Air Force sent into combat a unit like the 581st Air Resupply and Communications Wing—nor would it ever do so again. Its long-range bombers, amphibians, and helicopters roamed the night skies over North Korea virtually at will during the last year of the war, while its "Flying Boxcar" transports supported the beleaguered French army in Indochina. And its Georgetown University–trained PsyWar operators, using state of the art commercial printing presses, printed millions of propaganda leaflets that rained down like a ticker tape parade on huge blocks of North Korea. Still other 581st officers, trained by U.S. Army and CIA guerrilla warfare specialists, trained UN saboteurs and partisans in a variety of deadly skills. It was only natural that the CIA in particular help out, as the 581st (and its two sister wings) were activated at the specific request of the Agency.

The Agency's discrete involvement began in 1949, when "an agency outside the Department of Defense" approached the secretary of defense for covert air support similar to that provided to the Office of Strategic Services during World War II.[107] No such support then existed within the DoD and the Secretary's prompt decision to create this capability set off a bitter, three-way battle between the army, air force, and CIA. In the dawn of the Cold War each was fully determined to control unconventional warfare operations in the event of war with the Soviet Union. The advent of the Korean War the following year and the activation in 1951 of the first two "special operations wings," designated air resupply and communications (ARC) wings by the air force, only served to further fuel this heated interservice rivalry.

Less than two months after the activation of the first ARC wing the army made its move to wrest this air support away from its bureaucratic rival, the CIA. Brig. Gen. Robert McClure, the army's senior PsyWar officer in Washington in 1951, approached the air force in May 1951 with a request that it divert "the special air wings being organized to support CIA activities in Korea . . . for use by [army] psychological warfare."[108] What McClure appears not to have understood at the time was that the air force did not view its role as merely that of air support to the CIA, or anyone else. This misunderstanding appears to have been at least partially cleared up later that year, much to the general's dismay. After additional discussions with the air force the unhappy general reported to the army chief of staff that the air force "felt they [air force] had a major responsibility in the field of unconventional warfare, which did not exclude the actual command of guerrillas."[109]

The air force followed this unsettling bit of news up with a truly impressive display of gall by asking the army and CIA to train selected air force officers in guerrilla warfare tactics. Given this support the first 581st officers reported to Fort Benning, Georgia, to undergo an arduous stint of parachute, weapons, demolitions, and Ranger-type training. This training continued throughout the winter of 1951 as the major air components of the 581st completed their training at Mountain Home AFB, Idaho. By late spring of 1952 the wing had completed its training and received deployment orders to report to the Thirteenth Air Force, Clark Air Base, Philippines, by that July. Not surprisingly, it took the Thirteenth Air Force staff at Clark a little time to figure out just what it was that flew into town.

The 581st wasn't like anything the air force had seen before. Its composite force of several different types of aircraft was not unheard of, but with the ARC concept the aircraft were only one part of a multithreat system. The 581st combined a number of mutually supporting squadrons in a modular concept, of which three in particular formed the backbone of the unit's unconventional warfare mission:

1. 581st Air Resupply Squadron: The only squadron in the wing equipped with aircraft, it was trained to infiltrate agents and PsyWar leaflets into enemy-held territory with a combination of B-29 heavy bombers, C-119 heavy transports, SA-16 amphibians, and H-19 helicopters.
2. 581st Holding and Briefing Squadron: The army and CIA-trained airmen in this squadron supplied, trained, and briefed personnel assigned by other agencies for introduction behind enemy lines.

3. 581st Reproduction Squadron: Equipped with a printing capability equal to that found in all commercial presses in the four northwestern states of America, this squadron could produce four million PsyWar leaflets within a twenty-four-hour period, according to the Joint Printing Committee of Congress.[110]

Obviously the 581st was extremely flexible, shifting into whatever size and composition of elements best suited to accomplish a particular mission. And after explaining the advantages of this versatile and modular concept to the FEAF staff in Tokyo, 581st commander Col. John K. Arnold Jr. emerged with a war plan that spread the 581st from North Korea to Indochina:

1. Four of the twelve B-29s assigned to the 581st would be collocated at Yokota Air Base, Japan, with a conventional B-29 unit. Each crew was expected to fly once every four days, completing fifteen tactical leaflet drop missions over North Korea before returning to Clark Air Base.
2. All of the wing's four C-119 transports and crews were placed on ninety-day rotations for conventional troop carrier missions and resupply missions throughout the Far East.
3. Two of the unit's four SA-16 amphibians were sent on extended temporary duty to Seoul City Airport in Korea to fly with B Flight, another unconventional warfare unit. These black-painted aircraft specialized in night, coastal infiltration and exfiltration of agents behind enemy lines.
4. All four of its H-19 helicopters were collocated with an air rescue squadron at Seoul City Airport. With a primary mission identical to that of the SA-16s the helicopters also performed combat rescue of downed airmen as a secondary mission.
5. The wing's C-118 and C-54 transports (two each), were reserved for special missions in support of "an agency beyond the operational purview of the US Air Force."[111]

Beyond these deployments of its aircraft and crews the 581st kept a number of specialists and mission-tailored teams on continual rotations to Korea. One set of 581st orders dated 8 January 1953, for example, reads like a "who's who" list of unconventional warfare units operating behind enemy lines:

4 personnel from 581st Comm Sqdn to Detachment 2, 6004 AISS
1 person from 581st Resup & Comm Wg attached to "B" Flight
3 personnel from 581st Resup & Comm Sqdn attached to "B" Flight

In 1949 "an agency outside the Department of Defense" requested that the U.S. Air Force develop a covert air-support capability. Three air resupply and communications wings (ARCW) were subsequently activated, all of which used the B-29 Superfortress for long-range, low-level infiltration missions. The B-29 shown here was assigned to the 581st ARCW, the only such wing to fight in Korea. *Courtesy of Bob Brice*

> 1 person from 581st Hold & Brief Sqdn attached "B" Flight
> 5 personnel from 581st Hold & Brief Sqdn attached to CCRAK[112]

But for all the talent the 581st brought to the war it was still the flying squadron's aircrews that found themselves most in harms way, and their stories tell in graphic detail just how much harm there was out there for these airmen.

In the early morning hours of 13 January 1953 the Operations Center at Clark Air Base was notified that one of its B-29 Superfortress bombers, radio call sign "Stardust 40," had failed to return from a night leaflet drop mission fifteen miles south of the Yalu River. Included in the missing crew was the 581st wing commander, Col. John K. Arnold Jr. Nine days later Beijing Radio confirmed the shootdown and capture of the eleven surviving crewmembers, specifically mentioning Arnold's name in its list of prisoners. Following this brief announcement China's normally hyperactive propaganda machine lapsed into an uncharacteristic silence. Unknown to the UN Command, the airmen had already been transported to China when Beijing Radio announced their capture.

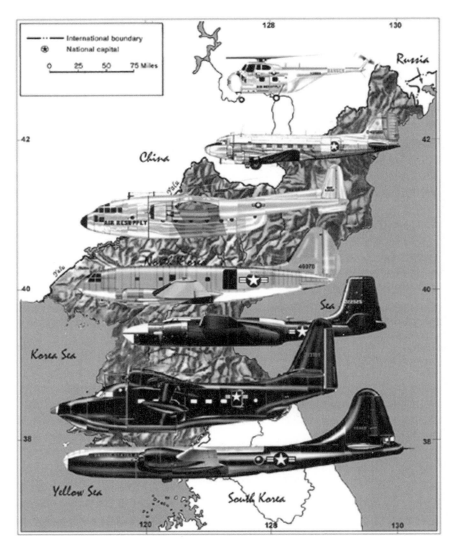

The U.S. Air Force roamed the night skies over North Korea and Manchuria in a variety of aircraft, parachuting Korean and Chinese agents and guerrillas into some of the most dangerous missions of the war. *Courtesy of Wayne Thompson*

Thus safely away from UN or Red Cross scrutiny they were kept handcuffed and chained in solitary confinement for months, while being subjected to grueling mental and physical torture. In a classified air force report on their ordeal, prepared after their release years later, the air force judged that the crew had endured "more brutality, tricks and contrivances" than any other American prisoners captured during the Korean War.[113] Arnold would later describe his response to such treatment with the terse statement, "I was in a state that I would classify as a complete nervous breakdown."[114]

In November 1954, nearly two years after their capture and nearly eighteen months after the war was over, the Chinese put the crewmen before a highly publicized military tribunal on charges of "espionage" and—to no one's surprise—declared them guilty. The effects of prolonged deprivation and torture showed on the crewmen during their show trial, however, and their haggard appearance generated considerable outrage throughout much of the Western world. The U.S. government and UN diplomats responded with increased efforts to secure the crew's release throughout the spring of 1955, but to no avail. Was it just coincidence that the massive Chinese political effort expended on this one aircrew just happened to fall on airmen from a special operations unit? Not according to the senior Chinese representative in these negotiations, no less a figure than Chou En-lai himself. In the minutes of a meeting with the UN secretary general on 8 January 1955, Chou En-lai states for the record, "According to material in our possession, the 581st air wing is a special operations wing with the *exclusive* task of carrying out operations for the Central Intelligence Agency. The wing works under cover of psychological warfare, such as leaflet operations [but] . . . its special task is to send agents and supplies to agents."[115]

The Chinese based their prosecution (and brutal treatment) of the 581st crew on the mission it was supposedly flying in support of the Central Intelligence Agency. U.S. Air Force records refute this claim in its entirety, but Chou En-lai's broad knowledge of the air resupply and communications wings, extracted in part from the badly abused prisoners, helped feed his highly publicized claims: "On Arnold's aircraft one person [twenty-two-year-old Airman 2d Class Harry M. Benjamin], was in charge of parachutes. The presence of this man in the crew is unusual. Benjamin had received special training at Fort Benning, Georgia, which was the same special kind of training as that given Downey and Fecteau. This fact proves that the persons involved in the two cases received the same training from the same institution."[116]

By linking the 581st crew to the CIA operation that resulted in the capture of Fecteau and Downey in Manchuria the previous November, Chou En-lai succeeded in further propagandizing China's illegal internment of the crew.[117] For all its displays of public indignation, however, China eventually concluded that the propaganda value of Arnold's crew wasn't worth the condemnation that continued to pour forth from a number of UN members. The Chinese finally released the crewmen in Hong Kong on 4 August 1955, the last American prisoners released after the Korean War.

The shootdown of Stardust 40 was neither the first nor the last of the B-29 losses during the Korean War. Most of the bomber losses occurred in air-to-air combat, as the enemy's agile MiG-15 fighters proved too fast for both the World War II–era armament still on the B-29s, and frequently even the jet fighter escort usually provided the bombers. Reasonably enough, the air force concluded that until the MiG threat could be neutralized, it had to be avoided. And because the MiG-15 was supposedly a "day-only" fighter with few of the electronic systems necessary to conduct night interceptor missions, limiting the B-29s to night missions seemed the obvious answer. The change in tactics seemed to work as the MiGs rarely chose to challenge night-flying B-29s. Lt. Col. George Pittman, the 581st Air Resupply Squadron commander at the time of the loss, still recalls the secret postshootdown briefing he received at Fifth Air Force headquarters in Japan: "The Fifth Air Force radar plots had shown twelve of the supposedly "day-only" fighters rising up to intercept Stardust 40. At approximately the same time, radar-controlled searchlights lit up the B-29, making it an easy target for the cannon-firing Migs."[118]

Stardust 40 was approaching its final leaflet drop pass for the mission at twenty-two thousand feet when the MiGs attacked just before midnight. Like all of the B-29s assigned to ARC wings, Stardust 40 had been modified with the removal of all gun turrets save the rear-facing guns below the bomber's vertical tail fin. Within moments three of the B-29's four engines were on fire. Capt. Wallace L. Brown, pilot of the bomber, recalls the crew baling out: "We landed safely in North Korean territory. . . . We were scattered all over the countryside."[119] North Korean militia troops rounded up the crew one by one the following day and after a short delay turned them over to the Chinese.

Official U.S. Air Force histories of the war reveal that the North Koreans possessed a rudimentary night-interceptor capability long before the shootdown of Stardust 40. But the officers of the 581st believed that the Chinese knew Arnold's B-29 was carrying leaflets, not bombs, as single B-29 leaflet missions had been flown recently in the same area. More disturbingly, the officers were also convinced that somehow the Chinese knew Arnold was on this particular flight. If true, the release of this information to Chinese agents represents one of the highest security breaches of the war. The 581st's suspicions were fueled by what happened within hours of the shootdown and days be-

Col. John K. Arnold Jr., 581st wing commander. To shoot down the B-29 carrying Arnold and his crew, the Communists used a combination of air-ground tactics rarely used during the war. Badly tortured during their postwar captivity in China, most—but perhaps not all—of the surviving crewmembers were finally released two years after the war ended. *U.S. Air Force*

fore Beijing Radio made its first announcement. Pittman recalls that "the early morning [13 January] edition of the Manila newspapers were highlighting the shootdown, quoting Hong Kong newspapers as their source. The newspaper stories were complete with the names and personal details of some of the surviving crewmembers, including their assignment to the 581st ARCW."[120]

The Communist Chinese links to Hong Kong newspapers did not surprise the air force officers, but how could such details of the aircrew have reached Hong Kong before the Stardust 40 survivors had even been captured? Or were these details already on file for use should the Chinese succeed in shooting down the B-29? Did the Chinese know Colonel Arnold was on the crew? Could they have known of its scheduled flight route that night? Was Arnold's presence aboard Stardust 40 the primary reason for what appears to have been a pre-planned aerial ambush? Or was the Communists' extreme sensitivity to the 581st's mission a major factor as well? How else could the near-instantaneous reporting of the shootdown be accounted for? The answers to these questions remain a mystery to this day.

Still other troubling mysteries surround the fate of the three crewman claimed by the Chinese to have died in the shootdown. According to a well-researched report on the shootdown released in 1998 by Associated Press journalist Bob Burns, Arnold himself believes that the two radar operators—1st Lt. Paul E. Van Voorhis and 1st Lt. Henry D. Weese—survived the shootdown and were later given to the Russians. While the ultimate fate of the two officers remains unknown, Arnold's suspicions are at least partially supported by statements in the report by surviving crewmember Steve Kiba that he saw Van Voorhis several times in prison during the following months.[121]

The 581st's plan to collocate its B-29s in Japan with a conventional bomber squadron had two advantages: it provided both the necessary maintenance support and the equally useful deception cover story for the ARC's unconventional warfare operations. This deception plan would be used elsewhere in Korea, notably with the 581st helicopters activated at Seoul City Airfield in December 1952. There they would blend in with the 2157th Air Rescue Squadron, another unit also flying the H-19 helicopter. There were, however, some awkward adjustments to be made as the conventional air rescue crews made room for the unconventional special operations pilots suddenly thrown into their midst.

Like owls, bats, and other aerial "things" that go bump in the night, the 581st aircrews flying behind enemy lines did their best work in the dark. And this fact did not sit well with the commander of the 3d Air Rescue Group (ARG), the headquarters tasked with providing maintenance support and living arrangements for all helicopter units stationed at the airfield. The air rescue commander made no bones about his views as he told the visiting Pittman, then the 581st deputy commander, "helicopter flying at night is too dangerous."[122] In a tense face-off Pittman came back at the group commander with the reminder that his responsibilities ended with "house keeping" support for the special operations crews, adding, "It's none of your business, don't worry about what they're doing."[123]

Back at Seoul City Airfield, however, the 2157th commander did succeed in having the big RESCUE markings removed from the sides of the 581st helicopters. To the 581st pilots it seemed the more conservative air rescue pilots didn't want the North Koreans confusing them with a 581st crew should they go down while on a combat rescue mission in North Korea.[124] And considering the fate of the 581st B-29 crewmen told on the previous pages, the air rescue concerns were not totally without merit.

The first group of special operations helicopter pilots to arrive in Korea had a few adjustments of their own to make, beginning with the basic fact that they arrived in Korea with no helicopters and no idea as to the nature of their assignment. And when the newly arrived pilots approached Fifth Air Force headquarters staff officers asking for both their aircraft and the location of the 581st ARCW, the initial staff response was denial that the 581st even existed. But it did of course and within a month of their arrival in Seoul six pilots, one sergeant, and twelve airmen fresh from technical training schools composed the 581st Helicopter Flight, commanded by Capt. Frank Westerman. And with four brand-new H-19A helicopters now in their possession the "helo" pilots finally got some answers to the questions the Fifth Air Force had been so reluctant to discuss.

The answers that came forth were, like the mission and even the unit's existence itself, buried in layers of deception plans and intentionally misleading organizational charts. And with these complex answers came their unavoidable realization of just how far the Fifth Air Force was prepared to go to hide from public scrutiny virtually everything about their activities. For the first time the pilots learned that their collocation with the air rescue squadron at the airfield was not simply a matter of administrative and maintenance support, but the necessary background to the cover story that they too were air rescue pilots. But their association with air rescue stopped there because in reality the flight could expect to receive its missions from another classified operation at the airfield. These mission orders and briefings came from B Flight, except when Fifth Air Force Intelligence officers chose to bypass B Flight by using still other classified channels. One can hardly fault the Communists (or the Fifth Air Force staff) if questions regarding the Helicopter Flight often generated blank faces and not much else.

The Helicopter Flight was activated to carry out one of the most sensitive missions of the war, the nighttime insertion and extraction of Korean agents behind enemy lines. And as its pilots would soon learn, the enemy's coastal radar coverage demanded that these missions be flown at the lowest possible altitudes, slipping undetected beneath the coverage as they flew into their blacked-out and (hopefully) deserted touchdown point along the coast. Without the benefit of today's reliable radar altimeters, night-vision goggles, and sophisticated navigation equipment, these missions demanded superb airmanship at the rawest "stick-and-rudder" level. Close calls were inevitable, and then—2d Lt. Robert Sullivan vividly recalls one night mission during which he felt the nose of the helicopter tug and dip slightly as he flew the helo's nose wheels into the frigid ocean waters; it would happen again to others.

The UN-controlled islands off North Korea's west coast were the launching points for most of these agent insertions into North Korea. Flying during daylight hours from Seoul to islands such as Cho-do, the flight's pilots fueled their aircraft immediately upon landing, then took a final mission brief before settling down for a few hours sleep to await darkness. For security reasons in the event of their capture, the pilots were not encouraged to look at the agent boarding their helicopter later that night. Following takeoff and flying in complete radio silence to avoid betraying their presence to the enemy's radio intercept teams, they could only hope North Korean coastal security forces were not waiting to ambush them at the drop-off point.

Not all threats came from the ground, however, and sometimes the threat started long before they crossed the coastline. Sullivan recalls one mission in which the helo launched with the radio call sign "Treefrog 33": "Flying an insertion mission north along the coast in total darkness the crew heard 'Kodak' (the radar-tracking site on Cho-do) ask 'Treefrog 33, how many treefrogs are out there?' Maintaining radio silence the special operators refused to respond. Kodak then announced 'Treefrog 33, I am painting five, repeat five, slow moving targets near your vicinity.'"[125] Without a word in response, Treefrog 33 banked out to sea, disappearing silently over the dark horizon en route back to Cho-do and safety. On a subsequent night mission it got trickier still, when "Kodak" asked Sullivan his distance from the drop-off point. This time Kodak's voice came with a faint Asian accent.

As dangerous as the night missions were the special operators at least had the elements of surprise and safety of darkness on their side. But both these elements were usually lost before the mission ever began when the crews were called upon to fly their cover mission, the combat rescue of downed pilots. When called into this type of mission the 581st crews preferred to launch the mission immediately, hoping to reach the downed pilot before the enemy had a chance to prepare an antiaircraft ambush for the rescue attempt it knew the Americans would inevitably make. In contrast to this approach the more conservative air rescue service philosophy called for more thorough, if time-consuming, mission planning. Although the former approach was unquestionably riskier to the helo crew, the latter also had a major drawback—the Communists got the same additional time to prepare for the Americans' arrival.

Whatever the choice of tactics, there was simply no way out of a knock-down brawl if the North Koreans were ready and waiting for the sound of an approaching helicopter. Most nerve-wracking for the helo crews was the Communists' tactic of waiting until the helicopter was committed to the most vulnerable part of the mission, hoisting the downed pilot aboard the helicopter, before revealing the full extent of their ambush. In a fight in which speed and movement were the keys to survival, the helo pilots hovering in midair over the downed pilot were little more than sitting ducks. And once having committed themselves to the hover they could do little but hold the helicopter motionless in midair and take their beating. And take a beating they did on the morning of 14 January 1953 when 581st pilots Frank Westerman and Lawrence Barrett fought for the life of a fighter pilot downed near one of the most deadly pieces of real estate in the world.

The main supply routes (MSRs) feeding the Communists' largest troop concentrations were dreaded by both the infantrymen and the combat pilots who fought and died with such depressing regularity in their proximity. But when F-51 Mustang fighter pilot Charles R. Cottrell Jr. baled out of his aircraft that cold January morning, the winds carried his parachute to the very edge of one of the most dangerous MSRs in North Korea. Already airborne over the Yellow Sea farther to the west, Westerman and Barrett listened on the air rescue radio frequency as the drama unfolded. If Cottrell stood any chance of rescue, it had to happen fast, and this time the mission planning came down to a quick coordination call to the fighter pilots fighting to buy time for any helo crew in a position to help. The citation to the Distinguished Flying Cross subsequently awarded to Barrett for the mission provides the official explanation for what happened next:

> In an unarmed, unescorted H-19A helicopter . . . [Barrett] plotted a course to the downed pilot's location and, without fighter escort or a known, flak-free route, started inland. Despite heavy flak and intense ground fire from enemy troops . . . the helicopter maneuvered into a hover and the downed pilot was hoisted [into the helo]. . . . While enroute back to the coast, [Barrett] directed a fighter attack on the positions of the enemy troops concentrated in the pick-up area. . . . The helicopter then proceeded safely to home base even though great battle damage had been sustained.[126]

Years later, Barrett recalled the unlikely rescue in slightly less official terms and with slightly more detail:

> No one screwed about with the MSRs in Korea! That's where all the B-26 drivers bought it. Mucking about in the Chinnampo River area [the helo's entry and exit point from North Korea for this mission] was also very hazardous. [But as we approached Cottrell that day] we executed a low, fast,

ground-hugging 180-degree approach to a quick stop to hover over Cottrell. . . . The North Koreans and Chicoms let loose with everything they had in the way of firepower—evidenced by the bullet holes in the tail rotor, tail cone, tail boom, and the transmission greenhouse. . . . Plenty of irritating skin damage, but nothing that threatened our safe flight . . . back to Cho-do.[127]

The following month yet another combat rescue made the 581st pilots begin to wonder whether their cover story was more dangerous than their primary mission. Things were not going particularly well for the Marine's Maj. Dave Cleeland on 24 February. His one hundredth combat mission had left him wounded, freezing, and lying next to the fuselage of his crashed F4U Corsair fighter, in the middle of the frozen Haiju reservoir surrounded by North Korean troops about to take him prisoner, if not kill him outright. A lack of local maps and subsequent confusion over the radios had already deterred two Air Rescue Service helicopters, before 581st pilots Joe Barrett[128] and Frank Fabijan were scrambled from Seoul. Time was running out fast for Cleeland, and the bad news outweighed the good.

The good news was that Barrett's helo was approaching the reservoir and had the crashed Corsair in sight. The bad news was that the North Koreans, upon hearing the approaching helicopter, were charging out onto the ice from their positions along the shoreline in a last-ditch attempt to capture or kill the pilot. Whether what happened next is good or bad news has a lot to do with whether the reader is American or North Korean.

As the North Koreans rushed out toward the wounded Cleeland, a combination of just-arrived Corsair and U.S. Air Force F-80 fighters orbiting overhead reacted instantaneously, raking the exposed enemy on the ice with heavy machine-gun and cannon fire. In response, the entire rim of the reservoir seem to explode with blinking lights as the North Koreans opened up on the now dangerously low flying fighters. In the midst of this air-ground frenzy, the helo swooped through a hail of ground fire seemingly coming from every direction. Picking up Cleeland, several bullet holes (including one to a fuel cell and another through the hand of the crewman, forty-six-year-old Airman 2d Class Thornton), and most of all a good fright, the H-19 crew fled to safety and some well-deserved recognition.[129]

Sometimes the collocated special operations and air rescue crews crossed paths on the same mission. This happened with a special twist on 12 April 1953, when two F-86 fighter pilots baled out of their battle-damaged jets over the Yellow Sea. One of the two, Capt. Joe McConnell, was already an ace and well on his way to becoming a national hero. With one special operations and one air rescue service helo searching the seas below for the two pilots, McConnell splashed into the near-freezing waters less than four hundred yards in front of Sullivan's helicopter—and a quick pickup courtesy of the special operations team. Sullivan recalls that "McConnell's first words on the helicopter's inter-phone, after 'Thanks,' were that he had a mission at 1530 hours later that same day and did I think he would be back in time for that one? The day after the pick-up he made a low pass . . . down the valley floor on Cho-do. [His] F-86 pitched up off the valley floor looking like it was moving at the speed of light."[130]

In the process of flying innumerable special operations and combat rescue missions during the war, the six special operations helo pilots put nearly a thousand flying hours on their stable of four helicopters. It remains a matter of considerable (and justifiable) pride to the flight's veterans that these missions were completed without a single accident, combat loss, or fatality. Sullivan's recently offered assessment of these operational accomplishments were succinctly put with a single rhetorical question: "Not too shabby for a bunch of beginners, eh?"[131]

While the 581st bombers, amphibians, and helicopters roamed the night skies over North Korea, the wing's C-119 Flying Boxcar transports made their mark fighting communism farther south—a lot farther south. For the transport crews this journey south began in earnest in 1953, as France neared the high-water mark of its bloody and ultimately futile battle to maintain control of its colonies in Indochina. To wage this battle the overextended French army needed both strategic airlift to ferry supplies into the region and tactical airlift to relay those supplies to its remote outposts spread throughout Vietnam. It was precisely the kind of sensitive, political-military mission the air resupply and communications wings were created to execute, and the 581st was soon tapped for the duty in Indochina.

Following the U.S. decision to discretely support the French effort, classified orders soon sent the ARC's heavily laden C-119s into Haiphong Airfield, a major supply hub for French army units operating in the northern half of Vietnam. Ammunition, vehicles, and in particular rolls of barbed wire, became high-priority cargo for the workhorse transports. But as the combat in the rice paddies and mountains of Vietnam continued to escalate so too did the difficulty of keeping the United States' low-profile involvement away from the attention of the American press. French demands quickly outstripped what the 581st alone could support and even as President Dwight D. Eisenhower sought to downplay America's growing commitment to the French, other U.S. Air Force transport units were added to the aerial pipeline into Vietnam. Looking back on this messy political situation, Grover Ensley, one of the C-119 pilots sent to Vietnam during this period, recalls, "Congress said we weren't there; the French said we don't want you here; the United States Air Force said *stay there!*"[132]

As still more demands for airlift escalated beyond what the United States was prepared to support publicly, the Eisenhower administration intensified its search for less obvious ways of supporting the French. The search eventually produced Operation Swivel Chair, two mutually supporting plans involving 581st personnel.[133] The first plan aimed to reduce the too-high public profile created by the increasing numbers of air force transports flying into Indochina, the second at providing the French with C-119-qualified aircrews from what was tactfully referred to simply as "other sources."

To accomplish the first plan the 581st helped coordinate a larger air force effort to fly a number of conventional C-119s from troop carrier bases in Japan to the 24th Air Depot Wing, collocated with the 581st at Clark Air Base. After their arrival at Clark the Japan-based transports were towed into one end of the depot's huge maintenance facilities, only to emerge shortly thereafter from the other end of the facilities with French national markings on their fuselages. Voilà! The 581st and conventional aircrews then flew the badly needed supplies into Vietnam aboard these "French" transports. In return the worn-out transports already in Indochina were flown back to Clark for refurbishment. These "French" C-119s exited the maintenance depot this time as U.S. Air Force aircraft, shortly to be flown back to their bases in Japan.

To accomplish the second plan of training pilots from other sources, the 581st developed an ad hoc training program for qualifying C-119 aircrews. This discrete program had a particular twist of its own, as the pilots they were training for combat in Indochina weren't French but rather American civilian employees of the Civil Air Transport (CAT) company, a CIA proprietary airline.[134] Unknown to the 581st instructor pilots there was still another twist to their program, one they wouldn't discover until they went out to the airfield to meet the first group of eight CAT pilots arriving at Clark for their C-119 conversion training.

Advised in advance that time available for training was short the 581st had organized an intense three-week course that could, with good maintenance and equally good weather, get the job done. But on meeting the CAT pilots for the first time the instructors learned they had exactly three *days* to complete the required training. In a fitting testimony to the professionalism of all, the incredibly high flying experience levels of the CAT pilots,[135] and the sturdiness of the C-119 itself, the much-abbreviated training was completed on time and without accident. It was by all accounts, however, a program that left both pilots and C-119s panting like winded ponies at the end of the seventy-two hours.

The CAT pilots did their 581st instructors proud, especially during the last stages of the war in which the Americans flew through intensive antiaircraft fire to parachute supplies to the paratroopers and Foreign Legionnaires in the doomed garrison at Dien Bien Phu. Its loss in May 1954 signaled the end of France as a colonial power in Indochina. But by this time the air force had already begun downsizing from wing to group status all of its ARC units. In 1954 the 581st Group left Clark for its final home on Okinawa, to be disbanded with little fanfare the following year. The end of the trail for air force special operations in the Pacific had come to an end four very eventful years after the arrival at Clark Air Base of a special operations unit the likes of which would never again be raised by the U.S. Air Force.

U.S. Navy
Special Operations | 3

The advent of the Korean War found the Navy in the midst of a shaky recovery from the tumultuous months of debates on its roles and missions, the "Revolt of the Admirals," and the extensive downsizing of naval forces after World War II.

Dr. Richard P. Hallion

It was a shaky recovery indeed. Beyond the organizational havoc caused by a five-year-long demobilization that stripped its fleet by 90 percent, the navy had lost a particularly acrimonious "roles and missions" battle with the air force only months earlier. In the fall of 1949 this bitter debate over the relative merits of and funding priorities for naval aviation versus land-based strategic air power, erupted into full public view in what the news media soon dubbed the "Revolt of the Admirals."[1]

Ultimately, the navy "revolt" failed, and amid considerable media and political criticism for the public manner in which the naval aviators had pursued their goals, the effort was judged by many at the time to have culminated in "a serious defeat for the navy."[2] Eight short months later President Truman stunned virtually everyone, especially the Department of Defense, with his directive to commit America's enfeebled military forces to combat in Korea. Not surprisingly, the navy found itself, as did the air force and army, with few forces in Asia prepared to support this directive.

At the outset of war, the Naval Forces, Far East (NAVFE) staff—the naval component to MacArthur's U.S. Far East Command—numbered a minuscule twenty-nine officers, and ComNavFE (commander, NAVFE) himself, Vice Adm. C. Turner Joy, was actually in Washington, D.C., the day the North Koreans attacked. Mirroring the command's limited responsibilities at this time, NAVFE's fleet totaled only one cruiser, four destroyers, four amphibious ships, one submarine, ten minesweepers, and a frigate attached from the Australian navy.[3] This situation changed dramatically within forty-eight hours, however, as the commander in chief, U.S. Pacific Fleet, transferred operational control of the Seventh Fleet—essentially all of the navy's ships in the western Pacific—to ComNavFE. The following month all United Nations naval forces committed to resisting the North Korean aggression were also placed under the operational control of ComNavFE. This international mix was quickly organized into four separate task forces (TF): TF 77, the carrier strike force; TF 95, the blockade-and-escort force; TF 96, Naval Forces, Japan, and, of particular importance to the special operations forces that would soon raid the North Korean coastline, TF 90, the Far East Amphibious Force.[4]

The two most urgent challenges facing NAVFE in the summer of 1950 required that it both support the Eighth Army's battered forces on the Korean peninsula and neutralize the North Korean People's Navy. The first task was begun that July with a massive, if poorly coordinated, navy–air force campaign to support the Eighth Army's fighting retreat southward before the North Korean People's Army.[5] The second was effectively accomplished early that same month after NAVFE ships sank three of four North Korean torpedo boats during a single battle. Following this loss, North Korea withdrew the remainder of its naval offensive power to the protection of Soviet and Chinese territorial waters for the remainder of the war.[6]

Unfortunately for the overall UN campaign in Korea, the navy's quick neutralization of the seaborne threat to its ships did little to help the rapidly deteriorating situation on the peninsula where, it appeared, the Eighth Army might be driven into the sea within a matter of weeks. So grim was the situation that many in FEC thought the Communists would likely overrun the three American and five South Korean army divisions—about ninety-two thousand troops[7]—making a final stand along the 145-mile-long Pusan perimeter, the last UN toehold in Korea. Only the U.S. Navy, it seemed, had the power to reverse the situation, if indeed it could be reversed, but what more could the navy do?

The navy's answer to that question was to begin an interdiction campaign against the vital lines of communication that carried the trains and truckloads of ammunition and fresh troops to the bulk of the North Korean army then attacking the Pusan perimeter. Facing the distinct possibility that the worst military defeat in American history was imminent, ComNavFE ordered TF 95 to bombard the important railway lines running the length of North Korea's eastern seaboard. As a wartime navy source noted, "Down this funnel, fed by the six rail lines from Manchuria and the connecting Trans-Siberian line, flowed all the war material for the Pohang-Taegu front [two major approaches to the Pusan perimeter]."[8]

To its dismay, however, the navy quickly found that its shipboard radar technology was not sufficiently developed to detect the nightly trains moving through mountainous terrain. Nor did daylight air strikes prove any more effective, as the alert train crews responded to the mere sight or sound of approaching aircraft by immediately hiding in the many tunnels cut by the railways through the granite mountains.[9] These evasive tactics were made still more effective by the North Koreans' use of locomotives at both ends of each train, thus allowing movement of the all-important cargo cars even when on the odd occasion air or naval bombardment crippled the lead or trail locomotive. Even when rail lines were damaged, repair crews frequently returned them to use in an amazingly short time. As Rear Adm. J. J. Clark, CTF 77, observed at the time, "Destroying enemy communications was simple enough, but the Reds built up a fabulously successful technique of repairing bridges and railroads. With pre-bolted ties and rails they could repair normal bomb damage to a railroad in four hours or less. The Reds soon poured in about eighty thousand Chinese coolie laborers to keep the railroads operating and supplies moving, with the result that our interdiction campaign did not interdict."[10]

In reviewing both the desperate situation on the peninsula and the failure of air-sea interdiction efforts to date, Admiral Joy faced three inescapable realities. First, Pusan's defenders were too weak to counterattack in the near term. The UN's best, if not only, hopes for reversing the tide of battle thus lie lay in action by its naval forces. Second, an air-sea interdiction campaign mounted by these naval forces was the strategy most likely to relieve the growing enemy pressure against the Pusan perimeter. Third, attempts to execute this strategy by air and naval bombardment had proven ineffective for the reasons already given. It was a discouraging dead end for the senior NAVFE officers, who realized how badly the soldiers and marines at Pusan were counting on the navy to get the NKPA off their backs.

Responding to these realities and the still-urgent need for an effective interdiction campaign, Joy called a meeting with the navy's acknowledged expert on amphibious warfare, Task Force 90 commander Rear Adm. James H. Doyle.[11] By sheer chance, Doyle's Amphibious

Group 1 ships had begun amphibious familiarization training in Japan with the U.S. Army's 35th Regimental Combat Team, only the month before the war started. At this meeting Joy assigned Doyle's TF 90 a role in the interdiction effort, personally suggesting in the process that Doyle form a raiding group from among the marine reconnaissance and navy underwater demolition team (UDT) personnel inbound shortly from California.[12] To assist Doyle with implementing his suggestion, Joy made available to Doyle's staff a combat-experienced raider and reconnaissance specialist, Maj. Edward P. Dupras of the Marine Corps. Already in Japan teaching amphibious tactics to U.S. Army troops when the war broke out, Dupras would soon figure prominently in TF 90's raiding war.

Doyle's command was the obvious choice to execute this type of raiding strategy, though the money needed to organize and maintain such a specialized raider force had simply not been available in the lean prewar military budgets of the late 1940s. To conduct the proposed raids, Doyle would have at any one time beginning that August at least one and usually two high-speed transports designed to carry raiding teams. But as the admiral quickly learned, there were no raiding teams in-theater, and the 1st Provisional Marine Brigade—not due to arrive in Korea before 3 August—was to be fully committed upon its arrival to the Pusan perimeter.

The oncoming marine brigade did have within its ranks one company of infantry with extensive prewar raider training aboard the U.S. Navy's only Pacific Fleet submarine dedicated to the special operations role. But while this submarine would arrive in Japan less than a week after the brigade, the infantrymen with whom it had trained so arduously would not be released from the brigade's total commitment to the defense of Pusan. NAVFE also had a ten-man detachment of UDT personnel in Japan at the time—working with Dupras to train army soldiers—but the navy had neither trained nor equipped its frogmen for onshore raiding missions.

Beyond what the navy-marine team could provide, MacArthur's headquarters was quickly assembling an ad hoc army team for the raiding role. But as this all-volunteer group did not come from those who had received prewar training from Dupras's team, its lack of amphibious proficiency was a critical defect in light of Doyle's need to produce immediate results.

The problems and worries hung over Doyle's planning group that July like some endless dark cloud. But help was on the way, literally, in the form of a handful of unique ships and crews that were already steaming toward that Japan that month.

High-Speed Transports

> The sailors became very protective, possessive even, of "their" raiders.
> To the ship's crew it became a matter of pride, if not outright honor, that
> the ship not let the raiders down when the going got tough on the North
> Korean coastline. This principle was irrevocable, whether the raiders be
> American, Korean, or British Royal Marine Commandos, all of whom
> entered the unique world of APD operations.

The navy called them "high-speed transports," or APDs, though
there was certainly much more to both the ship and its mission than
this simple title suggested. Operating singly or in pairs at different
times during the war, four of these highly specialized ships provided
the operational catalyst for the multinational raiding force that repeatedly struck North Korea's railway system.

Rotating from other Pacific Fleet bases into Yokosuka Naval Base,
Japan, the *Horace A. Bass* (APD-124), *Begor* (APD-127), *Diachenko*
(APD-123), and *Wantuck* (APD-125) constituted Transport Division
111. Because their raiding missions were most effective when these
ships operated singly or in pairs, commander, Transport Division 111
usually flew his flag aboard one of the ships then engaged in combat
operations. In order to oversee as much of the combat action as possible, he shifted his flag after each operation in order to assume tactical
command of the operating ships and raiding force committed to the
following mission.[13]

Built during World War II, these high-speed transports combined
the hull of a warship, a destroyer escort, with the superstructure of a
troop transport designed to both carry and launch amphibious landing
forces. To accomplish this dual role, a substantial length of the main
deck was enclosed to house 160 troops, while a cargo hold fitted with
a crane capable of handling light vehicles and equipment was added
further aft. In addition, the three-tube centerline torpedo station found
on the destroyer escort class was removed to make room for port and
starboard boat stations capable of launching and recovering four
thirty-six-foot landing boats.[14]

To make room for these structural modifications, each high-speed
transport featured only one 5-inch gun for its main armament, rather
than the two such weapons found on a destroyer escort. Both this
5-inch gun and the six 40-mm cannon (placed in three gun mounts)
could be aimed either optically or through the ship's fire control radar
system. The eight 20-mm cannon (placed in four gun-mounts) were
aimed optically by their gunners. Thus modified, these high-speed
transports were usually called APDs.[15]

During World War II the navy had found the versatile APD to be a
flexible and potent weapon. Moreover, this wartime experience re-

Versatile World War II–era fast transports, such as the USS *Horace A. Bass* (APD-124) shown here, combined the hull of a destroyer escort with the super-structure and landing-craft stations of a troop transport. *U.S. Naval Institute*

vealed that the key to its effectiveness lay in the teamwork developed between the ship's crew and the raiding forces it carried and launched into combat. Not surprisingly, this teamwork and sense of common purpose between the two groups led to a camaraderie that soon became recognized as a hallmark of the best APD operations.

It says a great deal about human nature that this teamwork and camaraderie remained a hallmark of APD operations in Korea, overcoming centuries-long cultural barriers and the mutual surprises that surfaced as tough Korean guerrillas boarded the APDs for their raids. And some of these surprises also brought their share of humor, as Lt. Hilary D. Mahin, gunnery and boat officer aboard the *Bass,* recalls from his ship's first mission with the Koreans:

> The *Bass* was fitted with larger shower stalls to accommodate the troops that we carried on our missions. Nevertheless, our shipboard evaporators could produce only so much fresh water and all ships practiced strict fresh water rationing. No one thought however to mention this to the Koreans as we departed from their base on Yong-do Island for our first mission up north with them.
>
> We had barely cleared the island harbor when the Koreans discovered the troop shower stalls, and they took to them like ducks to water! Before we caught on they had drained the ship's supply of fresh water to such an extent that we diverted into Pusan harbor to have a water tender refill our tanks. By then they had also discovered the food served in a U.S. Navy ship's galley![16]

Korean bliss aboard the *Bass* took a momentary dive after the guerrillas discovered the way American cooks "ruined" rice, the Korean dietary mainstay. But the APD's skipper resolved the issue quickly with a nice combination of cultural sensitivity and common sense by allowing the guerrillas into the ship's galley to prepare their own rice. In return, the grateful Koreans kept their large crocks of kimchee, the fermented, pungent end product of vegetables and garlic used in virtually all Korean meals, on the ship's fantail, as far away from American noses as possible. Now it was the crew's turn to be grateful, as kimchee exudes a powerful odor that invariably stuns the American sense of smell.

Underlying these humorous moments was something much more fundamental at work, something that turned duty aboard an APD into something very special. As the sailor-raider camaraderie developed, the ship's crew became very protective, possessive even, of "their" raiders. To the sailors it became a matter of pride, if not outright honor, that their ship not let the raiders down when the going got tough on the North Korean coastline. This principle was irrevocable, whether the raiders be American frogmen, CIA-led Korean guerrillas, or British Royal Marine Commandos. And as the commandos in particular would discover, this American sense of protectiveness extended both on and below the ocean's surface.

The *Perch*

The numerous drills and dives had convinced the crew that the *Perch* was not the left-handed, dangerous freak that she was once thought to be. Experience showed that the ship dives faster than a normal submarine (40 seconds) and can take and recover from large angles easily.

When the war started there were only two such submarines in the entire U.S. Navy. One conducted training exercises in the Atlantic Ocean, after which its crew sailed in broad daylight to the friendly ports found throughout the Americas and Europe. The other prowled the Sea of Japan by night, surfacing from its cold depths only long enough to unleash black-faced British Commandos against the North Korean coastline. Well-skilled and still better-rewarded would be the North Korean gunners who could send these raiders to a watery grave in the freezing black waters offshore. Moreover, in October 1950, the crew of this submarine began giving NKPA gunners just the opportunity they needed to collect such a reward.

The USS *Perch* (SS-313) was one of two World War II–era fleet-type submarines to undergo extensive modifications in 1948 for adaptation to the amphibious raiding role.[17] While at the Mare Island Naval Ship-

The USS *Perch* (ASSP-313), with its thirty-six-foot-long, airtight after-deck hangar. Extensively modified in 1948 for the raiding role, the submarine could carry 110 raiders and their equipment. *U.S. Navy*

yard in Vallejo, California, its two forward-most engines and generators (of four total) were removed to provide cargo and troop space amidships. Still additional room was created in the forward and aft compartments with the removal of all ten of the boat's torpedo tubes.[18] Altogether these modifications created sufficient space for 110 raiders and their equipment, plus 35 to 50 crewmen. And with the adaptation of the wardroom into a standby surgical ward, space was also created for the emergency surgery that would likely be needed by wounded raiders. But these changes were only the beginning of the boat's makeover for its specialized role.

A special snorkel system was added to the superstructure to induct fresh air from the surface, thus allowing the *Perch* to run submerged on its diesel engines instead of its batteries, as required by other submerged submarines. Engine exhaust gases were expelled underwater, dispersed by a special plate designed to avoid leaving a telltale trail of bubbles that could be seen from the surface.[19] This unique snorkel system allowed the submarine to approach the intended landing area submerged, in order to conduct a much longer than usual periscope reconnaissance of the target.

Behind the snorkel, a sixteen-foot-wide and thirty-six-foot-long cylindrical hangar was mounted to the boat's after deck. This airtight hangar carried an LVT (landing vehicle—tracked), an amphibious vehicle large enough to carry a jeep as well as a pack howitzer and its crew.[20] Thus modified, the *Perch* was recommissioned on 20 May 1948. Nearly eighteen months of sea trials and evaluations of the submarine-raider concept followed, the latter with B Company, 5th Marines, 1st Marine Division.[21] With the navy largely satisfied with the results of these evaluations, the *Perch* was redesignated yet again on 31 January 1950, as ASSP-313 (Submarine Transport-313).[22]

During its months of arduous amphibious training with the marine infantrymen, the *Perch* conducted intensive training drills along the California coastline adjacent to the large naval port at San Diego. These early drills went well, as both submariners and marines became proficient in the surface launching and retrieving of the inflatable rubber rafts used for the exercises. During this same period, the *Perch* also conducted joint training with frogmen assigned to UDT-3; the latter were anxious to test a submerged submarine's capability to launch them through its escape trunk for beach reconnaissance operations. In this aspect of training they were disappointed, however, for the *Perch*'s intensive training program was dedicated exclusively to its surface raiding role.[23]

The wisdom of committing to this emphasis on surface warfare training would be revealed far sooner than any could know in the late spring months of 1950, for this was precisely the wartime role immediately assigned to the *Perch* when war in Korea broke out. Three weeks after the war started, the boat was en route to Japan, the marines from B Company sent ahead of them on surface transport. The submarine arrived at Yokosuka Naval Base on 8 August 1950, and as a subsequent ship's report notes, morale aboard the ship was high: "The numerous drills and dives had convinced the crew that the *Perch* was not the left-handed, dangerous freak that she was once thought to be. Experience showed that the ship dives faster than a normal submarine (40 seconds) and can take and recover from large angles easily. All the training and experimenting instilled a tremendous 'can do' attitude."[24]

The submariners were, however, dismayed to learn soon after their arrival in Japan that the B Company marines with whom they had trained so hard and developed such proficiency would not be available for combat operations with them. Desperate for every rifleman that could be mustered in Korea, marine commanders committed to the last-ditch defense of the Pusan perimeter had wasted no time in pulling B Company's "submarine-raiders" into the meat grinder of combat on the peninsula.

As former *Perch* crewman M. E. Kebodeaux recalls, "We later learned that B Company had been shot up so bad at Pusan that even the few survivors were in various hospitals. The unit existed on paper, but not the marines we had trained with for so long."[25] Despite their disappointment, however, the enthusiastic crewmen produced some innovative improvements to their equipment during their first weeks in Japan.

The basic four-step attack maneuver developed by the *Perch*-marine team off the California coastline had the merit of simplicity. It required that the submarine approach the target beach while submerged, surface at night to launch the raiders in their inflatable boats, submerge again to minimize the likelihood of detection by coastal defense forces, then surface a final time to retrieve the returning raiders. Though fundamentally sound, the maneuver did not allow the submerged *Perch* to communicate with the raiding force ashore.

This lack of ship-to-shore communications represented a potentially serious flaw should the raiders encounter unexpected problems or enemy opposition. From four miles offshore—the range from which it normally launched the inflatable boats—the *Perch*'s periscope would be virtually useless for viewing the action ashore, especially on the dark nights preferred by the raiders. This problem was corrected in Japan, however, after the crew installed a short whip antenna on the snorkel-head valve, which would remain just above the surface while the submerged *Perch* awaited return of its raiders. Another problem overcome during this period involved the four-mile open-ocean distance the raiders would have to cover twice during a raid.

While the large LVT carried in the after-deck hangar was capable of towing a number of inflatable boats to the beach, its noisy engine precluded any chance of the raiders maintaining the surprise on which a successful mission—indeed their survival—was dependent. Searching for a less-noisy alternative during their stay in Yokosuka, the crew obtained a twenty-four-foot plywood boat powered by a six-cylinder Chrysler-Crown engine that could push the boat along at fifteen knots with no rafts in tow.[26] Christened *Suzuki* (the Japanese name for the perch fish), the boat—or "skimmer" as it was called—proved its worth in combat later that year, carrying the mission-necessary explosives while towing the raiders in seven inflatable rubber boats to within five hundred yards of the beach.[27]

To launch and retrieve the skimmer, the *Perch* flooded its aft ballast tanks, in the process partially submerging only the stern of the submarine to the minimum extent necessary to guide the skimmer on or off the special carriage on which it rode in the hangar. The crew soon became proficient in accomplishing this seemingly awkward maneuver in two to three minutes.[28] Satisfied with its new arrangement, the *Perch* never carried the LVT into combat.

Far less satisfying to the crew, however, was the emotional yo-yo it was undergoing as it trained in Japan with first one, then another, group of potential raiders, none of which stuck around long enough to put their training to the test with a combat patrol aboard the sub-

marine. A report of their training activities in Japan that August describes the problem:

> We embarked Underwater Demolition Team One [for] . . . the roughest
> week of training they or the *Perch* had seen. The morale of the crew and
> UDT were terrific. It was a blow to have to deliver the UDTs to an airplane
> for some other mission. We proceeded to Camp McGill on 22 August to
> pick up Major J. H. Ware, U.S. Army, and sixty-seven men from a Special
> Activities Company. On 29 August we embarked Captain D. H. Olson and
> the remaining fifty-six men from Major Ware's company. By 30 August we
> had trained 125 army men. We found at this time that we were not to land
> these troops either.[29]

Despite the obvious heart-and-soul effort put into the training by
both submariners and would-be raiders, it appears that the real problem—the obviously higher priority of simply maintaining a UN
foothold in Korea—led to the repeated, frustrating events experienced
by the *Perch* crew.

Though badly disappointed by this seemingly endless cycle of
training then losing a potential raiding force, crew morale shot up
again in mid-September with the arrival aboard their boat of yet another set of exuberant visitors, these from England's 41 Independent
Commando, Royal Marines. Training with these newcomers began immediately, and the youthful enthusiasm of each group, fueled by the
prospect of immediate action, quickly created the same kind of camaraderie between crew and raiders as that aboard the APDs. And, just as
with the earlier example, the humorous side of their meeting came together in the ship's galley as the submariners introduced the "Brits" to
submarine food, reputedly the best to be found in the entire U.S. Navy.

The young stalwarts who manned the 41 Independent Commando
carried vivid memories of the World War II–era food rationing system—meat and eggs in particular had been in short supply—that had
so severely tested British morale. In the process of "familiarizing
themselves with the submarine and American procedures" the
marines attacked the *Perch*'s food budget with the same enthusiasm
they would soon show for raiding the North Korean railroad system.
As the *Perch*'s skipper noted, "One of our steaks is a week's meat ra-
tion in England, and they had been in US territory only two weeks.
One morning they averaged six eggs per marine for breakfast."[30] To the
navy's credit, it somehow found the funds to feed its enthusiastic
guests, in the process creating yet another colorful story in the history
of the "Silent Service."

Frogmen

We were ready to do what nobody else could do, and what nobody else
wanted to do.

U.S. Navy underwater demolition teams were thrust into a new role in Korea, though trained and equipped only to the same standard as their World War II–era predecessors. Their services as scout swimmers and demolitions experts were particularly valued by the British Commandos and CIA guerrillas they led ashore on night raids into North Korea. *National Archives*

Exhausted from their two-hundred-yard-long swim through the cold, swift current that sweeps around the southern tip of the Korean peninsula, the two men crawled out of the ocean onto a deserted beach deep behind enemy lines. Too tired for the moment to care or even notice the small beach stones cutting into their bodies, the U.S. Navy's Lt. (jg) George Atcheson and BM3C Warren Foley shivered and sucked the cold ocean air into their lungs. It was close to midnight as the two frogmen lay exposed under the glow of a nearly full moon, both distinctly possessed of that terrible apprehension so well known to intruders suddenly caught in the beam of an inescapable light.

Their apprehension was well justified, for in fact these intruders were intent on committing an act that would sorely antagonize a North Korean army already credited with committing a number of atrocities against UN prisoners of war. Launched from the high-speed transport *Diachenko* earlier that night,[31] the two men had just begun the reconnaissance phase of TF 90's first sabotage mission of the war.[32] It was 5 August 1950, and other than their courage, the total weaponry carried by the two intruders included one .45-caliber pistol, one K-Bar combat knife, and a small number of grenades.[33]

The presence of the two men on the beach that night represented both the fortunes and misfortunes that had befallen the navy's elite underwater demolition teams since the end of World War II. The courage and determination displayed by their wartime predecessors had clearly survived the postwar years, as reflected by Atcheson's remarkable statement some years later that this particular mission had been undertaken "[because] some of the other targets would have been suicidal."[34] But on a less salutary note, the desperate effort also underscored the results that invariably follow when suddenly hard-pressed commanders attempt to overcome years of command neglect with the raw courage of an elite few.

Salutary or not, Doyle's TF 90 had little operational choice in the matter of UDT employment that August, given the interdiction mission and its critical time constraints. For, regardless of the morality or tactical wisdom of thrusting these few into such extreme danger, the simple truth was that the navy simply had no one else—beyond a handful of reconnaissance marines and frogmen—capable of attempting such high-risk missions. As another Korean War frogman succinctly put it, "We were ready to do what nobody else could do, and nobody else wanted to do."[35] The comment wasn't a complaint but rather a statement of professional pride that went well beyond Atcheson's inaugural 5 August mission into enemy territory. But if the pride was obviously still there, the same could not be said for the UDT's training and equipment, or even the manpower necessary to support a large-scale raiding campaign.

The numbers alone provide a sad commentary on just how much of the UDT capability had been lost during the demobilization programs of the late 1940s. With the onset of war in 1950, the four remaining teams present for roll call were a mere shadow of the thirty-two combat-experienced teams that supported the major amphibious landings throughout the Pacific during World War II.[36] These bleak numbers were even worse than they looked on paper, however, for the overall reduction in force was exacerbated still further by additional postwar reductions that cut nearly in half the manpower authorized each of the remaining teams. The cumulative effect of these reductions over the five years from 1945 to 1950 cut navy-wide UDT strength by nearly 95 percent.[37]

Beyond the scarcity of combat veterans in the remaining UDTs, operational capabilities and morale were further impaired as overall personnel shortages throughout the navy led to the assignment of non-

UDT officers to the proud teams. Of the four UDTs on active duty in 1947, for example, an experienced UDT officer commanded only UDT-2.[38] And beyond the difficult organizational reductions that affected virtually every command at the time, the teams also suffered from the animosity felt toward them by many conventional officers of the period. In what was not likely an isolated incident, one non-UDT officer selected to command a UDT was told in no uncertain terms by his superiors to "get that bunch of rag-tags straightened out as quickly as possible."[39]

Although the UDTs conducted some valuable training during the interwar years—including that previously described aboard the submarines *Perch* and *Sea Lion*—the navy's lean postwar budgets severely restricted the development of new concepts, or for that matter, even new equipment. As a result the Korean War found the understrength UDTs still woefully unprepared to conduct the two new missions—onshore raiding and the detection/destruction of moored antishipping mines—that would take them far beyond the limits of their World War II–era training and equipment.

Very few senior officers serving on either the Pacific Fleet or Amphibious Forces Pacific Fleet staffs during the war were enthused with the prospect of committing scarce UDT resources for these two new missions, and not without reason. Perhaps the best explanation for this point of view was that provided in a Pacific Fleet study prepared in early 1952, which concluded that "UDTs PACFLT are not adequately prepared by training or with equipment for operations more advanced or different from those of World War II."[40] And it was the experience derived from those World War II–era operations that dictated the navy doctrine limiting UDT operations to obstacle demolition and beach reconnaissance between the three-fathom curve line and the high-water mark found on the target beach.

The major problem with the Pacific Fleet report was that, despite the soundness of its rationale, NAVFE had nonetheless committed the UDT to "more advanced or different" combat operations from the very beginning of the war. Moreover, the frogmen were still conducting these special operations missions when the Pacific Fleet report was published eighteen months later, certainly sufficient time for the navy to have delegated the mission elsewhere had it chosen to do so. Between this report and battlefield reality something was clearly amiss; oddly, the navy was slow to look further into the discrepancy.

Perhaps some on the Pacific Fleet staff attributed the small UDT casualties to date—two killed and less than half a dozen wounded—to the World War II–era training in "operations beyond the high-water mark" provided to selected frogmen at the UDT Advanced Training Base established on Maui, Hawaii. Even this training, however, did not envision the kind of combat undertaken in Korea in 1950, and much of the expertise gained on Maui was lost during the huge demobilization programs that followed the Japanese capitulation in 1945. Thus UDTs 1 and 3 went to war with training and weapons that made them virtually indistinguishable from their World War II–era predecessors.

For the UDTs, the operational pace in the combat zone frequently found two of their platoons—approximately thirty men—forward-deployed to a particular APD for periods of six to eight weeks. The platoons usually ran between ten and twenty demolition or beach reconnaissance missions while aboard the APDs, depending on weather and enemy activity.[41] In addition, individual UDT personnel were often away on temporary duty with other military or CIA units, usually for advisory and training duties. This included the forward-basing of small teams on islands close to the North Korean coastline, where they stood alert duty with UN Escape and Evasion organizations assisting in the recovery of downed airmen.

The individual weaponry taken by the frogmen behind enemy lines was usually limited to the submachine guns, pistols, and knives found most useful for the close-quarters combat that characterized most raiding missions. Though presumably available, sound suppressors for the weapons are not known to have been used. UDT-1 veteran QM2C James Short recalls that on the few occasions when frogmen were required to eliminate North Korean sentries, the task was usually accomplished with a knife.[42] But few frogmen had undergone training for this kind of closeup killing, and the dangerous business was usually accomplished with a combination of "on the job training" and the hope that a dozing sentry would make the bloody job easier.

The frogmen used a variety of demolitions in their work, but the standard UDT charge was the Mark-135 Demolition Pack, which contained twenty pounds of C-3 plastic explosive. Though aqua-lungs had been introduced to the UDT community by this period, they were never used in combat during the war.[43]

Three Pacific Fleet UDTs served in the Far East during the war, with elements of one and usually two of the teams always present in the combat zone. As described earlier, UDT-1 shipped out from the Coronado Amphibious Base aboard the *Bass* following Truman's decision to intervene in Korea. Arriving in early August, this UDT absorbed UDT-3's ten-man detachment, the latter having been sent to Japan prior to the war to provide amphibious training to U.S. Army units.

The majority of UDT-3 departed Coronado in mid-August for a non-stop sailing that brought it to Japan later that month.[44] Neither of these UDTs arrived in the Far East at their authorized strength, but the buildup continued so that by late November 1950 both were reported at 140 percent of their wartime complement.[45]

As earlier noted, the Pacific Fleet responded quickly in getting both of its west coast UDTs to Japan, realizing in the process that fully half of the navy's entire UDT force had been committed to the war in less than six months. The navy didn't know what direction this new war might take or how long it might last, but it did know that any further requirements for UDT support in Korea would leave it with no option but to begin stripping the Atlantic Fleet UDTs of their personnel.

Faced with the obvious drawbacks of such a move, the navy re-called a number of UDT reservists to active duty, running them through an abbreviated refresher course before commissioning UDT-5 at Coronado in September 1951. UDT-5 arrived in Korea the following spring and, although employed primarily in beach survey operations, the enthusiastic reservists were evidently ready for any "special operation" that came their way, as a former officer aboard the *Bass* recalls: "In July 1952 we were working with UDT-5 on a beach survey near the island of Cheju-do southwest of Pusan. Here our froggies soon discovered that someone else was in the water with them, bare-breasted female Korean pearl divers! In a remarkable display of United Nations teamwork the UDT began diving with their newfound 'friends,' helping them recover pearls until we left the island a few short days later. UDT-5 always had high morale."[46]

UDT-5 was the third and final UDT to serve in Korea during the war. By the fall of 1952 all UDT raiding missions had ceased, and with the signing of the armistice in July 1953 all combat operations were terminated.

Marine Reconnaissance

Both [Dupras's] close-quarters combat experience and the expertise found in his exceptionally well-trained reconnaissance platoons would soon be tested in Korea, where the marines were committed to their first raid scarcely a week after their arrival in Japan.

As with the other uniformed services, Marine Corps manpower dropped sharply during the postwar years, from a wartime high of 485,833 to 74,279 in June 1950.[47] Despite this precipitous fall in numbers, however, the warrior spirit apparently remained high, for the marines responded to the onset of war with an enthusiasm unique to their traditions. Nor was this enthusiasm limited solely to the active duty force, for many individual reservists and former marines voluntarily reported to the Marine Corps staging base at Camp Pendleton, California, without bothering to wait for their official recall to active duty.[48]

Chaos reigned at Pendleton as active duty cadre worked around the clock, unpacking mothballed World War II equipment and organizing individuals and small units into a provisional brigade, the first elements of which sailed from San Diego, California, on 14 July 1950. The brigade's departure was an impressive response, considering that only twelve days had passed since the Pentagon first received a request for marine reinforcements from MacArthur.[49] And sailing with the ships carrying the marine brigade westward across the Pacific Ocean was the high-speed transport *Bass*, aboard it a company of marines to be disembarked at Pusan, as well as UDT-1 frogmen destined for subsequent delivery to Japan.

Following their arrival in Yokosuka, Japan, *Bass* skipper Lt. Cdr. Alan Ray and his crew would soon meet Major Dupras, a battle-hardened marine with a fighting history unusual even by Marine Corps standards. Dupras, a veteran of the 1st Raider Battalion's bloody fighting on Guadalcanal in 1942 and a survivor of the Corps' pyrrhic victory on Tarawa the following year, had later served in China, where he trained, then fought with, Chinese guerrillas.[50] While waiting in Japan for the arrival of the *Bass*, Dupras had already achieved considerable progress in melding together the UDT and 1st Marine Division Reconnaissance Company elements that had been flown out to Japan as part of the proposed raiding campaign. The *Bass* arrived in Japan too late to play a role in TF 90's inaugural 5 August raiding attempt aboard the *Diachenko*. But immediately following the ship's arrival at Yokosuka the following day, Ray, along with Cdr. Selden C. Small, then commanding Transport Division 111, met Dupras and UDT-1 boss Lt. Cdr. David F. "Kelly" Welch aboard Doyle's flagship, the USS *Mount McKinley*.

Within a matter of days, twenty-five frogmen from UDTs 1 and 3 and sixteen of Dupras's reconnaissance marines were merged on 6 August into the ad hoc Special Operations Group (SOG).[51] Following just two nights of rehearsals, the SOG departed Japan aboard the *Bass* on 9 August. Three nights later the SOG struck the railway system running along Korea's eastern coastline north of the thirty-eighth parallel, some two hundred miles behind enemy lines. During the three demolition missions that took place between 12 and 15 August, Dupras's marines provided beach security while the UDT placed their standard Mark-135 satchel charges under railroad tracks and bridges. As Dupras later recalled, "The hardest part of my job was continually to impress the boys that our job was demolition, not fighting. If possible, we tried to avoid any firefights. If there was any interference, or if our party was detected, we withdrew and hit 'em someplace else."[52]

These three raids represented NAVFE's first successful amphibious interdiction missions of the war and were credited with severely damaging the targeted segments of the railway system.[53] Later that month the SOG also conducted beach reconnaissance operations along Korea's western coastline.

The SOG's efforts that month provided an impressive display of navy-marine professionalism, the group having attained a level of performance far beyond that which could reasonably have been expected from its drastically abbreviated joint-training schedule. An appreciative Lt. Gen. George E. Stratemeyer, Far East Air Forces commander, was so impressed he sent a letter of congratulations to ComNavFE Joy, noting that "the damage reported resulting from the raids conducted is an excellent testimonial to the ability and the high state of training of the units involved."[54]

In further recognition of its achievements the SOG was later awarded a well-deserved Navy Unit Commendation for "outstanding heroism in support of military operations against enemy aggressor forces in the Korean Area from 12–25 August 1950 . . . 200 miles behind enemy lines on the east coast . . . destroying bridges and tunnels, disrupting enemy lines of communications . . . hydrographic surveys of three enemy-held beaches, despite opposition encountered the last night which forced the recon party to withdraw under fire."[55]

The recognition was certainly well deserved, though the SOG was disbanded at the end of August as its marines rejoined the 1st Marine Division then preparing for Operation Chromite, the major amphibious assault at Inchon two weeks later. Less than thirty days after it began, the U.S. Marine Corps involvement in coastal raiding was effectively terminated for the duration of the Korean War. It was an odd ending for the military service whose very existence itself was so closely linked to the strategy of amphibious warfare, especially considering the small number of marines involved in the SOG.

Even as the marines moved out to join the Inchon landing force, however, their replacements were familiarizing themselves with American weapons and amphibious tactics. These, too, were high-spirited marines, and bearing the proud traditions wrought from countless battles since their establishment in 1664 as the Duke of York and Albany's Maritime Regiment, they carried the modern-day title of Royal Marine Commandos.

Royal Marine Commandos

> MacArthur openly questioned whether the results that could be expected from the proposed raids justified the risks inherent with such operations. When Admiral C. Turner Joy voiced his confidence, MacArthur pushed his point with terse questions: "Can you prove?" and "Why is the Navy so keen to use Brits, but not UDTs?"

Few combatants moved out to war in the summer of 1950 with more speed and élan than did Britain's Royal Marine Commandos. Following the government's short-notice decision that August to activate a special raider unit for duty in Korea, the Royal Marines quickly selected Lt. Col. Douglas B. Drysdale to raise and command the 41 Independent Commando, Royal Marines. A highly regarded officer who had served with 3 Commando Brigade in the Far East during World War II, Drysdale moved immediately to fill the ranks of his new command.

Blessed with a surplus of highly trained and eager volunteers looking for some action, the Commando leader soon gathered an elite group of combat swimmers, demolition experts, and heavy weapons specialists.[56] Included in Drysdale's pick—and not atypical of the superb quality and spirit in those volunteering for the adventure—was Sergeant Major Trevor-Dodds, the European kayaking champion.[57] As Drysdale well knew, such skills were more than mere sport for the marines, who would later use their two-place Klepper kayaks for combat reconnaissance missions along the North Korean coastline.

With some 150 officers and men thus assembled, the group, dressed in Admiralty-provided civilian suits, boarded commercial airliners for transport to the Far East under what British historian Max Hastings describes as "melodramatic and wholly ineffectual security restrictions."[58] Once there, the Royal Marine Commandos were bolstered with the addition of a further 150 volunteers—diverted while en route to duty with 3 Commando Brigade in Malaya—to Camp McGill, Japan. At McGill they were completely resupplied with American equipment, weapons, and clothing, keeping only their distinctive green berets to denote their proud Commando lineage.

Immediately beginning an intensive, around-the-clock training program aboard Doyle's APDs and the recently arrived *Perch,* the Commandos quickly impressed the Americans with their enthusiasm and skill. As a report from the *Perch* observed, "These [Commandos] were experienced raiders with a 'can do' attitude comparable to that of the *Perch*'s. They seemed to enjoy having more thrown at them than they could possibly assimilate in the short time available, and rose to the occasion by becoming a well-trained and coordinated submarine raiding team in a remarkably short time."[59]

North Korea's mountainous interior dictated that its major railway system run along the relatively flat eastern seaboard, the rails frequently within sight of the shoreline. With numerous tunnels protecting military trains from air and sea bombardment, the UN turned to amphibious night raids to help destroy this vital line of communications. *National Archives*

It was indeed a remarkably short time—little more than two weeks—for the American sailors and British marines to develop the team cohesiveness necessary for survival in combat. Royal Marine Fred Heyhurst describes this period in the same excited tone felt by all at the time: "There was a tremendous spirit, to learn all we needed to know and get on with the job. We would get the hang of one [U.S.] weapon and go straight on to another, whatever the time was. . . . It [41 Commando] was the best unit anyone could have joined."[60]

The mutual respect that developed overnight between the Brits and Yanks was an intangible, yet critical, element of the strike force. Like their SOG predecessors, the raiders had precious little time to train together—less than a month—to develop the skills that would help ensure their mutual survival in the face of a disciplined, well-armed, and unforgiving enemy. Moreover, this enemy would be expecting their arrival, having been alerted to the UN raiding threat posed by the SOG missions. But just as the Commando training at McGill drew to a close with the men preparing for their first combat mission, the navy learned that its raiding plans had obviously raised some pointed questions in the mind of MacArthur himself.

In a series of messages to ComNavFE, General MacArthur openly questioned whether the results that could be expected from the proposed raids justified the risks inherent with such operations. When Admiral Joy voiced his confidence in the minimal risks to be taken and the destructive potential of the raids, MacArthur again pressed his doubts on the admiral with terse questions, "Can you prove?" and "Why is the navy so keen to use Brits, but not UDTs?"[61] Sticking to his guns, Joy replied, "Request reconsideration. The 41 Royal Marine Commando was formed and trained especially to conduct commando raids. Plans are ready for destruction of several key points between latitudes 40 and 41 on east coast. Believe they can be executed without serious risk. Submarine crew and commandos are keen to fight and gain experience for evaluation of this type of operation."[62]

MacArthur did reconsider, finally relenting in a 20 September message to ComNavFE authorizing raids by the *Perch* and "a detachment not to exceed seventy individuals of the 41 Royal Marine Commando."[63] Less than a week later, the *Perch* quietly crept out of Japan in the dead of night, its adrenaline-filled crew and sixty-seven Commandos eager for their first taste of combat in Korea.

The CIA's Special Missions Group

Most of the guerrillas inserted across North Korean beaches were sent ashore in small teams, at night, to conduct limited reconnaissance missions, establish Escape and Evasion networks, or collect local intelligence, particularly on the railway system. According to CIA records however—still partially classified nearly a half-century later—the Agency decided in 1951 to add a bigger punch to its amphibious operations.

Commander in chief MacArthur's strong antipathy to a CIA presence in his theater of operations inevitably influenced a number of early-war decisions taken by the Agency's senior officials in Japan. And among the most important of these decisions was their commitment to field their own intelligence networks and guerrilla forces in North Korea, independent of similar efforts undertaken by MacArthur's Far East Command. An effort of this magnitude still required military support, however, and this reality frequently led to acrimonious fights when Agency representatives approached MacArthur's army-dominated headquarters to ask for such support. Though in most cases the requested support was eventually provided, this continuing acrimony led in turn to the Agency's preference for working whenever possible with the two uniformed services with which it enjoyed much smoother relations, the U.S. Air Force and Navy.

Naval special operations—through Task Force 90—supported the Agency with both UDT and APD elements, the former training, then leading ashore, guerrillas launched from the APD providing the necessary transport and firepower. Unlike the U.S. Army, which used the term "partisan" when referring to the Koreans it employed behind enemy lines, the CIA and the navy used the more traditional title "guerrilla." As might be expected, these bureaucratic differences in terminology were of little interest to the frogmen and APD crews who risked their lives to deliver and retrieve the Koreans along the always-dangerous North Korean coastline. What did interest the sailors, however, were the rugged Korean raiders themselves, their temporary shipmates for the seven to ten days the two groups lived together during a typical mission north of the thirty-eighth parallel.

To the surprise of everyone and yet the surprise of no one, a tight camaraderie quickly sprang up aboard ship between American sailors and Korean guerrillas. This camaraderie often found form in the poker games that transcended substantial cultural and language barriers or, more notable yet, in the Koreans' noisy enthusiasm for the always popular "shoot 'em up" Hollywood westerns viewed nightly on the fantail of an APD at sea. Despite such light moments, however, the trips "up north" were anything but a light-hearted adventure, especially to the guerrillas, for whom the missions represented little more than a dangerous change of pace to their otherwise bleak existence.

For the most part, the guerrillas were North Korean civilians, screened and recruited by the Agency from among the large populations of pathetic, hungry refugees that filled the numerous camps around Pusan. As Hans Tofte, then the senior CIA officer in Japan, described them, "The refugees were down-in-the-mouth, bored with nothing to do. Joining the guerrillas would give them a chance to get out, to eat three meals a day, to have something to do. They would be buddies with a purpose, rather than shuffle around the camp."[64]

During the first six months of the war the Agency recruited several hundred refugees from such camps. Those selected were taken to the CIA's guerrilla training base, a tent city situated within a twenty-acre site on the small island of Yong-do, located some ninety miles south-southwest of Pusan.[65] There the Koreans were put through an accelerated training program by a small number of American military personnel (commanded by a marine, not an army officer) "on loan" to the CIA from their respective services.

The courses taught included the use of various weapons, sabotage techniques, and small rubber-boat handling for night insertions of small teams. The UDT were initially tapped to run the small boat training, but as the frogmen soon learned, they were also expected to take their "guerrilla graduates" on the dangerous insertions into North Korea. As Tofte himself later recalled, "I wanted it known [by the Koreans] that the Americans [UDT] took the guerrillas in by hand. This gave the Koreans respect for us and the military services also."[66]

Most of the guerrillas inserted across North Korean beaches were sent ashore in small teams, at night, to conduct limited reconnaissance missions, establish Escape and Evasion networks, or to collect local intelligence, particularly on the railway system. According to CIA records however—still partially classified nearly a half-century later—the Agency decided in 1951 to add a bigger punch to its amphibious operations: "A . . . raider team was recruited and trained by a Navy Underwater Demolition Team (UDT) specialist during July and August 1951. Between August 1951 and October 1952 this team carried out amphibious reconnaissance and raider operations along the east coast of North Korea. [A number of] successful landings were made."[67]

This team would almost certainly be the forty-to-fifty-man Special Missions Group (SMG) formed at the direction of the CIA by Lt. Atcheson (the same UDT officer whose 5 August 1950 mission west of Pusan is described earlier in this chapter).[68] If the numbers involved were admittedly modest, so too were the numbers advisable for the kinds of hit-and-run missions for which these raiders were organized. In any case, the SMG certainly fit in with TF 90's continued commitment to interdict the enemy's coastal railway system. These high-speed transport sailors and frogmen were going forward with whatever raiders—military or CIA—the UN would entrust into their care.

The *Perch* at War

> [Watching from the conning tower] wasn't exactly conducive to our peace of mind. We could see the gun flashes and moving lights. We could hear the crack of rifles and the stutter of machine guns and yet we were just sitting there, powerless to help. Finally we saw a blinding explosion followed by instant shock waves that reached far out to sea. We knew the mission was completed, but we didn't know at what cost.

On the night of 30 September 1950, the *Perch* rose silently out of the cold, dark depths of the Sea of Japan, its steel-gray conning tower cutting through the water like a dorsal fin. Some 150 miles behind enemy lines, the submarine broke the surface into the three-quarters moonlight that covered the sea. Scarcely a month had passed since the SOG's marines were pulled out to support MacArthur's dramatic invasion at Inchon, and only five days since the *Perch*'s stealthy night departure from Japan.

As the submarine surfaced four miles off North Korea's eastern coastline this night, its crew and Royal Marine Commandos gratefully took in the fresh air pumped below deck. For the last fourteen hours the boat's atmosphere had become increasingly foul with the exhalations of crew and raiders—despite use of the snorkel—while the boat's skipper, Lt. Cdr. Robert D. Quinn, conducted a thorough periscope reconnaissance of the target area.[69] In a scene that would be repeated many times in the future, this raid targeted a section of the north-south railroad track that came within a short distance of the shore.

As the Commandos spilled out onto the forward deck to inflate their black rubber rafts and *Perch* crewmen dragged the skimmer from the partially flooded after-deck hangar, lookouts stared intently through binoculars for signs of enemy activity ashore. Working rapidly in blacked-out conditions, seven rafts were quickly inflated and launched within the next thirty-two minutes.[70] But to the submariners' dismay, the skimmer's engine refused to start, its ignition system grounded out by the excessive humidity built up in the hangar during the prolonged dive.

Without the skimmer to tow the Commando-laden rafts the mission was finished before it started, the distance to the beach precluding any chance of paddling to and from the shoreline. But even as the submariners worked frantically on the engine, sick with the thought that failure on their part could force the cancellation of the eagerly awaited first raid, the submarine's radar detected a patrol boat maneuvering in the target area. The already tense situation worsened shortly thereafter when lookouts spotted two sets of vehicle lights moving into the target area before being extinguished—an ominous sign. With little choice, Quinn prudently concluded that the enemy had most likely been alerted to the submarine's presence and was attempting to set a trap for the Commandos. Quickly ordering the return of the rafts and skimmer to their storage areas, Quinn turned the big submarine out to sea. Staying on the surface for the next several hours to recharge the submarine's batteries, the *Perch* returned to the safety of the depths with the arrival of dawn.

Surfacing later that same day, the *Perch* completed a rendezvous with the destroyers *H. J. Thomas* and *Maddox*, the latter carrying commander, Destroyer Division 92. In a hasty conference aboard the *Maddox*, Quinn, along with the *Perch*'s embarkation officer (responsible for towing the rafts to/from the beach), and the Commando leader worked quickly to plan a raid that night against a secondary target in the area. As the enemy was obviously alerted to their presence, the plan entailed a diversionary attack by the *Thomas* on the previous night's target, while the *Perch* surfaced farther south to launch the Commandos against the secondary target. For its part, the *Maddox* would close protectively to within four thousand yards of the *Perch* after it surfaced, should the destroyer's firepower be needed.[71]

At 7:45 P.M. the *Perch* again broke the surface four miles off the coastline, having completed another submerged reconnaissance of the beach earlier in the day. This time the skimmer started without hesitation, towing seven rafts—six filled with Commandos and a seventh with explosives—to within five hundred yards of the shoreline. Releasing the tow ropes, the skimmer waited at the five-hundred-yard mark while the Commandos paddled the remaining distance to the beach and immediately fanned out to establish a defensive perimeter for the demolition teams.

But even as the covering force raced into position, the first of several firefights broke out when its lead elements encountered small groups of enemy soldiers. With the element of surprise obviously gone, the Commandos forming the defensive perimeter fought off the growing pressure on their position while the explosives were quickly planted in a culvert and railroad tunnel. Back on the *Perch*'s bridge, Quinn watched the fireworks through binoculars with increasing anxiety: "It wasn't exactly conducive to our peace of mind. We could see the gun flashes and moving lights. We could hear the crack of rifles and the stutter of machine guns and yet we were just sitting there, powerless to help. Finally we saw a blinding explosion followed by instant shock waves that reached far out to sea. We knew the mission was completed, but we didn't know at what cost."[72] The charges exploded at 1:15 on the morning of 2 October, much to the satisfaction of the Commandos. With the culvert and tunnel destroyed, they withdrew quickly to the landing beach to board their rafts for the tow back to the *Perch*.

The Commandos had not returned unblooded from their first successful combat mission of the war, however, as Royal Marine P. R. Jones had been killed during the fighting ashore. He was buried at sea with full honors aboard the *Perch* later that day, as the *Thomas* and *Maddox* trailed in formation behind the submarine with UN flags flown at half-mast.[73] The two destroyers made a high-speed departure following the firing of a twenty-one-gun salute by the *Maddox,* leaving the *Perch* to return alone to Japan three days later.

Following the return of the *Perch* to Yokosuka, Quinn completed a short "lessons-learned" report that clearly reflected both the anticipation and apprehension he felt regarding additional raiding missions for his boat. Some of his comments suggested mechanical improvements to the *Perch,* such as an access door between the submarine hull and the after-deck hangar that would allow crewmen to enter the airtight hangar while the submarine was submerged. Such access might have, for example, allowed the crew to detect and repair the skimmer's faulty engine before the submarine surfaced on the night of the aborted 30 September mission. Other suggestions involved tactical improvements, particularly those regarding the submarine's vulnerability on the surface in the target area.

The *Perch* had remained on the surface under a bright moon for nearly two hours on the night of 30 September, as the Commandos were first launched, then retrieved after the faulty skimmer engine could not be made to start. Moreover, the *Perch* remained on the surface in the target area for nearly seven hours the following night while the Commandos fought off the North Koreans attempting to thwart their demolition mission against the railway. It was on the second night that Quinn discovered (as would the APD skippers in future raids) that the submarine crew needed a bright moon both to guide the Commandos to the exact landing site and effect assistance should the raiders ashore need help.

But to remain essentially motionless on the surface for so long, within range of the enemy's coastal artillery, obviously put the submarine and crew at considerable risk. Further complicating attempts to judge the risk factors was that the skipper could not discount seaborne threats as well. A surprise attack by one of North Korea's fast patrol boats, for example, would have left the skipper of the lightly armed *Perch* with the cruel choice of either risking his entire boat and crew, or abandoning the Commandos to a bloody fate ashore.

In fact, it was precisely this potential seaborne threat that drove the decision to bring the *Maddox* to within easy rescue distance of the surfaced submarine on the second night's raid. Unfortunately, the unusual presence of a warship so close to shore also tipped off alert coastal defenses that something, probably an amphibious operation, was likely in progress. A final obstacle was the winter weather itself, which often turned the Sea of Japan into a submariner's nightmare: "The water became so cold and the sea so unpredictable in December 1950 that submarine patrols were abandoned because the snorkels froze up and endangered those vessels. The patrols were not resumed until April 1951."[74] For all of these man-made and weather-related reasons, NAVFE terminated submarine-raider operations following the *Perch*'s safe return to Yokosuka on 5 October 1950.[75]

Like the SOG, the *Perch*-Commando team had come and gone in less than a month. So much had happened in so little time that for some it was hard to remember that the war was scarcely ninety days old. This latest turn of events with the *Perch* did, however, stabilize the raiding lineup that would essentially continue in place until such missions wound down sharply in the final year of the war.

The Dangerous Ride to Work

No matter how many times we took a raiding party ashore, I could still feel the apprehension sweep through the boat as the *Bass* gradually disappeared into the darkness behind us. We couldn't even see the beach, only the dark vagueness of the coastal mountains a couple of miles ahead. I had to concentrate hard on the immediate task of keeping the boats in echelon formation and staying on course to the right beach.

From October 1950 forward, the UDT, British Commandos, and Korean guerrilla teams raiding North Korea's railway system were carried aboard the four APDs that formed the backbone of TF 90's fast-transport strike force. Moreover, it was from within this small group that the *Bass* had developed such a combat reputation that it came to be called "the Galloping Ghost of the Korean Coast."[76] The moniker may have sounded "Hollywood" to some, but as the ship's war records and interviews with its crewmen have since revealed, the raiding war was anything but glamorous.

It certainly hadn't been glamorous the previous August, for example, when the *Bass* took the SOG on its first forays into enemy-held territory. This first APD-UDT team had cut its teeth on those three missions, with all involved painfully aware that they were "winging it" in the face of an alert and well-armed enemy. Even at this early stage of the war, few of the raiders or commanders held any illusions that these raids could seriously interdict the enemy's overall campaign.

Nevertheless, such attacks could still be useful to the UN effort when they compelled the NKPA to divert even a few of its front-line combat units from the decisive fighting along the Pusan perimeter. With the outcome of the combat around Pusan seeming to hang in the balance with every daily attack and counterattack, the NKPA was desperate for every rifleman and artillery piece it could muster to finish a battle that many on both sides thought might well end the war.

The primary significance of the SOG's mid-August raids was twofold. First, they did in fact force the NKPA to divert scarce resources for the defense of the railway system that kept its army fueled,

Few combatants arrived in Korea with higher spirits than did those of the 41 Independent Commando, Royal Marines. These hand-picked volunteers were issued American equipment and weapons upon their arrival in the summer of 1950, keeping only their distinctive green berets to denote their proud lineage. *National Archives*

fed, and armed. Second, the amphibious assault methods tested during the SOG's brief tenure were further refined into the two beach-landing tactics practiced by the APD-raider teams for the remainder of the war. Both tactics had advantages and disadvantages, and, after considering the relative merits of each, the two raiding groups—British Commandos and Korean guerrillas—chose a different tactic for their operations.

For the Commandos it was the familiar, World War II–era "dry ramp landing" approach, in which the forward half of the LCPR's (landing craft, personnel–ramped) hull was beached ashore, the bow ramp dropped, and the raiders disgorged at a dead run for the nearest cover. In contrast, the guerrillas cut loose their seven-man inflatable rafts from the LCPR, towing them up to the surf line, then paddled through the surf to the beach. While the Commando approach[77] had the advantages of a quicker and safer passage through the surf line, the placing of one-third to one-half of the entire assault force in a single LCPR could lead to disaster if the boat overturned in the surf or was hit by enemy fire. In either event, the three-quarters-inch plywood hull of the LCPR provided precious little protection for its occupants.

As important as these beach-landing tactics were, they were still only one part in a very complex, choreographed play—a play in which even the slightest mistake in any of the other parts could reduce the entire show to shambles in a matter of minutes. And for both British and Korean raiders, the "show" began with an APD launching its LCPRs within two to four miles of the coastline. This considerable difference in distance was driven in turn by ComNavFE orders that kept the APDs outside the one-hundred-fathom curve, a line at variable distances from the shore that kept the ships in water at least six hundred feet deep. This order followed the loss of one ship and heavy damage to another four, all due to shallow water mines, during the last week of September 1950. It was the most costly week of the war for UN naval forces.[78]

For the Commando operations, the launched LCPRs immediately moved alongside the ship's fantail, where raiders waited to scramble down the big cargo nets hung minutes earlier from the main deck. In contrast, the guerrillas first lowered their rafts by rope into the sea below the cargo nets, moved down the nets into the rafts, then paddled off to hook up to the LCPRs waiting a short distance away.

The deliberately slow and carefully choreographed movement to shore that began with the embarkation of the raiding force—always conducted at night—was indeed a "dangerous ride to work." From the moment the boats began slowly moving forward at a snail's pace in total, blacked-out conditions, the APD's boat officer assumed tactical command of the raiding party from his position aboard the lead LCPR. Regardless of the beach-landing tactics employed, the boat officer halted the LCPRs just outside the dangerous surf line while he anxiously peered through the darkness attempting to judge whether the force had arrived at the right beach and whether the treacherous waves and tides would permit a landing.

Trying to watch, listen, and feel the sea conditions around him while ignoring the freezing cold cutting through his clothes, the boat officer was under enormous pressure to think quickly as his vulnerable force floated nearby, awaiting his decision. If his call was affirmative, a single UDT scout-swimmer clad in a rubber dry suit was dispatched into the icy black waters to swim ashore for a quick beach reconnaissance. Only after receiving an "all-clear" light signal from the beach, usually some thirty minutes later, would the boat officer commit to either taking the Commandos ashore in the LCPRs or cutting the guerrillas loose to paddle their rafts through the surf.

For nearly twenty of these nerve-wracking missions conducted by the *Bass* during its second combat tour in Korea, the heavy responsibility of making these quick life-or-death judgments fell on the shoulders of the previously introduced Lt. Hilary D. Mahin. Moreover, his vivid memories some forty-five years later reveal the intense concentration required of the boat officer on every one of these missions:

No matter how many times we took a raiding party ashore, I could still feel the apprehension sweep through the boat as the *Bass* gradually disappeared into the darkness behind us. We couldn't even see the beach, only the dark vagueness of the coastal mountains a couple of miles ahead. I had to concentrate hard on the immediate task of keeping the boats in echelon formation and staying on course to the right beach.

As the Boat Officer, I rode in the lead LCPR, taking navigation guidance over the radio from the ship, which had both the shoreline and our boats on its search radar. In addition to the boat crew of course the Commando leader and the UDT scout-swimmer were usually with me, as were the explosives we carried for the job. We had two .30-caliber machine guns in the bow, and if it were a Commando operation, twenty to twenty-five of them aboard as well. If we were taking guerrillas in, we usually towed three of their rafts behind each LCPR.

By using the boat's underwater exhaust system we kept the exhaust sound pretty low, which usually enabled us to get within two–three hundred yards of the beach where the surf roar would mask the sound of the engine from ashore. Here I had to decide whether the surf conditions would allow us to proceed in. If I did, the troop leader released the scout-swimmer into the sea for a cold swim to shore to perform a quick reconnaissance of the area. It was at this time that I released tactical control of the mission to the Commando leader.

For the next half-hour or so there was little we could do but hold position in the dark beyond the surf line, listening for the sound of a train or perhaps an enemy patrol craft. If the coast were clear we got a small green light signaling "come ashore." If the surf conditions were bad or the enemy was present in strength, our UDT would swim back out to us for the return to the ship.[79]

With British Commandos aboard, the light signal from the beach called in the waiting LCPRs to beach, drop the raiders off, and then back out quickly through the surf to await a "mission-accomplished" call from the raiding party. The boat officer responded immediately to this call by moving the LCPRs forward again as the Commando leader ashore fired a prearranged flare signal high into the night sky over the target—the signal for all raiders to return immediately to the beach. Given the unreliability of radios exposed to salt air and water, the confusion that inevitably accompanies night combat, plus the language problems when Korean guerrillas were employed, the simple flare signal was the key to ensuring that no raiders were left behind.

British Commandos engage in disembarkation drills from the *Bass* to their landing craft. Col. F. N. Grant, officer-in-command, is standing on deck, with hand on a vertical pole. *National Archives*

With the guerrillas, the "mission-accomplished" signal from shore also sent the LCPRs waiting beyond the surf line onto the beach for the pickup. While designated guerrillas helped strap the rafts outboard of the LCPR, the main party boarded the boat, which then backed out (as with the Commandos) through the surf. Regardless of the makeup of the raiding party, however, the passage back out through the pounding surf could prove more dangerous than the mission itself, and, as Mahin recalls, men sometimes died in the attempt:

> Getting back out through the surf usually proved more difficult than getting in, as the boats backed out to avoid being capsized by breaking waves while attempting to turn around in shallow water. In April 1952 four of our Koreans, fully loaded with combat gear and weapons, were swept into the waves as they attempted to climb into our LCPR after securing their raft to its hull.
>
> Without thinking, I jumped in to grab one of them, followed immediately by Bosun's Mate MacDonald. I grabbed one guerrilla, but was going under myself as I wore no life jacket. MacDonald, who did have a lifejacket,

grabbed me and another guerrilla, keeping us all afloat just long enough for other hands to drag us back over the gunwale into the boat. Unfortunately, the two other guerrillas drowned. We returned the following day to retrieve their bodies.[80]

Given the inevitability of casualties among the raiders during these hazardous missions, either from enemy action or accidents, Mahin added an emergency medical team to the raider force. This team was placed in a third LCPR, a combination backup boat and seagoing ambulance. Trailing behind the assault force by some five hundred yards, this LCPR carried two corpsmen and their supplies, plasma, medical stretchers, and so on.

Medical help was bolstered aboard the APD as well, with the addition of a physician to the ship's crew for each combat mission. As Mahin recalls with a laugh, however, this otherwise-welcomed assistance took an unexpected turn with the arrival of the first doctor. Anticipating an emergency room specialist or at least a general surgeon, the crew was astonished to learn that the U.S. Navy, in its infinite wisdom, had sent them a gynecologist!

No doubt the raiders, even given the occasional odd choice of specialists sent to the APDs, appreciated this increased medical support. However, the LCPR crews endured another problem, one found in the psychological dimension but potentially more devastating than a physical wound. Unlike individual Commandos or guerrillas, few of whom would participate in every mission undertaken by their unit, the boat crews aboard an APD went on every raid conducted by every raiding party carried aboard their ship. Thus the individual boat crewman's exposure to death, crippling injury, or capture was—by this one statistic alone—higher than that faced by any single Commando or guerrilla. And it was a statistic rammed home by such heart-stopping close calls as that experienced by Mahin and Boatswain's Mate Ken Eckert on the night of 23 June 1952, when a stream of machine-gun slugs slammed into their LCPR, sending hot bits of shrapnel into their faces.

Unlike the Commandos or guerrillas, these sailors were not selected from an all-volunteer pool that had been physically and psychologically screened before being put through a punishing selection course designed to weed out all but the most aggressive. Beaching their LCPRs under enemy fire at night, deep behind enemy lines, was only a part-time job for these seamen, who held full-time duties aboard ship. Under such circumstances, the emotional stress on the LCPR crews in general, and the boat officer in particular, could only have a cumulative effect as the missions wore on throughout the war.

The "catch of the day": North Korean fishermen, dressed in white, wait passively aboard the *Bass* during their journey to South Korea and subsequent interrogation. Captured the previous night, the fishermen provided invaluable information on the location of antishipping minefields in their area. *Courtesy of Hilary Mahin*

It is a well-known axiom within the profession of arms—borne out through centuries of warfare—that each individual has only a limited supply of courage. Moreover, each frightening experience endured by the individual dips into that supply of courage, much like someone drinking from a cup holding only a finite amount of liquid. And to those repeatedly subjected to the test of combat, few experiences in life are more frightening than the shock of realizing that the cup of courage is finally and suddenly empty. For Mahin this shock hit home on the final raid conducted by the *Bass* on its second combat tour in Korean waters:

> The missions never got easier, although the competence of our boat crews increased with every raid, because no amount of raiding experience changed the critical conditions beyond my control. The surf and the enemy's reaction were always unpredictable in the dark, and there was always that fear that the wrong decision on my part could get people killed.
> You just wondered how long competence and especially luck could carry you. In the end my courage deserted me on a mission, somewhere

near my twentieth raid, and I can never forget that indescribable apprehension that overwhelmed me. I seemed to be frozen physically and mentally; even calling out a command was a major effort that took all my willpower. In short, I'd run out of gas.[81]

As Mahin's candid account of his experience attests, the burden of combat rarely falls equally on all those involved. Almost by definition, the bravest are inevitably consumed in body and spirit by the near-inhuman demands placed on those who willingly position themselves again and again on that lethal edge of human performance found in combat behind enemy lines.

The Raids

One of the most dangerous and successful special operations missions of the entire war had already taken place in the spring of 1951, when one of these navy-CIA raiding parties escorted a U.S. Army general, a doctor, into enemy-held territory south of Wonsan.

The chronological progression of NAVFE's raiding activities during the war was fairly straightforward—dramatic to be sure, but still relatively simple from the headquarters viewpoint. Following the termination of the Special Operations Group and submarine-raider operations in September and October 1950, respectively, the U.S. Navy provided the transportation (APDs) and scout-swimmers (UDTs) for the British Commandos until the withdrawal of the Commandos from combat in December 1951.

During the following year the same APD-UDT combination carried CIA guerrillas ashore, with individual frogmen commanding the raids ashore in all but name. This U.S.-Korean teamwork tapered off sharply in mid-1952, no doubt reflecting the American realization that, at this late stage of the war, such raids were virtually meaningless in determining the final outcome. There was a time, however, in the fall of 1950, when the fires burned bright in the hearts of raiders intent on taking the war back to the North Koreans' homeland.

This time came right after the navy withdrew the *Perch* from combat, when C Troop, 41 Commando, boarded the *Bass* for a strike against the North Korean coastline on the night of 6–7 October 1950, their target a railway tunnel 150 miles north of Hungnam. This raid took place only some 80 miles south of the Soviet border and was the first British Commando raid launched from an APD. It and the raid the following night were the first in a series of attacks over the next several months against the railway system which ran along a 120-mile stretch of coastline located between forty and forty-two degrees north latitude.

This first raid was more complicated than most that would follow, as the surveillance radar on the *Bass* failed just before its boats were launched, forcing its raiding partner, the *Wantuck,* to assume control and guidance of the boats on the long, slow approach to the beach.[82] A British journalist accompanied this mission all the way ashore, subsequently publishing his experiences in vivid detail:

> The umbilical towrope [attaching the black rubber raft to the LCPR] has been unhitched. We are twelve men . . . gliding quickly by paddle towards . . . the hills which loom nearer (I never before felt the full menace of the verb "loom"). One officer—Lieutenant Peter R. Thomas—has swum ahead alone: a tiny winking red light tell us that he has got there, that it is at least possible to land.
>
> The silence grows half-perceptibly into sound, the rhythmical swish of surf. . . . For a second or two we are caught violently in a chaos of foam. We hit something solid: "Out, quick, get out. . . . Come *on,* for Christ's sake!" It is an urgent but not quick task to drag the boat up to [the beach]; no tug-o'-war team ever heaved so desperately. . . . This patch of sand becomes Commando H.Q. A new, temporary bridgehead is established in North Korea . . . less than a 100 miles from the Soviet frontier.
>
> Troop Commander Lieutenant Derek Pounds had told the troops: "Civilians are to be left alone if they stay indoors; if they interfere, they get rubbed out." A [Korean] man came out, and wandered about. . . . Some were for shooting him; but it was less noisy to knock him on the head. ("I was sorry for him in a way," the marine who did it said afterwards, showing me the teeth-marks on his rifle-butt, "but he oughtn't to have been out there.").
>
> The long tow back to the ship was an agreeable anti-climax; the marines' wet clothing clung icily about them, yet there was sense of fulfillment and of intense relief. . . . On board there was a miniature bottle of brandy for each man (strictly medicinal, for U.S. Navy ships are dry). The *Bass* is a fast armed troop carrier. . . . Her youthful, smilingly taciturn captain, Lieutenant Commander Alan Ray, presides over her with unruffled equanimity.[83]

This raid and the one that followed appear to be the first and last missions in which the Commandos went ashore in rubber rafts towed behind LCPRs, the tactic used exclusively by the Korean guerrillas in 1952. Following these two missions, the Commandos reverted to the dry ramp landing tactics with which they were more familiar.

The raiders had the satisfaction of watching their demolitions explode against the targets on both missions, the second night's explosion setting off a large fire that was still burning as the APDs prudently left the area. The North Korean reaction to these early raids was surprisingly light (though one Commando was killed during the first mission), and the APDs returned to Sasebo, Japan, on 9 October to replenish and stand by for further duty as directed by Task Force 90. This standby period proved shorter than expected, as the APDs were dispatched almost immediately for the kind of special operations duty that made their crews claim—half in tears, half in laughter—that what "APD" really stood for was "any purpose designated"!

The last three months of 1950 became the "mine season" for APDs *Begor, Diachenko,* and *Bass,* as well as the frogmen of UDTs 1 and 3. Always sensitive to the UN naval dominance of the waters surrounding North Korea, the Communists fought back with virtually the only weapon at their disposal: extensive mining of the major harbors within their control. In particular, this included the east coast ports of Wonsan and Hungnam as well as Chinnampo, the west coast port of entry for the North Korean capitol city of Pyongyang. Sweeping for 250-pound mines moored just below the surface was a dangerous business, even for minesweepers built for this sole purpose. So dangerous, in fact, that in Wonsan Harbor the minesweepers *Pledge* and *Pirate* were sunk on 12 October by the very mines they were attempting to sweep.

The frogmen found Wonsan particularly difficult, as one veteran of the UDT mine-sweeping effort notes:

UDT was rushed into the destruction of loose surface mines. . . . UDT men were placed in whale boats, given M1 rifles with armor-piercing shells, and the go-ahead to sink or detonate the mines. What a zoo! In rolling, pitching seas, here were the gunners on a bobbing cork, taking aim on another bobbing cork. Another mission for UDT? What the hell, we're flexible!

It wasn't over yet. Wonsan, *always* the mines. What a nightmare—cruising around with our four-foot draft LCPRs was no picnic, even with the mine watch on the bow. On 17 October another minesweeper sank, and another on 18 October, both of which had Korean crews to be rescued.[84]

That December a ten-man UDT detachment boarded the *Begor* for a demolition mission that would later be described as the single largest nonnuclear explosion to date. Having earlier evacuated the port of Hungnam just ahead of the advancing Chinese army, the UN moved to deny use of the harbor facilities to the Communists for the duration of the war if possible. That goal was accomplished quite handily the day before Christmas, 1950, when Hungnam harbor rocked with an explosion generated by a substantial combination of UDT explosives as well as "400 tons of frozen dynamite, five hundred 1000-pound aerial bombs, and about two hundred drums of gasoline."[85]

The Hungnam fireworks display was a fitting, as well as impressive, culmination of the overall UDT performance during the first six months of the war. For the UDTs to have taken and survived

The APDs were noted for their versatility. The USS *Begor* (APD-127) supported the ten-man UDT detachment that demolished Hungnam harbor the day before Christmas, 1950, with four hundred tons of frozen dynamite, five hundred 1000-pound aerial bombs, and some two hundred drums of gasoline. *U.S. Navy*

such extraordinary risks in raids, minefields, and other dangerous tasks so far beyond the scope of their World War II–era training and equipment—without a single death—seemed to many at the time to be too good to be true. As events were soon to prove, it was.

Typical of these hair-raising experiences was that experienced by a UDT-3 element on the night of 23–24 September 1950, as an LCPR from the *Bass* towed five inflatable rafts full of frogmen toward the beach approach to Taechon, just north of the west coast port city of Kunsan. What was supposed to be a "routine combat recon on an enemy beach" revealed virtually all the weaknesses of the still-infant APD-UDT program. With tongue-in-cheek humor, one participant describes the operation:

> In the briefing prior to launch, all crews and swimmers were given the latest intelligence . . . including the fact that a tourist who had been on the beach in 1949 had seen no soldiers or guns there. What more could we ask?

A piece of cake! Right on schedule, *Bass* steamed into the area and sounded General Quarters, which could be heard for miles, and with a nearly full moon we didn't have any vision problems finding the beach—a stroke of luck!

Within minutes the [enemy] guns started blazing, tracers everywhere! Boat #1 hit, eight men in the water[,] . . . four men in the water from the other boats. For what seemed like hours, the LCPR fished around for swimmers.[86]

In his official after-action report for this mission, the UDT-3 commander on the scene describes, with considerably less humor, the subsequent recovery of the men in the water, most of which took place under enemy fire: "Small arms fire from hill on left flank of beach. . . . Men missing: 10 . . . recovered one swimmer off center of beach . . . recovered two swimmers off right flank of beach. . . . Small arms fire from the right flank of beach. . . . Recovered another swimmer off center of beach . . . recovered one swimmer off right flank of beach . . . recovered one swimmer 1000 yards off beach . . . recovered one swimmer 1200 yards off beach . . . recovered one swimmer 3000 yards off beach . . . recovered two swimmers 4000 yards off beach. All men accounted for."[87]

But the good luck that always seemed to favor the UDT in such close calls came to an end on 19 January 1951, when a similar beach reconnaissance farther south resulted in the deaths of two UDT-1 swimmers, the only such combat casualties of the war. In addition to the two killed, two other UDT were wounded, as were two LCPR crewmen from the *Bass*.[88]

The details of the terse after-action report reveal the chilling drama played out in the cold dark waters that night, when the North Koreans got a rare opportunity to catch the frogmen in their gunsights:

About ten men came over the dune line, assumed prone firing positions and commenced firing at the beach party. Immediately all of the [beach party] took to the water and commenced swimming with the rubber boat. . . . Lt (j.g.) E. I. Frey was swimming to [a tow line] when he was hit twice in the head. . . . Lt (j.g.) Pope and QM2 Boswell attempted to keep the body afloat but, due to the strong current, they were dragged under the LCPR and were forced to let go. The body of Lt (j.g.) Frey was never again seen [Frey's body was, in fact, subsequently recovered].

Due to the extreme cold, the swimmers were unable to help [pull other swimmers aboard]. . . . Lt (j.g.) Satterfield was boosted to the gunwale where he was shot in the back and died immediately. During this action, the coxswain [BM3 Sidney A. "Swede" Petersen], was shot in the left knee but continued to man his station. He finally collapsed and his job was assumed by a UDT 1-man. The boat's radioman [SM Frank D. Prosser] was shot through the left elbow as he helped to pull Satterfield aboard.[89]

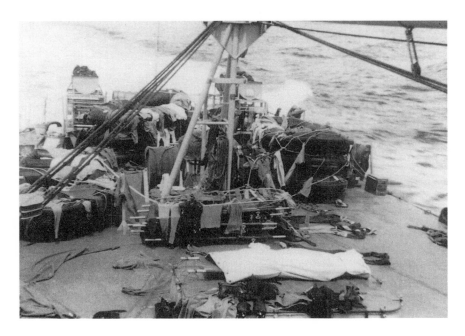

On board the *Bass,* the body of a CIA guerrilla lies on a stretcher under a white tarp (*foreground*) while the rubber rafts and equipment used by the raiders the previous night dry out. *Courtesy of Hilary Mahin*

Two dead and four wounded were not large numbers by the standards of combat in Korea, but the losses cut especially deep into the small APD-UDT community. This one mission incurred the single largest casualty rate among the UDT throughout the entire war, a deadly reminder of the danger inherent in these operations.

Despite their losses, there was little time for mourning as the entry of the Chinese army into the war the previous November had an immediate impact on the raider community. In response to an urgent request that same month from the hard-pressed 1st Marine Division, the 41 Independent Commando was dispatched to join the Americans fighting near the Chosin Reservoir in North Korea. With the Commandos' departure, coastal raiding virtually ceased until the spring of 1951, when the British returned to Japan to reequip and absorb the new replacements that returned its strength to near that of the original three hundred with which it had started the war.

The Commandos resumed coastal attacks in April 1951, when the British teamed up with the UDT in a raid that ripped up large sections of railway track north of Hungnam. That July and August, B and C Troops of the Commando set up forward bases on two small islands in Wonsan harbor. From these islands further raids were conducted, as were a number of small reconnaissance missions, the latter often undertaken in two-man kayaks. Raiding casualties during 1951 were relatively light—one officer and sergeant killed and twenty other ranks wounded—due in no small part to the commonsense approach to the raiding role as expressed by their senior officer on the scene, Lt. Col. F. N. "Chips" Grant: "On each [raid] I pulled my men out when the opposition got serious. I did not consider a ten-foot bridge worth serious casualties. Our main aim—that of keeping up the threat to the coast—was achieved. We could have maintained ourselves [against heavy opposition], but only at a cost not commensurate with the value of the target."[90] This pattern of coastal raiding continued until the Commandos were permanently withdrawn from Korea on 22 December 1951.[91]

While the departure of the Commandos from Korea broke up an effective UN raiding team, it also demonstrated the adaptability of the APD-UDT concept to function just as effectively with other UN raiders. This critical point was reaffirmed that winter by the relative speed and effectiveness with which the Korean guerrillas of the Special Missions Group replaced the Commandos.

Also assisting in this midwar transition was the earlier APD-UDT experience with other CIA-sponsored guerrillas, many of whom had already proven their effectiveness on a number of special operations missions. In fact, one of the most dangerous and successful special operations missions of the entire war had already taken place in March 1951, when one of these CIA raiding parties escorted a U.S. Army general, a doctor, into enemy-held territory south of Wonsan.

The U.S. Army rarely sends its generals behind enemy lines, especially if indigenous guerrillas recruited for the most part from the roster of the opposing team are providing this senior officer with his only protection in such dangerous territory. It's a scenario not unlike that of throwing a forward pass in a football game in which two of the three subsequent possibilities are bad news for the offense. Had the Communists succeeded in killing Brig. Gen. Crawford F. Sams during his clandestine intrusion into North Korea on the night of 13–14 March, they would have achieved a victory of significant proportions. However, capturing FEC's surgeon general would have been a propaganda coup of immense proportions. Even more important than his general officer status was the fact that his mission had as its goal nothing less than puncturing a hole in one of the Communists' most treasured propaganda programs:

In February 1951 both Peking Radio and the *People's Daily* reported that Koreans had witnessed American aircraft drop insects that resulted in cases of cholera. In March, the Communists alleged that American artillery had been used to shoot typhus germs across the Imjin River, and that the U.S. Army had sent infected animals and [infected material] to four locations.

The North Koreans stated that the U.S. was responsible for 3,500 cases of smallpox in civilians and demanded that UN commanders Mathew B. Ridgway and Douglas MacArthur be tried for these "crimes." [North Korean leader] Kim Il Sung issued an emergency decree, calling for the National Extraordinary Anti-Epidemic Committee [and other bureaucracies] to destroy insects.[92]

However fallacious the charges sounded to American ears, they were not claims that could go unanswered, especially because in at least one area highlighted by the Communists there did indeed appear to be an epidemic of some kind.

The problem for the UN was that the territories allegedly affected were all under Communist control, and the Communists refused to allow health inspectors from the International Red Cross or the UN World Health Organization into the areas. What Communist leaders would not admit was that in the face of widespread epidemics stemming from displaced refugee populations, contaminated water, and a variety of other factors, its rudimentary medical system had collapsed.

The UN Command suspected as much, but in the face of Communist propaganda charges of germ warfare, Headquarters, Far East Command developed an audacious plan to put proof behind its suspicions. Evidently (and no doubt reluctantly) concluding that its public rebuttal to the Communist allegations would require the firsthand report of the most senior medical authority possible, FEC authorized the insertion into North Korea of General Sams. Perhaps considering the political fall-out should Sams be killed or captured, the wily MacArthur allowed the navy and CIA—the latter still his least-favorite intelligence organization—to conduct the high-risk mission. Two separate postwar CIA reports are combined here to describe the mission:

This mission was more dangerous than usual because the Wonsan area was on the alert, having detected lights at sea. The [CIA–guerrilla team] operating from a U.S. destroyer took Brigadier General Crawford F. Sams . . . by whaleboat and raft . . . into an enemy fishing village at night, outposted the area, made contact with the village chiefs, and returned the Surgeon General to the destroyer. The mission was successful and the disease was identified as hemorrhagic smallpox. Both Sams and the commander in chief, Far East Command, were impressed by the speed and efficiency of the CIA operations.[93]

Returning to Tokyo immediately, Sams subsequently presented his medical findings before the UN and various other public forums, effectively dispelling for the moment the credibility, if not the zeal, of the Communist propaganda.[94] An appreciative General MacArthur later awarded Sams the Distinguished Service Cross for his unique and dangerous mission.[95]

On the night of 25 January 1952 the SMG continued the creditable performance of its predecessors with one of the more successful hit-and-run raids of the war, an assault on the railway line some nine miles south of Songjin. Departing from the *Wantuck,* the guerrillas struck a train sitting between two tunnels. In addition to derailing the locomotive and tender, one small railroad trestle was destroyed, and eleven North Korean soldiers were killed and one captured. The attacking force suffered no casualties.

U.S. records of these raids, found primarily in the war diaries and memoirs of the APDs and their crews, suggest that such forays dropped off sharply in the summer of 1952. In a scenario eerily prescient of one that would follow nearly two decades later in Southeast Asia, the U.S. strategy at this stage of the war concentrated almost wholly on minimizing its casualties and withdrawing most if its forces from the region with some form of "honorable peace." And just as they would again some twenty years later, the negotiations with the Communists were moving forward at an agonizingly slow pace.

Perhaps to help nudge the Communists along, the navy sent its APD-UDT team north for one final series of operations, this time against the enemy's food supply. From July to September 1952, elements of UDT-5 and UDT-3 from the *Diachenko* and *Weiss* (APD-135), respectively, began destroying fishing nets and sampans in the Sea of Japan north of Wonsan. Though the results from these net-destruction missions were "below expectations," the navy planned further such operations in the spring of 1953 before finally being ordered to cease its planning in light of the belated progress then being made at the negotiation table. From this period until the signing of the armistice on 27 July 1953, the APD-UDT teams were committed to beach survey and harbor cleanup duties requiring their demolition skills.

After the war the APDs were steadily retired, without fanfare, to Fleet Reserve moorings at various locations around the U.S. The UDTs, on the other hand, had begun a philosophical and operational evolution from its World War II beginnings from which they would not turn back. Its onshore raiding experiences in Korea would underpin a slow but steady growth in such capabilities until the early 1960s, at which time President John F. Kennedy set the UDT on the irreversible path that led to the present-day SEAL (sea-air-land) teams.

CIA Covert Warfare | 4

I wonder if there is any foundation for the rumors that have come to me to the effect that through this Central Intelligence Agency, they are contemplating operational activities.

Congressional representative Fred Busby, 1947

Approved by Congress on 26 July 1947, the National Security Act remains one of the most powerful legislative actions ever taken by the U.S. Congress. Driven largely by Cold War fears of Soviet aggression, the act called in large part for a massive reorganization of the nation's military institutions, including the establishment of the U.S. Air Force and a cabinet-level secretary of defense to manage all three military services.

Moving beyond military matters, the act also created the powerful National Security Council (NSC) to assist the White House in coordinating defense and foreign policy issues. In addition, as almost a last-minute thought, the legislation called for the transformation of a small and ineffectual intelligence organization—the Central Intelligence Group—into a national-level intelligence apparatus unprecedented in American history.[1]

This last piece of legislation created the Central Intelligence Agency, an organization that generated from the very beginning a distinct sense of unease among a number of thoughtful politicians and senior government officials. To soothe congressional misgivings concerning the CIA's potential to become an "American Gestapo," the Truman administration emphasized the proposed Agency's lack of police and subpoena powers, or a domestic security mission.

Despite such reassurances, however, it appears in retrospect that even at this early stage the administration had plans for the new CIA that, if made public, would likely have upset Congress still further. One CIA historical report supporting this suspicion of presidential subterfuge notes in part that "for [political] tactical reasons the White House had kept the Act's section on the CIA as brief as possible, and postponed a full enumeration of the Director's powers."[2]

In the end, however, their apprehensions were overcome by the much more visceral fear that the Soviet subversion and occupation of Eastern Europe were precursors to similar incursions in Western Europe. Their fears were not entirely misplaced. As Congress and President Truman—not to mention Soviet premier Joseph Stalin—well knew, the ill-advised political stampede to demobilize America's military forces at the end of the World War II left the United States stripped of any credible military deterrent to Stalin's threats. To be sure, America still possessed sole ownership of the atomic bomb when the NSC and CIA were created. Even that psychological security blanket, however, was stripped away two years later, when in August 1949 the Soviets demonstrated that they, too, possessed the evil genie of nuclear destruction.

With America's conventional and nuclear military deterrents virtually impotent in countering a major Soviet thrust into Western Europe, the NSC's quest for alternative responses became an all-consuming search. And that search soon led the council to take a second look at the fledgling CIA, whose deliberately vague legislative charter described its duties as "coordinating the intelligence activities of the several departments and agencies in the interest of national security."[3] The vague wording had been sufficient to assure passage of the act in 1947, while still leaving considerable latitude for subsequent expansion. And given the Cold War pressures that led to its creation in the first place, it was inevitable that the CIA's expansion into "operational activities" would come sooner rather than later.

This, in fact, is exactly what happened, when less than six months after its own creation the NSC met in December 1947 to modify the CIA's charter. Noting "the vicious psychological efforts of the USSR, its satellite countries and Communist groups," the council issued National Security Council Directive (NSCD) 4/A, directing the CIA to carry out "covert psychological operations designed to counteract Soviet and Soviet-inspired activities which constitute a threat to world peace."[4]

The CIA was not the NSC's first choice to carry out 4/A-type operations. Only after both the secretaries of defense and state declined earlier NSC overtures, on the basis that public exposure of 4/A's quasi-legal actions might embarrass their departments, did the NSC turn to the Agency. Overriding the legal objections voiced by Rear Adm. Roscoe H. Hillenkoetter, the Agency's third director (DCI) in as many years, the NSC assigned 4/A to the Agency for implementation.

This apparent progress was not what it seemed, however, for during the ensuing six months DCI Hillenkoetter antagonized the NSC as well as Defense and State with his reluctant and sluggish implementation of the 4/A mandate. In response to growing Cold War tensions—the Soviet blockade of West Berlin had just begun—and to fire Hillenkoetter's lukewarm enthusiasm, the NSC issued NSCD 10/2 in June 1948. Remarkable in its aggressiveness and wide-ranging scope, 10/2 proved a major watershed event in the history of the CIA. The directive greatly expanded the Agency's charter for covert operations, to include "any covert activities related to propaganda; preventive direct action, including sabotage, anti-sabotage, demolition and evacuation measures; subversion against hostile states, including assistance to underground resistance movements, guerrillas, and refugee liberation groups; and support of indigenous anti-communist elements in threatened countries of the free world."[5]

NSCD 10/2 was even more of a hammer than this wording alone suggests, a fact due in no small part to the subsequent interpretation put on the directive within the intelligence community. In his history of the early Cold War era, author William R. Corson notes, "The intelligence community's reaction to the NSC's apparently unanimous endorsement and support of 'dirty tricks' was swift. In their view, no holds were barred. The NSC 10/2 decision was broadly interpreted to mean that not only the President but all the guys on top had to put the brass knuckles on and go to work."[6]

That same summer an increasingly frustrated NSC moved again to deal with Hillenkoetter's passive resistance by creating a new organization, the Office of Policy Coordination (OPC), to execute 10/2 operations. A hybrid organization administratively subordinated to the CIA but more responsive to the State Department, OPC was headed by Frank G. Wisner, an OSS veteran of Eastern Europe and former assistant secretary of state for the Occupied Territories. Armed with the powerful 10/2 as his mandate and with the whole world subject to his intervention, the intense and creative Wisner soon began giving the NSC the response that Hillenkoetter could not or would not provide.

Typical of Wisner's enthusiasm and interpretation of 10/2, for example, was the support he soon solicited and received from the Department of Defense. An important demonstration of his effectiveness in this role occurred the following year, when he persuaded the secre-

The CIA training facility at Ft. Benning, Georgia, was housed in a former hospital complex. Designated Training Center One, its CIA and military instructor staff conducted a variety of courses in guerrilla warfare, demolitions, weapons, and intelligence tradecraft. *Courtesy of Edward Joseph*

tary of the army to provide guerrilla-warfare training facilities for the Agency at Fort Benning, Georgia.[7] Operating from an inactive military hospital subsequently redesignated Training Center One, CIA and army instructors soon began conducting a wide range of weapons, demolitions, and guerrilla training to OPC, as well as carefully selected U.S. military students.[8]

The NSC's decision to integrate OPC's operational aggressiveness into the CIA's conservative corporate philosophy proved a mixed blessing within the Agency. Internal dissension and resentment quickly broke out between OPC's well-funded covert operators and the longtime espionage agents entrenched in the Agency's Office of Special Operations (OSO). On the other hand, much of the Agency's growth during this period was due almost entirely to OPC's incredible expansion.

From 1949 to 1952, OPC's staff mushroomed from 302 to 2,812 employees (plus 3,142 overseas contract personnel), while its budget expanded from $4.7 million to $82 million.[9] By the time OPC and OSO were belatedly merged on 1 August 1952 under the Deputy Director for Plans—the covert operations directorate—operational activities accounted for 60 percent of the Agency's total personnel and 74 percent of its overall budget.[10] Traditional intelligence tradecraft such as that envisioned by Congress in 1947 had clearly taken a back seat to 10/2-type operations by this stage of the Agency's existence. This overly rapid expansion brought with it a number of problems, including the need to bureaucratically mask a budget now running into many millions. This particular problem was largely resolved with congressional passage of the Central Intelligence Agency Act of 1949, which allowed the CIA to bury its budget within those of several other federal bureaucracies.[11]

The outbreak of war on the Korean peninsula found the Agency two years into this tremendous but uneven growth spurt, its erratic effectiveness limiting the confidence with which its reports were read by Washington's senior political leaders. In a 28 February 1949 intelligence estimate, for example, the Agency was something less than helpful in predicting that the withdrawal of American military forces from South Korea later that year "would probably be followed *in time* [emphasis added] by an invasion."[12] Further damaging its already-shaky credibility was the postinvasion revelation of a CIA estimate, prepared just before the war, that put the number of North Korean troops at thirty-six thousand; fully one hundred thousand lower than the actual number that attacked shortly thereafter.[13]

Thus the political shock waves generated by North Korea's surprise attack hit CIA headquarters—indeed all of Washington—like a stinging slap to the back of the head. In Washington, all eyes had been looking apprehensively across the Atlantic to the seemingly inevitable showdown with Stalin over the future of a Western Europe still politically and economically shattered in the aftermath of World War II.

Perhaps the first U.S. casualty of the Korean War was DCI Hillenkoetter himself. The admiral's credibility had declined steadily over the preceding two years, following the Agency's failure to provide adequate advance notice of revolution in Guatemala (1948) and the Soviet explosion of an atom bomb (1949). By June 1950 Hillenkoetter's star had sunk so low that Truman didn't even bother to request his presence in the series of emergency staff meetings held immediately after the North Korean invasion.[14] The DCI was an easy target for Washington's inevitable search for a scapegoat, though left unharmed were the careers of others whose misjudgments were equally to blame. Maj. Gen. Charles A. Willoughby, for example, then the senior U.S. intelligence officer in Japan, predicted in March 1950—only three months before the outbreak of war—that "there will be no civil war in Korea this spring or summer."[15]

The political sacking of Hillenkoetter deflected some embarrassing questions away from the State and Defense Departments as well as the White House, but it was done at the expense of the Agency. If the CIA had any room for optimism in the next several weeks, it came with the new credibility the Agency soon accrued in Washington's power circles with Truman's shrewd selection of Hillenkoetter's successor. As the new DCI, Gen. Walter Bedell Smith, Eisenhower's former chief of staff during World War II and more recently ambassador to Moscow, soon took control of the Agency in a manner that left no doubt in anyone's mind as to who was in charge.

Conflict in MacArthur's Court

It was an ugly environment that drove Tofte to the bitter observation, "MacArthur has three enemies: the Russians, the Chinese, and the North Koreans. I have four, those three plus MacArthur!"

For the CIA, the Korean War posed three distinct challenges. To meet the first challenge, it had to keep the Cold War's only hot war in perspective. Who knew if Korea wasn't simply one of Stalin's diversionary tactics before the main blow fell on Western Europe? The Agency's global mission, including 10/2 operations, did not allow the CIA the luxury of concentrating the majority of its resources in Korea. The second challenge was more difficult, as it called for effective tactical and strategic intelligence support to MacArthur's military campaign on the Korean peninsula. And therein lay the third and most difficult challenge, the crux of which was the CIA's major problem in the Far East: How to support MacArthur in a war in which the only force more opposed to the CIA than the North Koreans was MacArthur himself!

MacArthur's intense and longstanding objections to a CIA presence in Japan can be judged in part by the fact that he relented on this issue only after prolonged and combined pressure from both the Joint Chiefs of Staff and the NSC. Only the month before the war broke out did the general permit a minuscule presence in Japan: three OSO agents working largely from their hotel rooms in Tokyo. Run by George Aurell, a former insurance executive who had lived in Japan prior to World War II, the OSO cell maintained at best a strained relationship with MacArthur's headquarters. This relationship changed rapidly less than a month after the war broke out, however, when, with all the subtlety of a brick flying through a plate glass window, OPC chief Wisner's first OPC operative arrived in Tokyo.

Wisner's choice was a certain Hans Tofte, an OSS veteran of the European Theater of Operations and a naturalized American of Danish origin. Though difficult to verify from sources other than Tofte himself, he was reputed to have studied Chinese in Peking, spoken several languages, worked in Northeast Asia for the East Asiatic Company prior to World War II, and held a sea captain's certificate and an airplane pilot's license. But if in 1950 Tofte appeared to be the right man at the right time for the job, the dominant reality for both Tofte and the Agency was that the three-year-old CIA had never been to war before. Moreover, neither Tofte's nor Wisner's experience against the Nazis had prepared them for anything like the sheer ruthlessness with which Asian Communists ruled the populations under their control.

If OPC's guidance for conducting covert operations in support of the U.S. military in times of war was vague, it also allowed plenty of freedom for operatives with imagination and drive, two characteristics often used to describe both Wisner and Tofte. But before Tofte could bring these characteristics to bear on the enemy, he had two more immediate tasks to accomplish in Japan. The first required that he find suitable bases, preferably near Tokyo, to establish covert training facilities for the North Korean refugees he would soon recruit for such missions. Even though the new program called for bases big enough to support one thousand people and a major CIA communications site, Tofte soon found the desired areas at both Atsugi Air Base, some forty-seven miles south of Tokyo, and Chigasaki, on the outskirts of Tokyo itself.[16]

Having quickly set the beginnings of his training program in motion, Tofte immediately turned his attention to one of those unpleasant tasks better undertaken sooner rather than later. In this instance the task involved "sorting out" Maj. Gen. Charles A. Willoughby, FEC's senior intelligence officer and MacArthur's most loyal supporter. Imperious and difficult to deal with even on a good day, "Sir Charles" Willoughby's reputation suffers with a rare uniformity of denigrations from virtually all who knew him at the time.[17] The confrontation between the two eventually escalated to the point where Willoughby actually ordered Japanese counter-intelligence agents to shadow Tofte's agents as the latter went about their business.[18] It was an ugly environment that drove Tofte to the bitter observation, "MacArthur has three enemies: the Russians, the Chinese, and the North Koreans. I have four, those three plus MacArthur!"[19]

Despite this bureaucratic war in Tokyo, the CIA presence in the Far East grew dramatically, if belatedly. Despite Willoughby's distaste for the CIA, he possessed few alternatives to seeking its help. By 1950 the catastrophic post–World War II cuts in defense spending had long since stripped FEC of the financial and trained human resources necessary to establish effective intelligence networks anywhere in the Far East.

Thus with pitifully few assets at his disposal following the North Korean invasion that June, Willoughby had little option but to seek Agency support for the Eighth Army's tactical battlefield intelligence requirements. Such short-range combat-support operations would normally be found far down on the priority list of OSO and OPC operatives attempting to run national-level intelligence and 10/2 operations on a global basis. But given the emergency in Korea, neither Aurell nor Tofte were in a position to refuse Willoughby's tasking.

A grudging accommodation between FEC and the CIA was eventually achieved, but only after both organizations tacitly agreed to avoid further confrontation by simply ignoring the duplication of effort as they ran their own intelligence and guerrilla operations in North Korea. On FEC's staff OPC operations were run under the cover name "Documents Research Section V," U.S. Far East Command.[20]

In the fall of 1951, six months after MacArthur's and Willoughby's departures from FEC, a subsequent attempt to coordinate their separate efforts erupted into a bureaucratic brawl that poisoned FEC-CIA relations for the remainder of the war. As these events would prove, MacArthur's dismissal did little to soften the bitter debate as to which organization—the military or the CIA—would control FEC's secret operations in Communist-held territory. And as events would soon prove, Tofte's days in Korea were also numbered by this time, as his fortunes with the Agency had already begun to wane.

In late 1950 Tofte's OPC staff produced and directed—under cover, of course—a popular, hard-hitting Japanese commercial film depicting Soviet abuses of Japanese POWs in Siberian prison camps. The film reportedly achieved a notable propaganda success in Japan. Too much success, in fact, as it forced the Agency's accounting department to deal with something unknown to federal accountants—a profit column. Seemingly emboldened by his producer's debut, Tofte moved onto another movie project that would ultimately contribute to his downfall. This second movie, including rare "combat footage" of CIA guerrillas operating in North Korea, was sent to the United States, where it was shown with much corporate pride to select audiences in Washington: "The film was widely shown in government circles, the CIA was pleased with its enthusiastic reception, and Tofte's reputation soared . . . until someone in a Pentagon audience noted a slight discrepancy in the CIA's—that is, Tofte's—claim that this was all actual footage of an actual operation, shot by intrepid CIA cameramen. Did the CIA send its paramilitary teams ashore, as depicted in the film, *in broad daylight?* Embarrassment all around. Tofte [subsequently] confessed that the film was, ah . . . simulated."[21]

Tofte was further tainted after the war, when an Agency operation in Latin America with which he was involved went sour. Things continued to go downhill for Tofte, and he was terminated in September

1966 following Agency charges that he had been found to have been storing classified documents in his apartment.[22]

Land of the Morning Calm

Adding to the mounting confusion, the U.S. Air Force and Navy continued running their own unconventional warfare campaigns against the enemy's rear sanctuaries, sometimes in support of the army or the Agency, sometimes on their own, and sometimes with British forces or the Korean navy.

The story of the CIA's field operations in Korea and China during the war is best understood from the perspectives of the Agency's two directorates that conducted these operations. This approach remains useful even after the two directorates were merged on 2 July 1951 under the cover name Joint Advisory Commission—Korea.[23] While the more violent covert operations run by OPC consumed the larger share of the CIA's resources in Northern Asia, the OSO's more subtle espionage activities were no less active in their own sphere.

These differences were, however, a moot point in the first weeks of the war, as George Aurell's tiny OSO cell stationed in Tokyo represented the Agency's only full-time presence in the Far East. As noted earlier, OPC's first entry into the war came with the arrival of Hans Tofte in Japan that July, almost a full month after the war's start. Until his arrival, Aurell's OSO agents, like everyone else, worked around the clock while awaiting reinforcements from the homeland. Especially hard hit by this reality in the first few days were the OSO communicators in Seoul.

It took nearly forty-eight hours for the American Embassy in Seoul to realize the full extent of the North Korean invasion. On 27 June, MacArthur was appointed commander of all U.S. Forces in Korea while the previous holder of this title—Ambassador John J. Muccio—was ordered to pack up the embassy staff and head for Suwon, some twenty miles to the south. With the American ambassador effectively on the run, OSO communicators became the mobile embassy's primary link to the outside world. Additional CIA communications gear and operators were flown into Suwon as OSO operatives were pressed into emergency duty as military intelligence officers. The pause at Suwon was short-lived, however, as the North Korean People's Army soon arrived to chase the embassy-OSO staff seventy miles farther south to Taejon, and thence into the tenuous security of the Pusan Perimeter. It had not been a dignified withdrawal.

Dignified or not, however, other OSO agents had made good use of the time consumed by the withdrawal to recruit and train Korean agents within the Pusan Perimeter. As the Agency archives note,

"OSO . . . personnel in Pusan also concentrated on forming and reactivating agent networks during the evacuation of Seoul . . . radio personnel . . . were dispatched to Pusan to serve as communications links with existing . . . nets in Seoul and Pyongyang. Efforts to contact stay-behinds in the North Korean areas continued."[24]

Still other OSO-directed agents were used extensively as battlefield line-crossers, traversing the always dangerous no-man's-land separating the opposing armies to bring in valuable front-line tactical information. Included in these fall 1950 successes was a noteworthy demonstration of OSO's intelligence-gathering techniques, one that took place near Inchon harbor prior to MacArthur's successful amphibious landing near that port city in September.

For this mission two OSO officers brought two Korean married couples together on an island off Inchon, then split them into two separate teams; the husband from one couple matched with the wife from the second couple. While the first team went ashore near Inchon, the second was held in "protective custody." The original couples were kept separated after the first team returned with its report. Only after the second team returned from the same area and the two reports were matched and corroborated were the spouses returned to their mates and sent back to their communities.[25] It was a period of frenetic growth for the OSO, and, as previously noted, an inordinate volume of its reporting was committed to Eighth Army tasking. Of the OSO reports disseminated between 1 November 1950 and 31 October 1951, "50 percent dealt with military or tactical information, 30 percent with North Korean political information, 15 percent with economic intelligence, and 5 percent with biographic data."[26]

While Willoughby may have had little alternative but to press the CIA for tactical intelligence, the general actually faced a much bigger intelligence collection problem than simply asking the civilians for help. Even before 1950 drew to a close, FEC had effectively lost control of the myriad military intelligence agencies operating in Communist-held territories. As noted in greater detail elsewhere in this history, every branch of the U.S. military was running its own intelligence operations with little regard to the efforts run by others.

Even within the Agency itself the semiautonomous OSO-OPC directorates found themselves crossing each other's jurisdictional boundaries to utilize assets each had established for its own purposes. This included the Agency's cover organizations within the military, the OSO's Department of the Army Liaison Detachment[27] and the OPC's Far East Air Forces Technical Analysis Group (FEAF/TAG).[28] In addition to their own cover organizations, both OSO and OPC went to the Fifth Air Force's Special Air Missions Detachment—later B Flight,

6167th Air Base Group—to have their agents parachuted into North Korea and China. Especially in the early war years, it was not unusual for agents from both directorates to be parachuted from the same aircraft at separate locations for substantially different missions. Worse still, other aircraft dropped a combination of agents, flares, and propaganda leaflets on a single flight. Beyond the potential for operational confusion, agent handlers were painfully aware of the gross security violations such practices entailed.

October 1950 was an eventful month for FEC and the Agency. While the Eighth Army established its headquarters in Seoul and the American Embassy reestablished its operations in the city, OPC set up headquarters at the Traymore Hotel in downtown Seoul.[29] It was a deceptive period for the Americans, for while UN field forces chased northward after the remnants of the NKPA, and headquarters soldiers, diplomats, and spies in Seoul hooked up their coffeepots, the first Chinese "volunteers" were already slipping southward into North Korea. In an ugly reminder of the cost incurred when people see only what they want to see, Willoughby discarded front-line reports of captured Chinese prisoners as he informed the Pentagon that "the most auspicious time [for Chinese military intervention] had long since passed."[30]

In a move more fortunate than they could have guessed at the time, OSO agents made good use of October by recruiting North Koreans for future penetration agents.[31] As some three hundred thousand Chinese soldiers were about to prove, the recruited agents would earn their pay not as penetration agents but as stay-behind agents. By January 1951 the Communists were back in Seoul, the battered Eighth Army regrouping farther south along the thirty-seventh parallel.

As a badly shaken and demoralized Eighth Army regrouped in January 1951, its headquarters staff concluded a postmortem of recent events, in particular the alleged failure of its major intelligence organizations to predict Chinese intervention in the war. A number of problems surfaced, many of which traced their roots back to the proliferation of military and civilian intelligence organizations either duplicating or leaving gaps in their collective efforts behind enemy lines. One of the first solutions offered and adopted as a remedy was the establishment of firm geographical boundaries separating OPC and military unconventional warfare in North Korea.

Working together effectively at least for the moment, OPC and the Eighth Army agreed to a north-south line dividing North Korea into western and eastern Areas of Operation (AO).[32] As OPC had already established the nucleus of a guerrilla movement in the extreme north-eastern mountains of North Korea, the eastern AO was given to Tofte while the Eighth Army maintained its control of the partisan force in the larger western AO.

Even this minimal agreement was substantially compromised with operational exceptions, however, as less than two months later Eighth Army staff officers announced their intention to begin partisan operations (Task Force Kirkland) from islands near the east coast port of Wonsan. Angry protests from OPC led to yet another confrontation, the outcome of which was that Kirkland's AO was subsequently limited that May to a semicircular area surrounding Wonsan, while OPC guerrillas operated from Wonsan north to the border with the Soviet Union. Adding to the mounting confusion, the U.S. Air Force and Navy continued running their own unconventional warfare campaigns against the enemy's rear sanctuaries, sometimes in support of the army or the Agency, sometimes on their own, and sometimes with British forces or the Korean navy.

The Agency took the lead in simplifying the confusion by merging its OSO-OPC assets in Korea on 2 July 1951, thus establishing JACK, the CIA's first combined Clandestine Services field mission.[33] As part of its deception plan intended to thwart Communist attempts to penetrate the organization, JACK employees were documented as members of the U.S. armed forces or Army Department civilians, while its vehicles were given a variety of markings.[34] The difficulty of protecting its installations and operations from enemy penetration grew in direct proportion to JACK's rapid expansion. By October 1952 JACK's facilities had grown to include four major facilities at Seoul, Inchon, and Pusan, as well as some seventy-seven training or launching or reception points, offices, safehouses, a number of vessels of varying sizes, and a [substantial] staff of indigenous employees."[35] It was a strong showing but still one that left begging the critical question: When would "someone" stop this behind-the-lines chaos that benefited only the Communists and put the scattered efforts under the command and control of one organization? The answer came later that year, and it was a bitter pill for the Agency to swallow.

"The sauce to cook the CIA goose"

A month later FEC-G2 announced its decision. Taken without further discussion with JACK, air force, or navy officials, it was a decision that poisoned FEC-CIA relations for the duration of the war.

During the same period that the OSO-OPC directorates were being merged in Korea, DCI Smith reached agreement with senior Department of the Army officials in Washington to place JACK under the operational control of MacArthur's replacement as CinCFE, Gen. Mathew B. Ridgway. In deference to the responsibilities attendant to on-scene commander in times of war, the Washington agreement left unspecified exactly how Ridgway was to integrate JACK into FEC's command structure. This task was undertaken on 21–22 October 1951, when FEC's Intelligence Directorate hosted a series of meetings in Seoul with senior JACK, Eighth Army, Seventh Fleet, and Fifth Air Force representatives.[36]

The document used as a base line for discussion at these meetings was a FEC-G2 proposal that a single executive agency be designated to run clandestine and covert activities throughout the Far East, to include Korea.[37] Supporting this general concept, JACK representatives at the meetings put forward a strong case supporting their contention that such wide-ranging activities would best be handled by the CIA. In doing so they cited in particular their successes in North Korea:

> By October 1951 the penetration of the North Korean Communist Party, Army . . . and governmental offices was well underway, as is shown by the subsequent record achieved by those nets during the months of November, December, and January, e.g., intelligence production of [JACK] increased by one-third during December. . . . 40 percent of that production was military intelligence in direct support of the Armed Forces of the United States in Korea, the remaining 60 percent being divided between political, economic, social, and counter-espionage reporting of a more long-range nature. In January, two specific reports covering the entire Order of Battle of the North Korean and Chinese Communist armies in North Korea were received.[38]

In presenting their case for CIA control of the proposed organization, JACK officers were speaking with the full support of, indeed at the direction of, their headquarters in Washington. However, as the following message to JACK reveals, CIA headquarters was operating under a premise that would soon be shown to be a gross fallacy: "Assumed that Far East Command proposal [for a single executive agency] is . . . intended to facilitate transfer of total responsibility for covert, clandestine and related activities to Central Intelligence Agency at an early date. Guidance which follows hereinafter based on this premise. At this instant we must depend for protection Central Intelligence Agency interests upon your assurance of continued validity of this assumption."[39]

Clearly, the Agency's enthusiasm for unifying the unconventional warfare program was predicated on its being unified under JACK, or at least some new organization run by the CIA from its Tokyo station. During the Seoul meetings several agreements further defining the organization and mission were agreed to: "The organizational integrity of Army, Air Force, Navy, and CIA units shall be maintained . . . and placed simultaneously under CCRAK [definition follows in text]. CIA operations of high sensitivity and/or with long-term characteristics which extend . . . into adjacent areas and are not in direct support of the Eighth Army shall be excepted from CCRAK control. CCRAK is a joint staff under one command."[40]

All signatories at the Seoul conferences agreed in writing to these stipulations, and, according to CIA archives, Fifth Air Force and Seventh Fleet representatives went on record expressing their views that JACK seemed best suited to run the proposed organization.[41] The meetings were subsequently adjourned to await FEC-G2's decision, with Agency participants clearly anticipating a favorable outcome.

A month later FEC-G2 announced its decision. Taken without further discussion with JACK, air force, or navy officials, it was a decision that poisoned FEC-CIA relations for the duration of the war. Established with FEC orders dated 28 November 1951, the new executive agency was designated "Covert, Clandestine, and Related Activities—Korea," with the cover name "Combined Command, Reconnaissance Activities—Korea," or CCRAK.[42] Almost every single point agreed upon by the signatories in Seoul, and almost every point insisted upon by CIA headquarters in Washington, had been ignored. Agency records express suspicion that FEC-G2's decision was made without the prior knowledge of Ridgway, but it is unlikely that the politically savvy general had not preapproved the announcement.[43] But if the expressed suspicion itself sounds naïve, the result was certainly a fait accompli that left FEC's army intelligence officers firmly in control of virtually all UN covert and clandestine operations in North Korea.

It was the poorest possible start for the new organization, a joint-endeavor organization dependent on the professional cooperation of all concerned. Worse yet, FEC-G2 limited CCRAK to operational control—not command—of the air force, navy, and JACK units submitted to it by the other Seoul conference signatories. It didn't take long for trouble to erupt within CCRAK, and one of the first fights occurred between the army and air force.

In a February 1952 meeting of CCRAK's senior staff, army Col. Washington M. Ives, the new Chief, CCRAK, announced his plans for sending CCRAK operatives "beyond the Yalu and into China."[44] A number of unit commanders present voiced their strong doubts that CCRAK had such a capability. In particular, CCRAK's Deputy for Air, Lt. Col. George Budway, made no bones that CCRAK "would be going way over its head" in attempting such missions.[45] It didn't help matters that Colonel Ives was the former deputy for administration, FEC-G2. Though spoken well of by those who knew him, Ives's lack of intelligence collection and unconventional warfare experience inevitably left many in CCRAK to conclude that the colonel's selection for the job was based largely on his willingness to follow instructions from FEC-G2 officers.

As part of CCRAK's charter, its deputy chief position was reserved for the senior JACK officer, someone selected by Agency headquarters in Washington. And, initially at least, JACK's chief of station in Seoul filled CCRAK's operations billet.[46] While on paper these two positions would seem well placed to protect Agency interests, JACK officers soon found themselves increasingly tasked with tactical intelligence duties that detracted sharply from their ability to prosecute their national-level missions. As Agency archives note, "Inasmuch as the desires of General Ridgway [FEC], General Van Fleet [Eighth Army], General Everest [Fifth Air Force], and Admiral Briscoe [Seventh Fleet] can only be met through long-range sensitive operations, the Chief/CIA Mission, Korea [JACK] must spend time within CCRAK and then go back to his own Mission where the [primary CIA] work must be performed."[47] While the FEC commanders who succeeded MacArthur gave the Agency relatively more latitude in prosecuting its national missions in the Far East, JACK officers continued to chafe under the tight rein imposed by CCRAK supervision.

JACK morale sagged as its officers watched with growing dismay the manner in which army officers assigned to FEC-G2 increasingly asserted their authority in Agency operations. As to why CIA headquarters in Washington chose not to fight this growing encroachment on its charter, CIA records of this period suggest one possible answer: "With MacArthur's G2 (Willoughby) gone, the CIA Chiefs . . . while skeptically remembering that not long ago General Willoughby put CIA activities under surveillance . . . cautiously agreed not to fight 'city hall.'"[48]

Ironically, army control over CIA activities was exactly what both MacArthur and Willoughby had always sought, after having failed to keep the CIA out of Japan altogether. In the words of one CIA historian, "Clearly, CCRAK was sauce to cook the CIA goose."[49]

It is interesting to note that throughout all of these trials and tribulations both provoked and endured by FEC-G2 and JACK officers, military-civilian working relationships at the field level were marked by a distinctly cooperative attitude among the case officers. Noting this welcomed relief from headquarters politics, one Agency archive observes, "CIA advisors worked with the Eighth Army west coast guerrillas from January to April 1952. Competition between the CIA and Army

Though the CIA's proprietary airline, Civil Air Transport (CAT), operated from South Korean airfields early in the war, the Agency's records note that CAT aircrews did not become engaged in agent drops behind communist lines until the tenth month of the war. *Hans Tofte Collection via Joseph Goulden*

guerrilla warfare efforts was keen but wholesome, with no real problems at the operating level. The over-all CIA/Army relationship at that level was eminently satisfactory and mutually advantageous."[50]

As FEC-G2 slowly strengthened its grip on intelligence and special operations resources in Korea, CIA leaders in Washington quietly conducted a reassessment of their own on these resources. The Agency had earlier committed three of its best senior clandestine services officers to JACK, two to work within CCRAK as deputy chief and chief, counter-intelligence, and the third as head of foreign intelligence activities.[51]

Concluding that the highly restrictive environment within CCRAK was essentially wasting the talents of the three promising officers, the Agency reassigned all three from Korea in the following months. Relatively inexperienced officers were sent in their place, and as the Agency historian candidly notes, "A regrettable side effect of the control exercised by CCRAK is that the Agency did not put its best foot forward in Korea in the last year of the war."[52]

Air Operations

The Agency had been using air force crews for a considerable time before either service became aware of a major disconnect in communications that was costing the Koreans dearly. Time after time the B Flight aircrews reported a successful resupply drop, while the agents on the drop zone were radioing back at virtually the same time to base station asking what happened to their resupply.

For the first ten months of the war all CIA agents dropped into North Korea were flown in by the U.S. Air Force, in particular a small C-47 transport-equipped Special Air Mission Detachment (SAM) from the Fifth Air Force's 21st Troop Carrier Squadron.[53] As the war progressed, this dependency gradually decreased as the CIA's proprietary airline, Civil Air Transport (CAT), gradually supplemented, but never completely replaced, air force support. This was especially true of the use JACK made of B Flight after it replaced the SAM in April 1952. A larger organization, B Flight was equipped with an aircraft of particular interest to JACK operatives: the B-26 medium bomber modified to carry parachutists. Interestingly, CIA histories of the war differ sharply among themselves in the Agency's appraisal of the air force support it used at different stages of the war.

The SAM Detachment flew the CIA's first airborne infiltration missions of the war immediately after the Inchon landings in September 1950, the OSO teams committed to the effort having trained since the previous July at the Agency's Pusan base.[54] The handful of teams were dropped into separate areas near Korea's northern border with China to establish observation posts in the mountains overlooking the main corridors of transportation from China and Russia. The results were disappointing, though OSO's agent handlers were pleased to see a number of the agents return through friendly lines weeks later. At this early stage of the war, the battlefield situation remained so fluid that rear-area security still remained a secondary mission for the Chinese and North Korean armies.

The Agency's airborne infiltration techniques varied from those of the military in several aspects. OSO-OPC agents jumped in civilian clothes, using the standard T-10 military parachute but without the standard chest-mounted reserve parachute. This was not the callousness it might appear, as most jumps were conducted at a minimal five hundred feet. From this low height, the jumper would have virtually no time to deploy the reserve chute if the main failed to open, thus making the reserve more a psychological comfort than a realistic option. These considerations for the safety of the agents were, of course, only relevant in the final stages of the infiltration, a process that had begun hours earlier back at the airfield in South Korea.

Immediately prior to takeoff, mostly likely from Seoul City Airfield, the all-Korean team was moved from a building on the airfield to a briefing hut near the aircraft's arrival point. The agent handler checked team equipment, went over the mission objectives and procedures one last time, and in general kept the team motivated and focused on their mission. At a signal, the team mounted a canvas-covered truck for movement to the airplane, which was parked at a remote section of the airfield. Once in the aircraft, neither the team nor the case officer talked to the aircrew.

For obvious reasons, drop zones were selected in remote areas, with the additional criterion that they be within three walking days of the target area. Whenever possible, at least one of the infiltrated team members would have friends or relatives within the target area. Teams frequently took a pair of air force-trained carrier pigeons for intercept-free communications, the birds carrying coded messages indicating the team's status after infiltration.

Even though agents were given false documents and cover stories should they be captured, the false identities reflected more their handler's faith in intelligence tradecraft than the Korean agent's confidence in their usefulness. The Koreans were right, for even the Agency acknowledged that trying to keep up with North Korean identity documents was a "major problem."[55] What the Korean agents did find useful, however, was the issuance of barter items such as gold rings, medical supplies, and other hard-to-get items in North Korean's war-torn economy.

The Agency had been using air force crews for a considerable time before either service became aware of a major disconnect in communications that was costing the Koreans dearly. Time after time the B Flight aircrews reported a successful resupply drop, while the agents on the drop zone were radioing back at virtually the same time to base station asking what happened to their resupply. The core problem was not discovered until the fall of 1952, when an investigation revealed that for many missions the marginally trained aircrews had not been briefed on the CIA drop zone markings taught to its agents. Agency records give a critical and more specific account of the problem: "Apparently only one technique was used, penetrating during the moon phase in clear weather, making the drop on a light pattern. Since the same technique was used during every moon phase by the Korean Mission [JACK] and other agencies in the area, a [North Korean] defense of hill watchers was set up, and numerous fires in various patterns appeared on the ground whenever a plane flew overhead. As a result, aircrews dropped supplies and even personnel without being absolutely sure that they were over the right drop zone pattern and that it was not a trap."[56]

That this deadly discrepancy existed for so long appears due largely to the strict security measures intentionally designed to minimize the risk of security leaks. In this case, however, such measures proved a tragic case of the left hand not knowing what the right hand was doing. While the CIA refuses to release its statistics on the number of agent and resupply drops made into North Korea and China, one candid assessment found in its archives provides a clue as to the magnitude of the tragedy: "The whole aim of the air activity in Korea seemed to be quantity, not quality. Tons and tons of rice and other commodities, as well as thousands of personnel, were dropped into North Korea during the war period from 25 June 1950 to 27 July 1953."[57]

Having clearly given the issue of air support considerable thought, JACK concludes in its report for the final year of the war that, had the Agency been given complete control of its air support during the war, it would have needed no more than three aircraft with CIA-trained aircrews to improve on the performance rendered by B Flight. This was a harsh judgment, especially considering that other JACK histories of the period show a more favorable evaluation of B Flight's performance. In retrospect, the harsher judgment may be closer to the truth, if only because B Flight archives are replete with many of the same complaints—lack of special operations aircrew training and general inexperience due to constant rotations—voiced by JACK officers.

While the Agency did benefit from the higher experience levels found within its own CAT aircrews, it would also receive a painful reminder that one danger in particular posed a threat that no amount of experience or courage could overcome. That reminder came in November 1952 on a long-range mission that took a CAT C-47 deep into northern China. As dangerous as the area was, the mission itself would go a step further in its daring.

Enemies of the People's Court

As the aircraft slowed to enter the most vulnerable stage of the operation, machine gun fire erupted from the darkness on all sides, slicing into the aircraft. Careening from the impact of so many hits at close range, the aircraft staggered through the air before plowing into the ground not far from the stunning ambush.

One of the most intractable problems facing both the CIA and FEC during the war was their inability to extract deep-penetration agents from North Korea or China. Once parachuted behind enemy lines, the Korean and Chinese agents were virtually trapped in the area, with the possible exception of those operations taking place near the coastline. In this event, there was at least the theoretical chance of pickup by one of the Agency's boats, or perhaps by one of the U.S. Air Force planes

The air-to-ground "All-American" retrieval system was designed for those in desperate straits, not those with any other option for escape. This demonstration took place in Japan in August 1952, only three months before the CIA sent a similar aircraft into Manchuria to attempt such a retrieval of one of its agents. Special operations soldier John Sadler wears a T-7 parachute harness attached to a nylon rope, held in a folded coil by rubber bands. The rope is attached in turn to the "snatch cable" strung horizontally overhead between the two vertical poles. The long-handled "hook" mounted from the aircraft snags the cable in much the same fashion as does the arresting gear used by naval aircraft landing on an aircraft carrier. Slowing to its absolute minimum stall speed as it approaches the cable with the hook, the C-47 snatches the cable (and Sadler) from the ground, simultaneously clawing for airspeed and altitude. The inherent stretch in nylon keeps Sadler from being torn in two by the sudden acceleration. Once in the air, Sadler is slowly reeled into the aircraft's open cargo door by an electric winch. The ill-fated CIA mission called for this maneuver to be performed at night. *Courtesy of John Sadler via John Plaster*

which occasionally operated in the area. This situation began to change for the first time only in the fall of 1952, when a new air-to-ground retrieval system was successfully tested in Japan.

The "All-American" system, as it was called, was normally mounted on a twin-engine C-47 transport and designed to retrieve from the ground one individual at a time. This was done by connecting one end of the retrieval line to an electrically driven drum mounted in the aircraft's fuselage near the main cargo door. The line was then run through a pulley out to the tip of a metal pole thrust horizontally out of the cargo door, much like a fishing pole arrangement. At the end of the line was a strong metal hook, lowered as the retrieval aircraft began a low-and-slow approach to the agent. On the ground, the agent sat in a special harness, which in turn was tied to a horizontal rope strung so as to be snagged by the hook as the aircraft passed overhead. Following a successful snag, the aircraft climbed for altitude while the electrical winch pulled the agent up to the cargo door to be pulled inside the fuselage by the cabin crew.

Though a relatively simply arrangement, it nonetheless required the aircraft to come within a few feet of the ground at speeds well below one hundred miles per hour. Obviously the aircraft would be extremely vulnerable to ground fire during its pickup run, should there be any enemy in the vicinity. As a result of all these considerations, both JACK and the military chose to limit its attempts with the All-American system to only "high-priority-minimal-risk" situations. In November 1952, Agency officers in Japan concluded that they faced exactly the sort of mission that met these criteria.

The officers had received a series of radio messages calling for help from a Chinese guerrilla-intelligence team it had parachuted into Manchuria the previous month. After discussing the situation, the commander of the Joint Technical Analysis Group (JTAG), an OPC cover organization, informed the Agency's newly established North Asia Command that it would dispatch a C-47 equipped with the all-American system to retrieve one of the team.[58] The attempt appeared to meet the minimal-risk criteria as the team, not believed to have been doubled (i.e., forced to work for the enemy), had radioed its assurances that no enemy would be in the vicinity of the pickup.

Chosen to operate the pickup system from the back of the JTAG aircraft's cabin were two newly arrived CIA employees, John T. Downey and Richard G. Fecteau. Downey describes what subsequently happened next with disarming understatement:

> The aircraft was a C-47 . . . that carried no markings, was "sterilized" as a security precaution to prevent tracing its origin. The purpose of retrieving the agent was to debrief him on the results of his mission. The aircraft took off from Seoul [Seoul City Airport, or "Spook City" as it was known, the primary special air missions field in South Korea] shortly after 9 p.m. [29 November]. Weather during the flight was clear and cold, visibility good. We followed a route that was generally used for . . . flights into China, that

is, from Seoul roughly east to the coast, then north over water. [We] crossed the Korean-Chinese border at 12 midnight and reached the pickup area fifteen minutes later.[59]

After establishing radio contact with the team and dropping the agent harness and gear needed for the pickup, the aircraft circled and began its descent for the retrieval. As the aircraft slowed to enter the most vulnerable stage of the operation, machine-gun fire erupted from the darkness on all sides, slicing into the aircraft. Careening from the impact of so many hits at close range, the aircraft staggered through the air before plowing into the ground not far from the stunning ambush.

JTAG officers in Japan were not aware of anything amiss until the C-47 failed to return to Seoul on schedule. Fearing the worst, JTAG immediately initiated a plausible denial operation with the support of Brig. Gen. Jacob E. Smart, Far East Air Forces deputy for operations: "The air force laid on a sea search between Japan and Korea under the pretext that an air force plane had possibly gone down on a trip between the two land areas. This was supported by a carefully devised flight by a second C-47 which, by suddenly diving below radar coverage, appeared to have crashed into the sea. The search lasted almost a week without, naturally, direct results. During [this week], Japan headquarters of FEC waited in trepidation for any word of survivors of the rescue operation."[60]

Fear turned to uncertainty regarding the fate of the aircraft and crew when China's normally hyperactive propaganda machine made no mention of shooting down a UN aircraft in China, a real propaganda coup by any standard. Perhaps the aircraft had hit a mountain in some remote area not yet discovered by security forces?

Two long years to the month passed before the Agency discovered what really happened in China that night, and only then after it was stunned to learn that Downey and Fecteau were alive and were to be tried as spies in Peking. Both had been in solitary confinement during the two years between their capture and trial. In November 1954 the two were tried and convicted of espionage activities, despite strong protests from the Eisenhower administration that the two were Department of the Army civilians lost on a routine flight from Seoul to Japan.

Twenty-two-year-old Downey received a life sentence, while twenty-five-year-old Fecteau got twenty years. Years of fruitless attempts by a succession of U.S. administrations failed to secure the release of the two. Fecteau was finally released in December 1971 and subsequently went on to become an assistant director of athletics at

Boston University before his retirement in 1989. Released two years later, Downey subsequently completed Harvard Law School and is now a judge of the Superior Court in the state of Connecticut. During their two decades in prison, the two were listed in the Agency's personnel files as serving on "Special Detail Foreign at Official Station Undetermined."[61] On 25 June 1998, DCI George J. Tenet awarded the two the Director's Medal, which was inscribed with the most appropriate words: "Extraordinary Fidelity and Essential Service."

Maritime Operations

> As subsequent experience was to show, the CIA's major problem was not so much acts of nature as it was a prolonged underestimation of the resources needed to establish a serious maritime campaign. As Agency records reveal, this underestimation of the difficulties involved in seaborne operations was due almost exclusively to the fact that the personnel assigned these operations were, to put it simply, landlubbers.

The Agency's covert maritime operations conducted four primary missions during the war: small boat movement of agents to and from North Korea; night coastal raiding with the Special Missions Group; covert escape and evasion (E&E) activities; and interisland logistical support. While it was an ambitious program that scored some notable successes, it was at the same time a program so plagued with major deficiencies that, according to Agency records, it never came close to meeting its operational potential.

Particularly disappointing was the program's inability to capitalize on the unparalleled opportunities for covert operations provided by the convenient location of the thousands of islands dotting the rugged Korean coastline. True, a number of natural factors—for example, the extreme tidal variations along Korea's west coast, fog, high winds and sea state, and winter ice—limited effective small boat operations. The Agency's commonsense operational precaution of limiting launch and recovery operations to dark-of-the-moon periods also limited the number of operations that could be mounted.

But as subsequent experience was to show, the CIA's major problem was not so much acts of nature as it was a prolonged underestimation of the resources needed to establish a serious maritime campaign. As Agency records reveal, this underestimation of the difficulties involved in seaborne operations was due almost exclusively to the fact that the personnel assigned these operations were, to put it simply, landlubbers: "The Korean seamen employed by the Korea Mission [OSO-OPC, subsequently JACK] had little or no technical maritime or naval training, and the Mission itself did not have properly equipped

American personnel to remedy the situation. Consequently, operations were marked by a strong lack of precision that was at all times dangerous and intolerable."[62]

In fact, many of these untrained boat crews and agents were in danger long before they encountered Communists and dangerous coastal waters. Also putting out to sea with these boats, as if members of the crew, were major problems stemming from a lack of security precautions in port and of maintenance on the boats themselves:

> Mission vessels never had a restricted berthing area in either Inchon or Pusan, which inevitably led to the loss of security and efficiency. On the east coast, no provision was made to ship supplies from the rear echelon to staging areas [on the islands]. . . . On the west coast, case officers were forced to spend four-fifths of their time on supply and repair problems because of the lack of a support section to handle the logistics of island bases. These conditions . . . were the results of extreme compartmentation and project self-sufficiency which Mission case officers found, without exception, a bitter experience.[63]

Such conditions crippled the maritime program for nearly all of the first two years of the war. Notable successes were achieved during this period, however, when the Agency used professional seamen—U.S. Navy sailors aboard high-speed transports and U.S. Air Force crash rescue boat crews—to carry its agents and guerrillas across the dangerous seas surrounding Korea.

In March 1951, for example, the U.S. Navy took Brigadier General Sams of the U.S. Army and an escort of OPC guerrillas into Communist-held territory for a highly successful mission (see navy monograph for a more detailed description of this mission). And that summer OPC developed a coastal raider force (the SMG) which operated successfully from the U.S. Navy's high-speed transports throughout much of 1952. On the west coast, air force "special operations sailors" took agents as far north as Manchuria in eighty-five-foot crash rescue boats, using only celestial navigation to land the teams with pinpoint accuracy on darkened beaches.

It took until 1952 before field complaints from maritime operatives succeeded in provoking a meaningful response from the Agency's management structure. That year the Agency sent a U.S. Navy admiral, along with the assistant deputies for OPC and OSO, to Korea to set up proper naval support for JACK's rag-tag fleet of small boats.[64] Improvements followed, and that November JACK moved to centralize control of its fleet through the creation of the Maritime Operations Section. But this too, failed, when—apparently for operational security reasons—JACK continued to leave most of its boats in the hands of individual case officers.

From an in-depth evaluation of its wartime travails with maritime operations, the Agency developed a "lessons-learned" report on the subject with a terse summary of the minimal requirements for future such operations:

1. A simple maritime technical training program to produce reasonably efficient skippers and seamen.
2. Centralized maritime administrative activities through the use of port coordinators who have been delegated substantial in-port authority and through a maritime administrative section at headquarters.
3. Assign to a single support authority the necessary number of vessels to coordinate and centralize maritime supply runs.[65]

Beyond these specific management conclusions the report reached out to identify the underlying conditions that stalled the program's development: "Although the maritime problems in Korea had been recognized for an extended period, the solutions had been rejected by higher authority because of security, compartmentation, and lack of qualified personnel. Some case officers also rejected assistance because they did not want to lose a part of their empire or be subjected to more control through a centralized system."[66]

Despite this generally dismal assessment of its covert maritime program, the fact remains that the Korea Mission did operate a considerable number of small boats and did conduct hundreds of agent insertions and extractions along North Korean coastlines, executing in the process an unknown number of successful operations. In comparison to airborne insertions, resistance movements behind Communist lines, the E&E program, etc., the amphibious operations run by both FEC and JACK still account for the highest agent-return rates and tactical successes of the covert war.

Yet even in retrospect it remains difficult to understand why JACK's senior officers struggled for so long to grasp such obvious fundamentals as the need for trained seamen and adequate logistics support. These same officers clearly understood the same fundamentals as they applied to air support, for example, or to guerrilla-warfare training programs. Moreover, these were the same management-level officers who successfully incorporated military skills into their organizations on a regular basis.

One partial explanation is likely found in an Agency observation that noted the operational zeal in JACK's field agents that "predominated consistently to the exclusion of support."[67] This overemphasis on operations may account, for example, for JACK's willingness to recruit UDT personnel for the dangerous raiding missions without also recruiting the U.S. Navy bosun's mates who essentially made their living by operating and maintaining the small craft on which the frogmen and raiders bet their lives. The significance of this problem wasn't so much that these deficiencies spelled the absolute difference between success or failure for any given mission, so much as how the courage and sacrifice of a few were expended in an effort that could have—but didn't—make a difference in the war's outcome.

Escape and Evasion

> These teams were dropped into the teeth of the Chinese offensive, without reception committees and sufficient operational data. A number of rescues were alleged to have been made during this second program, though all but one of the teams were either lost or exfiltrated.

As with so many other issues involving U.S. efforts to operate behind Communist lines in Korea, the E&E program became a major source of friction between the CIA and FEC. In researching this particularly troublesome aspect of unconventional warfare operations in North Korea, I uncovered one particular CIA document describing this program so comprehensively as to justify a rare near-verbatim recital. What follows therefore are the relevant sections of "Infiltration and Resupply of Agents in North Korea, 1952–1953." As some sections remain redacted by the CIA, I have taken the liberty to edit where necessary for the sake of continuity and clarity.

The first covert escape and evasion program in Korea was initiated in 7 September 1950 at the request of General Partridge, Fifth Air Force commander.[68] Some two hundred Korean troops were subsequently recruited and trained in E&E techniques, and, on 22 October 1950, a number of four-man teams were ready for launching into North Korea.[69] However, this E&E program was canceled on 27 October 1950, and a week later Gen. Charles A. Willoughby froze all E&E assets. Both of these actions were taken in the headquarters euphoria that followed the UN successes in North Korea, successes that seemed certain to fulfill MacArthur's 24 November pledge to "have the troops home by Christmas."

Scarcely days after Willoughby's decision, the intervention of Chinese troops in Korea sent UN forces reeling south. In response, the Agency sent new agents into E&E training while it attempted to reassemble the remaining assets of its initial program. These old-new

E&E teams were quickly transferred to Korea for launch preparations, and on 5 December confirmation was received that a number of these teams were operating in the Pyongyang area. These teams were dropped into the teeth of the Chinese offensive, without reception committees and sufficient operational data. A number of rescues were alleged to have been made during this second program, though all but one of the teams were either lost or exfiltrated.

In March 1951 the Agency dropped its use of four-man teams for E&E missions, assigning the role instead to the "general resistance warfare groups" it had by then begun deploying in Communist-held territory.[70] Fully ten months later these groups were credited with a paltry fifteen rescues of downed aircrew, and even then air force reports suggested that at least some of these rescues were due more to luck and circumstance than any planned E&E effort.

On 8 May 1952, FEAF announced its intention to take responsibility for the covert E&E program from the Agency, citing its belief that it could achieve better results than those obtained by resistance teams or by intelligence agents who viewed E&E as a secondary effort. To this end, the air force wanted to purchase fishing vessels, equipped with radios and manned by Koreans, to ply the west coast of North Korea to rescue and exfiltrate downed pilots. Brig. Gen. Charles Y. Banfil, FEAF's deputy chief of staff, Intelligence, informed the Agency that he had taken up the matter with Washington, and that the air force was going into the E&E business by default.

The CIA responded to this FEAF initiative by pointing out that, while CCRAK had assumed full responsibility for direction and control of the E&E activities in Korea, it had simply turned the mission over to JACK, which lacked the necessary experienced personnel. JACK representatives went a step further in stating that, if FEAF had the funds and personnel to take control of the E&E mission, it should make those assets available to CCRAK. The bureaucratic ill-will surrounding the establishment of that organization the preceding December surfaced again in this rare CIA–air force dispute, with JACK officers clearly believing that they were being blamed for CCRAK's failure to develop an effective covert E&E program.

A 19 May CCRAK meeting on the subject led the conferees back to the air force's original proposal to purchase indigenous fishing boats for E&E duty off North Korea's western coast, an area covering the route taken by UN fighters returning from combat in the notorious MiG Alley. The Agency proposed instead an alternative plan using smaller, faster craft, for which JACK would recruit the crews and indigenous radio operators and provide signal plans, equipment, and a fifty-ton mother ship. The Fifth Air Force was to provide technical assistance as needed. For their part the air force and navy would be responsible for air support, should protection be needed for the boats. CIA headquarters approved JACK's proposal on 27 May 1952, along with authorization to make the necessary expenditures if the military services concurred.

The headquarters approval arrived only three days after another message from headquarters, this one advising JACK that Britain's Royal Air Force was considering the possibility of moving a full-time E&E unit of its own into Korea. At the time of the offer, there were more than a thousand British POWs in North Korean camps. But the Royal Air Force proposal to parachute British officers behind enemy lines—a variation of the Agency's early-war use of four-man teams for such missions—was by 1952 considered unrealistic by JACK, and headquarters ultimately advised against the British initiative.

It took an additional five months before representatives from the Far East Command, Naval Forces Far East, Fifth Air Force, Seventh Fleet, and CCRAK met in Tokyo that October to further discuss JACK's proposal for a covert boat program under CCRAK. The conference began with navy representatives disclosing their receipt of a $2.5 million E&E fund intended for the purchase, maintenance, and operational supervision of the proposed fleet. In fact, NAVFE had already established Task Force 96.8 expressly for the program. The navy plan also put these boats under its control for the duration of hostilities, a period during which the CIA would have no responsibility for the program.

Having obviously put some thought and money into the proposed program, the navy representatives were nonplussed to discover that the Agency already had, during the previous four months, purchased, fitted, and placed into operation all the "covert boats" it deemed necessary for the program. In fact, JACK had also activated a maritime base nine miles southeast of Inchon on 16 June to serve as the primary control and logistical center for its E&E program on the west coast.[71] A secondary function of the base was its support of other Agency programs having maritime components, including an effort to develop and exploit contacts with Korean and Chinese smugglers.

JACK representatives did accept the navy's offer to provide the necessary maintenance for its boats—on a reimbursable basis from the Agency—but would not allow the navy to assume control of the boats.

Agency records do not include the navy's response to JACK's preemptive moves, but in fact JACK did, as promised, retain control of the boats for the remainder of the war.

A month after the conference in Tokyo, CIA headquarters cabled JACK to criticize its E&E operations in northwest Korea. In particular headquarters expressed its concern that JACK was engaging too much in semiovert activities, such as directing indigenous craft for sea rescue and coastal pickups instead of limiting its effort to CIA's charter for covert-only E&E. JACK officers found themselves caught between operational demands in Korea and bureaucratic expectations from Washington. Having suffered considerable criticism from FEC in general and the air force in particular for the lack of E&E rescues behind enemy lines, JACK was anxious to put some numbers on the board. And in North Korea such numbers were far more likely to come from semiovert or overt operations than any covert program.

The cease-fire of 27 July 1953 forced a complete reassessment and reorganization of covert E&E operations and personnel. The CIA's goal was to reorganize into a security-tight, efficiently run project capable of producing a higher-level intelligence product as its secondary mission. The primary effort was directed toward developing additional nets in the geographic areas into which the largest number of aircraft went down during the three years of hostilities in North Korea. In the event hostilities resumed, the project would be ready to continue its covert aircrew recovery program.

The proposed establishment of these new E&E nets was crippled by two armistice-related agreements. First, the withdrawal of UN navies from North Korean coastal waters and the evacuation begun two months earlier of all but five of the UN's partisan-held islands resulted in immediate evidence of increased enemy coastal patrol (specifically, high-speed) boats. The presence of these patrol craft essentially terminated any practical hope of inserting agents via amphibious means into the desired E&E areas. Another armistice prohibition against UN overflights of North Korea essentially ruled out airborne infiltration of the agents. Without seaborne or airborne assets, agents were left with no other option but to use overland routes through enemy lines, long since recognized by the Agency as the most time-consuming, arduous, dangerous, and least likely to succeed method of infiltration.

In December 1953 the Agency's North Asia Command candidly concluded that the E&E program in Korea had been of such magnitude and scope that it could only have been accomplished by a truly joint effort by all the military services and the CIA, a joint effort that never developed. The report went further in stating that, in retrospect, it was doubtful that the CIA could take credit even in small part for the rescue of the previously noted fifteen airmen brought back through friendly lines between March 1951 and January 1952. JACK's E&E program was terminated as of 30 September 1954.

General Resistance Warfare Groups

> Following JACK's decision to "terminate the contract," a special air resupply flight was scheduled for the team on 3 August 1952. One bundle contained the requested luxury items and women's clothing, which, when removed from the container, set off an explosion from the explosives buried underneath.

By the winter of 1950 Tofte's OPC had already begun Operation Blossom, the deployment of what the Agency referred to as "general resistance warfare groups."[72] As the Agency envisioned this program, selected North Korean refugees would be sent back home to form an underground resistance network capable of operating indefinitely in Communist-held territory by virtue of the support received from a presumably cooperative civilian population. Within a short period of time these groups evolved from a semipassive resistance network to that of a more heavily armed and aggressive force.

During the course of the following year, OPC infiltrated by both air and sea a number of Blossom teams into central and northeast Korea.[73] Contact with some of the teams was lost immediately, but other teams managed to survive and even consolidate forces in certain areas. Still effective at this stage of the war, these teams turned in some notable successes in October 1951, when they passed critical targeting intelligence to the JACK base in Pusan. The Agency's good relations with the U.S. Navy paid off immediately, as this time-perishable target data was immediately forwarded to Task Force 77 (TF 77), the navy's fast carrier task force operating in the Sea of Japan. Vice Adm. J. J. Clark, commander, TF 77, later wrote of the excellent results achieved through this cooperation:

> I had worked out a system whereby the carriers could attack and photograph promising targets suggested by JACK's North Korean agents. The most successful of these raids occurred at Kapsan, south of the Yalu River. JACK's guerrillas informed us that North Korean commissars from four adjoining districts were going to meet secretly at Kapsan on 28–30 October 1951. We took high-altitude photographs of the twelve major buildings and barracks beforehand. . . .
>
> On the morning of the 29th, eight Essex Skyraiders, loaded with 1,000-pound napalm and 250-pound general-purpose bombs, struck just as the commissars were meeting . . . three bombs hit squarely [on the main bomb

shelter] . . . then the planes strafed the compound with 20-mm incendiary cannon and high-explosive machine gun fire. The area was flattened into flaming rubble. JACK's agents moved closer to take a count: 144 party officials and 376 soldiers killed . . . all twelve buildings destroyed. Enraged, the North Korea radio announced a reward would be given for the capture of the "butchers of Kapsan."[74]

Such successes came at a high cost to the guerrillas, however, as by the following month the Agency was still in steady radio contact with barely half of the original teams inserted over the previous months.

The onset of Korea's notorious winter brought with it radio instructions from OPC to break down into smaller units and concentrate on survival until the following spring. However, even this wasn't enough for the beleaguered teams, for by January 1952, only a handful were still in communication. Two months later OPC concluded that virtually all of the remaining force had been captured and doubled. In April OPC attempted to resurrect the movement, using for the most part replacements trained at its guerrilla warfare facility on Yong-do.

In addition to those replacement personnel destined for the Blossom project, a number of other teams were organized under a single program to accomplish three separate missions:

1. Special action teams: Infiltrated by air and sea to conduct hit-and-run raids intended to acquire North Korean documentation and local-area intelligence, as well as to cache supplies for E&E requirements. These teams were to be extracted by sea after completion of their missions.
2. Special mission groups: Conducted amphibious commando raids for purposes of intelligence collection, kidnapping of local officials, and sabotage along the eastern coast of North Korea with which segments of the project had been involved since the summer of 1951.
3. Resistance cadre: Organized into small cells with the mission of establishing resistance movements in North Korea.[75]

The ambitious program ran into deep problems almost immediately, as by the summer of 1952 suspicions were already running deep that many of the teams infiltrated after training had already been doubled by the Communists. OPC itself judged that by this period the program had sunk to its lowest level of effectiveness in its one-year existence. Worse yet, it became clear to OPC officers that the Communists themselves were sufficiently aware of the program to attempt penetration of the organization with its own agents.[76] OPC agents captured and doubled earlier were sent back to Yong-do to learn everything possible about the organization before volunteering to return again to North Korea. Once back in their homeland, they could defect at the first opportunity to make their report.

There were many variations to the double-agent game, with perhaps the most common practice being that of a doubled guerrilla team sending low-level but accurate reports back to base. At least for a time, OPC could often be tricked into supporting this ruse by sending resupply and agent reinforcement to the doubled team; the reinforcing agents were either killed or doubled themselves after being captured on the drop zone. There were a number of solutions to the problem once the doubling was detected, and the Agency used one of its most effective methods on a doubled team in August 1952.

Some months earlier, radio operators at a JACK base were surprised to hear from two teams that had, without JACK authorization, joined forces in their operational area. According to the now-combined teams, one team had lost its radio but not its communications plan, with the all-important codes and frequencies. Apparently by sheer chance, this first team had encountered the second team, which had lost its communication plan but not its radio. Though suspicious, JACK authorized the two small teams to join forces as they were the only JACK agents in the area at the time. JACK's suspicions were further fueled by the team's failure to give correct responses to several test questions submitted to them, as well as the team's request for luxury items and women's apparel, both known to be high on the priority list of Communist officials in North Korea. The team's fate was finally sealed when a defecting Communist from the area in which the team was operating confirmed to JACK officers that the team had indeed been doubled.

Following JACK's decision to "terminate the contract," a special air resupply flight was scheduled for the team on 3 August 1952. One bundle contained the requested luxury items and women's clothing, which, when removed from the container, set off an explosion from the explosives buried underneath. Another bundle contained a note addressed to the Communist province chief, known by name to the Agency. The note stated that the chief's "southern neighbors" had known the team was doubled for some time and had profited well from what they had learned. Agency archives note cryptically that the team "was never heard from again."[77]

During the remainder of 1952 the Agency's airdropped teams were annihilated, taking 100 percent losses as many simply disappeared after parachuting into North Korea.[78] Agency records indicate a number of teams were successfully resupplied by air, with the odd note that the teams were issued radio receivers but not transmitters. From such reports it seems apparent that the teams were resupplied at prearranged times and locations for missions so dangerous that the Agency itself had little confidence in their completion. Whether the teams were even at the drop zones to receive the resupply can be little more than speculation. As noted elsewhere, North Korean and Chinese control of their territory by late 1952 was so complete that "guerrilla operations" could better be described as suicide missions for the teams.

As the war (and the armistice negotiations) wore on, the Korean agents in training took increasing notice of an obvious fact: those who had gone on operations before them were never seen again. None of the special action teams, for example, are known to have been exfiltrated after their missions. This lethal reality took its toll in the training camps, as formerly good relations between the Koreans and their American agent handlers began to deteriorate sharply. By this stage of the war it was painfully clear to the guerrillas that the risks they were being asked to take could have no real bearing on its outcome.

This tension and potential danger to the agent handlers located in the guerrilla camps continued to grow as the war itself wound down. A final Agency assessment, conducted in late 1952, concluded that its behind-the-lines operations "had been too thoroughly penetrated by the Communists, and would have to be abandoned, including all the personnel of the SMG."[79] The Agency would later judge the SMG and special action teams as "ineffective and wasteful of personnel and funds."[80]

The CIA's postwar assessment of its role in Korea and the impact of its operations in the later stages of the war is brutally candid in a number of conclusions:

> The large majority of the intelligence gathered in 1952 and 1953 through infiltration and exfiltration operations was fabricated or controlled by the North Korean and Chinese Communist Forces security services . . . [and as for the Agency's covert E&E program] no airman or POW was known to have been assisted by CIA-sponsored clandestine mechanisms. . . . E&E operations as conducted by CIA in Korea were not only ineffective but probably morally reprehensible in the numbers of lives lost, and the amount of time and treasure expended was enormously disproportionate to attainments therefrom.[81]

While, for the most part, Agency records restrict their internal assessments to their own service, their comments on the unconventional war behind Communist lines would ultimately apply to all such UN efforts: "Although in the early stages of the Korean War some operational successes resulted from activities carried on under OPC projects . . . after the battlefront solidified and enemy security increased, there was little appreciable effectiveness from the substantial sums spent and the numerous Koreans sacrificed in what proved to be a basically futile attempt to set up resistance cells and E&E capabilities in North Korea."[82]

For all of these reasons, the CIA terminated virtually all of its unconventional warfare programs with the signing of the armistice in July 1953.

Conclusion

> To be considered successful, partisan [special operations] action must produce a discernible and important influence, political or military, in the outcome of the battle, campaign, or war, that cannot be obtained by the use of regular military forces at comparable or less cost. In Korea, this criterion was not met . . . the circumstances that prevailed were such as to practically preclude realization of this criterion.
>
> *Frederick W. Cleaver et al., UN Partisan Warfare in Korea*

It behooves the would-be historian to show some humility when passing judgment on the previous endeavors of others, especially when such wisdom comes largely from half-century-old hindsight. This being said, it is one thing to acknowledge this potential ego trap, and quite another to use it as an excuse for dodging critical judgments on the human drama and sacrifice described in the preceding stories.

By itself, the sacrifice of the poorly trained Koreans sent behind enemy lines warrants such judgment, as their sacrifice remains the only legacy of their courage and effort. So many of them were sent into North Korea that both U.S. military and CIA records are frank in admitting that exact losses are unknown, largely because no one knows for sure just how many were sent. Also warranting such judgment is the courage of the American and British partisan advisors and raiders who took such incredible risks while deep in Communist-held territory. What did all their courage and effort come to, in the end? And to reverse this perspective, what impact did the war have on these U.S. special operations units, both during and after the conflict?

Regarding the first question, virtually all historians conversant with the subject agree that the special operations effort had no strategic impact on the outcome of the war, or even its major turning points. To be sure, opportunities to have such an impact did occur, as for example, the Far East Command's opportunity in early 1951 to form an effective command and control system for the burgeoning partisan movement. At this fluid stage of the war, there were still opportunities for partisans and coastal raiders to operate successfully in the enemy's rear areas. However, as would happen again and again throughout the war, conventional officers with neither the interest nor understanding of special operations necessary to exploit such opportunities frequently squandered them.

For the most part, such squandering emerged from amorphous headquarters bureaucracies in the form of decisions that neither terminated weak programs nor reinforced successful ones. The U.S. Navy, for example, tasked its UDT for raiding missions beyond the scope of their World War II–era doctrine, while at the same time using this same doctrine as the rationale for not providing the training and equipment needed for these dangerous raids. Not until 1963, when President John F. Kennedy personally directed the Department of the Navy to institute what became the modern-day SEAL concept, did the navy update its UDT doctrine to match what it had tasked its frogmen to do in the Korean War a decade earlier.

Perhaps one reason why so many opportunities were squandered with uninspired staff decisions was that for the most part, the consequences of these decisions were neither dramatic nor even noticeable in the day-to-day grind of the "big war." There were exceptions, however, and they could prove bloody for the United States and its allies. No better example of this situation can be found than in MacArthur's refusal to believe the special operations intelligence reports describing the massive Chinese army columns crossing into Korea in October 1950, weeks before their "surprise" assault shredded the UN's unprepared field forces. These unheeded warnings came from Operation Aviary agents parachuted into the North Korean–Chinese border areas by MacArthur's own command. But in the end, the failure of special operations forces to make a significant impact on the war was not a matter of a few dramatic blunders by senior U.S. officers, but rather a continual series of miscalculations that arguably can be brought down to just two issues.

The first of these two issues arrived in Korea in late 1950 in the form of some three hundred thousand Chinese army "volunteers." Their sheer numbers alone, with an inexhaustible supply of more to follow when needed, drastically altered the prospects for conducting unconventional warfare in Communist-held territory. The UN's lightly armed guerrilla and commando forces employed in North Korea were not trained, equipped, or organized to take on the Chinese and North Korean armies, but rather to divert the largest number possible of their troops from front-line combat to rear area security duty.

In this regard the UN generally got its money's worth. In the spring of 1951, for example, Eighth Army reports estimated that harassment operations conducted by UN partisans diverted two full North Korean army corps—some forty thousand troops—from a critical Chinese offensive. Other Eighth Army reports throughout the war list partisan claims of considerable casualties and damage inflicted against Communist targets.

While many U.S. officers viewed these partisan claims with suspicion, there can be little doubt that the collective UN partisan effort did succeed in tying down large numbers of enemy troops in rear area security programs. But in an eerie precedent to the "body-count" phenomenon that became a hallmark of U.S. miscalculations in Vietnam a decade later, American commanders in this Northeast Asian war grossly overestimated the military value of tying down large numbers of enemy forces behind their front lines. The irrelevance in Asia of what appeared to Americans to be a laudable military strategy—keeping enemy troops away from the front lines—emerges from the experiences of the UN forces that were keeping these troops away from the front lines. Three realities in particular are worthy of note.

First, China's assumption from North Korea of the main burden of front-line combat with the UN ensured that all the military and political forces necessary to assure rear-area security would be available for the task. Second, the vast Chinese manpower reserves and their willingness to absorb casualties made them virtually impervious to all but the most extreme casualty rates—rates the guerrilla/commando forces were incapable of inflicting. These first two realities created a third—the inability of UN guerrillas and commandos to penetrate beyond the coastline to disrupt the vital lines of communication that supplied the Communists' front-line forces.

In the face of these realities, the January 1951 decision by Far East Command staff officers to label an absurdly small staff element the "Attrition Section" simply underscores their misunderstanding of the partisan potential to have a "discernible and important influence" in North Korea. From this basic misunderstanding of the battlefield situation flowed a number of subsequent FEC decisions, for example, continuing an airborne partisan effort despite its 100 percent failure rate.

The second issue to cripple the potential impact of UN special operations in North Korea found its roots in the skepticism with which many senior U.S. military officers viewed special operations as a legitimate form of warfare. This skepticism was underscored at different times, for example, by the adamant refusal of both FEC and Eighth Army headquarters staffs to designate an appropriate command and support structure for the thousands-strong partisan combat force operating under its direction.

Even more puzzling were those decisions, made by combat-experienced infantry officers, that would have been unthinkable had they occurred in a conventional infantry command. One striking example of this phenomenon was the decision to continue with the parachute insertion of the doomed Operation Virginia I sabotage team, despite the last-minute decision to remove the team's leader and sole officer.

FEC's air and naval components struggled with ad hoc special operations as well, succeeding most often when individual creativeness and courage succeeded in overcoming a lack of systemic planning and support. A classic example of this situation can be found in the experiences of the Fifth Air Force's Special Air Missions during the first year of the war. So low was the priority assigned to its top secret night missions (Operation Aviary) into North Korea that its aircrews were released to perform these dangerous operations as an "extra duty," and then only after completing a full day flying routine cargo runs. Only after suffering considerable criticism from the army for its role in compromising Operation Spitfire did Fifth Air Force headquarters agree to dedicate a flying unit (B Flight) to the special operations mission. Even then, months passed before B Flight was finally activated.

For its part, the U.S. Navy committed its UDT to coastal raiding activities above the high water mark from the earliest days of the war. To their credit the aggressive frogmen carried out these missions with remarkably few casualties, despite a near total lack of training and equipment for the mission. Rather than reinforce this successful performance, however contrary it ran to the established World War II–era UDT doctrine, many in the navy discouraged the use of UDT as raiders.

For example, one Pacific Fleet staff study issued in 1952 argued against such employment on the grounds that the previously noted lack of training and equipment did not adequately prepare the frogmen for the very kind of success that they had achieved in the previous two years. Perhaps to bolster this curious logic and discourage the trend, the navy declined to establish a formal "UDT-raider" school during the course of the war.

Beyond these internal military problems, FEC's response to the CIA's special operations programs proved to be not so much that of skepticism, but of outright hostility. Much has been made of MacArthur's animosity toward the CIA, for example, but as this history makes clear, the critical antagonisms between FEC and the Agency lasted long after MacArthur's departure in April 1951. In fact, the watershed event that led the CIA—by its own admission—to begin withdrawing its best officers from Korea occurred with the establishment of the previously described CCRAK eight months after MacArthur's departure from the theater. MacArthur's replacement, General Ridgway, appears to have kept curiously distant from the critical decision as to which agency—FEC's Intelligence Directorate or the CIA—would control the controversial CCRAK. So distant, in fact, that CIA representatives subsequently voiced their suspicion that the general wasn't even made aware of FEC-G2's decision in its own favor until after the decision was made.

On balance, it is difficult to judge whether military or CIA special operations proved most effective in Korea. While the military certainly had the resources, numbers, and an undeniable baseline of military skills, its disdain for special operations and collective low opinion of unconventional warfare greatly diminished these inherent organizational strengths. The CIA, on the other hand, operated with relatively generous funding; the zeal of a new organization not yet hobbled by overly restrictive regulations; and the wide-open charter of the previously described National Security Council directives. Given these opposite characteristics, the FEC-CIA combination could only have had two possible outcomes. Either the two merged to create an incredibly potent special operations force or they fell into a counterproductive squabble from which only the Communists would benefit. Unfortunately, the latter outcome must be regarded as their Korean War legacy.

Since the Korean War, the American military establishment has made considerable, if erratic, progress in the evolution of its special operations forces. The U.S. Army's Green Berets, a few of whom were sent to Korea in the final stages of the war, have grown to become an accepted fixture in the army's force structure. The Vietnam War validated the usefulness of the U.S. Navy's SEALs, as well as U.S. Air Force Special Operations units. These forces waned in the post-Vietnam years until, as is often the case, a military disaster (Desert One in Iran, 1980) led senior civilian officials to demand restoration of this country's special operations capabilities.

On 16 April 1987, the United States Special Operations Command (USSOCOM) was activated as one of the nine unified commands in the Department of Defense. Army, navy, and air force flag-rank officers with career-long expertise in special operations now serve on its staff—as does a senior representative from the Central Intelligence Agency, who serves as a principal, and, by all accounts, valued advisor to the commander in chief, USSOCOM.

I wish USSOCOM well. So too, I suspect, would the unknown numbers of special operators who sortied into the dark mountains of North Korea . . . and never returned.

Notes

Introduction

1. J. Lawton Collins, *War in Peacetime: The History and Lessons of Korea* (Boston: Houghton Mifflin, 1969), 30.

2. Savada, *North Korea,* 51.

3. Goulden, *Korea,* 19.

4. Blair, *Forgotten War,* 43.

5. Hastings, *Korean War,* 33.

6. Because the Republic of Korea and the Democratic Republic of Korea are commonly referred to as South Korea and North Korea, respectively, in most literature, these terms will be used for these two countries hereafter.

7. Hastings, *Korean War,* 35.

8. Finley, "U.S. Military Experience in Korea," 51.

9. Hastings, *Korean War,* 45. See also Blair, *Forgotten War,* 45.

10. Finley, "U.S. Military Experience in Korea," 8.

11. Ibid., 166. See also Blair, *Forgotten War,* 45.

12. Sandler, *Korean War,* 166–67. See also Blair, *Forgotten War,* 45.

13. Collins, *War in Peacetime,* 42–43.

14. MacArthur's senior intelligence officer, Maj. Gen. Charles A. Willoughby, maintained a "surveillance detachment" in Korea that had in fact given several warnings of a North Korean attack in the summer of 1950—all of which were discounted by Willoughby (Sandler, *Korean War,* 354).

15. Collins, *War in Peacetime,* 77.

16. Though severely reduced during the winter of 1949–50, the North Korean guerrilla threat remained a potent problem in South Korea throughout the war. As a result UN forces were forced to commit no less than 30 percent of their total troop strength during the war period to deal with the guerrillas (Sandler, *Korean War,* 17).

17. Goulden, *Korea,* 42.

18. The United States provided more than 90 percent of the UN commitment to the war (Finley, "U.S. Military Experience in Korea," 15). To remain

consistent with most histories of the war, however, I will generally use "UN" when referring to the American forces in Korea.

19. Collins, *War in Peacetime,* 218.

20. Hackworth and Sherman, *About Face,* 53, 63.

21. Blair, *Forgotten War,* 6–11.

22. General of the Army Omar N. Bradley and Clay Blair, *General's Life* (New York: Simon & Schuster, 1983), 474, cited in Blair, *Forgotten War,* 8.

23. Collins, *War in Peacetime,* 67.

24. Bradley and Blair, *General's Life,* 474.

25. Blair, *Forgotten War,* 9.

26. Department of the Navy, *U.S. Navy Active Force Levels: 1917–95,* 4–5.

27. Paddock, *U.S. Army Special Warfare,* 23.

28. Ibid., 25.

29. Ibid., 31.

30. Central Intelligence Agency, *Directors and Deputy Directors of Central Intelligence,* 1.

31. The Official War Report of the OSS placed its maximum wartime strength at 13,000 in December 1944. By May 1945 the army, which provided the bulk of the military personnel assigned to the OSS, placed its strength within the OSS at 8,360 (Paddock, *U.S. Army Special Warfare,* 24–25).

32. Paddock, *U.S. Army Special Warfare,* 25.

33. Ibid., 34.

34. The National Security Act of 1947 included in its language the creation of the Department of Defense, U.S. Air Force, National Security Council, and the Central Intelligence Agency.

35. Fondacaro, "Strategic Analysis of U.S. Special Operations," 47.

36. Cleaver et al., "UN Partisan Warfare in Korea," 94.

37. Nichols, *How Many Times Can I Die?* 132–33.

Chapter 1. U.S. Army Unconventional Warfare

1. MacArthur did direct unconventional warfare operations in the Pacific during World War II, notably with the Australians under his command. The operative phase here, as it applied to all such operations, is "under his command."

2. Goulden, *Korea,* 38.

3. Kim, "Eyewitness," 162.

4. At the request of President-elect Manuel Quezon of the Philippines, and with the concurrence of President Franklin Roosevelt, MacArthur assumed the post of military advisor of the Philippine Commonwealth.

5. Futrell, *United States Air Force in Korea,* 44.

6. A small but revealing example of the army dominance in FEC headquarters during this period is found in MacArthur's insistence that his staff directorates retain the designation "G" (as used in an all–U.S. Army headquarters) rather than the U.S. military standard "J" denoting directorates in a joint-service command headquarters such as FEC.

7. Paddock, *U.S. Army Special Warfare,* 103.

8. Stevens et al., "Intelligence Information by Partisans," vol. 1 (confidential). Information extracted is unclassified.

9. Questionnaire completed by former LG officer Lt. Col. Harry F. Walterhouse, student, PMGS, Camp Gordon, Georgia, January 1952, in Stevens et al., "Intelligence Information by Partisans," 1:22 (hereafter cited as Walterhouse questionnaire).

10. Ibid.

11. Maj. Robert B. Brewer, USA (Ret.) (former FEC-LG officer) to Joseph C. Goulden (author, *Korea: The Untold Story of the War*), 12 December 1984, subject: "Unconventional warfare operations in Korea."

12. "Experience in Chorwon of a Radio Team," a special report prepared by the 442d CIC detachment, APO 301 (June 1951), in Stevens et al., "Intelligence Information by Partisans," 1:27.

13. Brewer's wartime experiences, in Stevens et al., "Intelligence Information by Partisans," 1:52.

14. During the Korean War the term "partisan" was used to describe North Koreans operating behind Communist lines on behalf of the UN forces. In contrast, the term "guerrilla" was used when referring to North Koreans operating behind UN lines on behalf of the Communists.

15. Far East Command Liaison Detachment to Vice Admiral H. M. Martin, Commander, Seventh Fleet, memorandum, 28 September 1951, subject: "Clandestine Activities, Korea," 1.

16. Each TLO team included approximately twenty-five Koreans led by a three-man U.S. Army element: one officer, two enlisted (Malcom, *White Tigers,* 138–39).

17. Malcom, *White Tigers,* 139.

18. Evanhoe, *Dark Moon,* 13.

19. Stevens et al., "Intelligence Information by Partisans," 1:21.

20. Malcom, *White Tigers,* 139.

21. Capt. Mel Gile, 3d Infantry Division TLO team leader (1951–52), telephone interviews, 1990–92, in Evanhoe, *Dark Moon,* 13.

22. Malcom, *White Tigers,* 138.

23. "Covert Activities in Korea," a special report prepared by Joint Special Operations Branch, Military Intelligence Section, General Headquarters, Far East Command, August 1950–June 1951, sec. 3, p. 5, in Stevens et al., "Intelligence Information by Partisans," 2:20–21.

24. Brewer, telephone interviews with author, May 1994; also Brig. Gen. Harry C. Aderholt, U.S. Air Force Oral History Interview, 36, 46 (hereafter cited as Aderholt oral history).

25. "Covert Activities in Korea," sec. 4, p. 1, in Stevens et al., "Intelligence Information by Partisans," 1:29.

26. Stevens et al., "Intelligence Information by Partisans," 1:29.

27. "Covert Activities in Korea," sec. 2, p. 2, in Stevens et al., "Intelligence Information by Partisans," 1:29.

28. Brewer, "Study Regarding Parachute Agent Problems," Joint Special Operations Center, FEC/LG, 3 September 1950, attached as Appendix 2 to vol. 2 of Stevens et al., "Intelligence Information by Partisans."

29. Ibid.

30. Stevens et al., "Intelligence Information by Partisans," 1:20, 31.

31. Brewer to Goulden, 12 December 1984.

32. Ibid.

33. Ibid.

34. Stevens et al., "Intelligence Information by Partisans," 2:43.

35. Ibid.

36. Ibid.

37. Aderholt oral history, 53.

38. Ibid., 46.

39. Brewer to Goulden, 12 December 1984.

40. Evanhoe, "Reported Alive: Three U.S. SpecOps Men Still Missing in the Korean War," *Behind the Lines* (November/December 1993): 42–43.

41. Was the Chinese interpreter lying or perhaps mistaken? Why was King taken back to the crash site? A pro-UN agent working in a nearby military hospital reported that shortly after the downing of the C-46, a wounded American "spy" had been brought to the facility. His description of the American closely resembled that of Sgt. George G. Tatarakis, the assistant jumpmaster on the doomed flight. Other agents subsequently reported that an American matching Tatarakis's description was put on a train bound for Siberia.

42. Stevens et al., "Intelligence Information by Partisans," 2:43.

43. The smaller cargo parachute dropped the agent at a higher rate of descent than the troop-type parachute, in turn causing a higher probability of injuries to the agent upon impact with the ground.

44. "Study Regarding Parachute Agent Problems," in Stevens et al., "Intelligence Information by Partisans," 2:207.

45. Ibid.

46. Ibid., 2:47.

47. Needless to say, this peninsular geography proved just as advantageous to North Korean spies and guerrillas infiltrating into South Korea. The difference during the war was that the U.S. and British navies were present in force, whereas the small North Korean navy was essentially a nonplayer in the conflict.

48. "Covert Activities in Korea," sec. 4, including 2, in Stevens et al., "Intelligence Information by Partisans," 2:49.

49. Ibid., sec. 4, p. 2, in Stevens et al., "Intelligence Information by Partisans," 2:49.

50. Malcom, *White Tigers,* 128.

51. "Covert Activities in Korea," sec. 4, in Stevens et al., "Intelligence Information by Partisans," 2:49.

52. ROK TF 95.7 message, 8 January 1951, U.S. Army Forces, Far East, 8086 Army Unit, MHD Report, USMHI Document Collection.

53. U.S. Army Forces, Far East, 8086 Army Unit, "UN Partisan Forces in the Korean Conflict," 10.

54. Day, "Partisan Operations," 17.

55. In American military terminology a combined command includes the forces of two or more countries.

56. Fondacaro, "Strategic Analysis of U.S. Special Operations," 64.

57. Cleaver et al., "UN Partisan Warfare in Korea," 34.

58. Ibid.

59. Ibid., 32. See also Fondacaro, "Strategic Analysis of U.S. Special Operations," 64.

60. Cleaver et al., "UN Partisan Warfare in Korea," 39–40.

61. Ibid., 36.

62. Fondacaro, "Strategic Analysis of U.S. Special Operations," 67.

63. Cleaver et al., "UN Partisan Warfare in Korea," 37.

64. Ibid., 44.

65. Day, "Partisan Operations," 40.

66. FEC-Intelligence estimates of North Korean army strength (136,000) just before the outbreak of war proved uncannily accurate. In contrast, the CIA estimate (36,000) was so far off as to damage the agency's already weak credibility (in the eyes of MacArthur, among others) still further.

67. Malcom, *White Tigers,* 28.

68. Central Intelligence Agency, *Secret War in Korea, June 1950–June 1952,* March 1964, 3. Secret. Washington, D.C.: CIA (hereafter cited as *Secret War in Korea*). Information extracted is unclassified.

69. Ibid., 74.

70. Ibid., 5.

71. Ibid.

72. *CIA in Korea* 3:98.

73. Fondacaro, "Strategic Analysis of U.S. Special Operations," 69. See also *Secret War in Korea,* 11.

74. *Secret War in Korea,* 6.

75. Ibid., 74.

76. Ibid., 74–75.

77. Singlaub, *Hazardous Duty,* 181.

78. Ibid., 181–82.

79. Malcom, *White Tigers,* 27.

80. Cleaver et al., "UN Partisan Warfare in Korea," 62.

81. Ibid., 77.

82. Ibid., 62–63.

83. Ibid., 62.

84. Ibid., 64.

85. Ibid., 3.

86. U.S. Army Forces, "UN Partisan Forces," 2.

87. Schuetta, "Guerrilla Warfare and Airpower," 66.

88. U.S. Army Forces, "UN Partisan Forces," 61.

89. Ibid., 80.

90. Ibid., 27.

91. First recruited by the British army in the early 1800s, the rugged Nepalese have since gone on to fight in Ghurka regiments in virtually every war undertaken by the British Empire. They are renowned for their loyalty, discipline, fighting spirit, and lethal effectiveness with the large Kukuri knives they carry into combat.

92. Former partisan "advisor" Dr. Muang Manbahadur, interview with author, 5 June 1998.

93. U.S. Army Forces, "UN Partisan Forces," 20–21.

94. Schuetta, "Guerrilla Warfare and Airpower," 81.

95. Malcom, *White Tigers,* 43.

96. Copy of Plan Able in Cleaver et al., "UN Partisan Warfare in Korea," 158.

97. Ibid., 159.

98. Of these eleven only two were committed to training the partisans. In addition, eight Korean marines functioned as assistant instructors and interpreters.

99. Col. George Budway, USAF (Ret.) (former chief, Air Operations, CCRAK) to R. H. Dawson, memorandum, June 1987, subject: "CCRAK: Covert, Clandestine and Related Activities—Korea" (hereafter cited as Budway memorandum), 6. Author's collection.

100. "Organization and Plan for Partisan Operations in Korea," Eighth Army, January 1951, in Schuetta, "Guerrilla Warfare and Airpower," 71.

101. Cleaver et al., "UN Partisan Warfare in Korea," 154. See also U.S. Army Forces, "UN Partisan Forces," 59–60.

102. Lt. Col. Archie Johnston, USA (Ret.), "FEC/LD (K)," from a photocopy of Johnston's article published in the U.S. Army magazine *Static-Line,* issue date unknown (hereafter cited as Johnston article).

103. Cleaver et al., "UN Partisan Warfare in Korea," 31.

104. Ibid.

105. Ibid., 39, 42.

106. Evanhoe, *Dark Moon,* 74.

107. Ibid.

108. Ibid.

109. Former Task Force Kirkland advisor Adam Dintenfass, memorandum, n.d. Author's collection.

110. Ed Evanhoe (former Kirkland advisor), telephone interview with author, 22 November 1997.

111. Former Kirkland advisor Col. Kingston Winget, USA (Ret.), telephone interviews by Ed Evanhoe, 1990–93, in Evanhoe, *Dark Moon,* 73.

112. Col. Nam Pyo Lee, ROKA (Ret.) (former interpreter with TF Kirkland), to Ed Evanhoe (former Kirkland advisor), 1 January 1999. Author's collection.

113. Budway memorandum, 6.

114. Cleaver et al., "UN Partisan Warfare in Korea," 155.

115. Pak Chang Oun, personal recollections of a Kirkland partisan, in letter dated 12 July 1985, Seoul, Republic of South Korea. Author's collection.

116. Cleaver et al., "UN Partisan Warfare in Korea," 155.

117. Malcom, *White Tigers,* 21.

118. Col. John McGee to Col. Rod Paschall, 24 March 1986, in Malcom, *White Tigers,* 24. On file at U.S. Army Military History Institute, Carlisle, Pennsylvania.

119. Ibid.

120. Cleaver et al., "UN Partisan Warfare in Korea," 10.

121. Fondacaro, "Strategic Analysis of U.S. Special Operations," 102.

122. *Fifth Air Force Intelligence Summary* 3, no. 5 (20 September 1952): 49–50, in Schuetta, "Guerrilla Warfare and Airpower," 89.

123. Malcom, *White Tigers,* 25.

124. Another U.S. report submitted two months earlier estimated that only 4,000 of the partisans were as yet armed with weapons (Cleaver et al., "UN Partisan Warfare in Korea," 44). As a matter of perspective, it is worth noting that of the total 8,333 partisans accounted for in the report, only 290 came from Task Force Kirkland.

125. *Fifth Air Force Intelligence Summary,* in Schuetta, "Guerrilla Warfare and Airpower," 89.

126. U.S. Army Forces, "UN Partisan Forces," 109.

127. Ibid., 81.

128. Ibid.

129. Cleaver et al., "UN Partisan Warfare in Korea," 51.

130. Ibid., 55.

131. U.S. Army Forces, "UN Partisan Forces," 41–42.

132. Ibid., 114–15.

133. Ibid., 18.

134. These two direct action and guerrilla warfare missions were distinct from the intelligence collection operations conducted by Operation Aviary agents.

135. Cleaver et al., "UN Partisan Warfare in Korea," 52. See also Evanhoe, *Dark Moon,* 52–53.

136. Evanhoe, *Dark Moon,* 53–54.

137. POW Debriefing Report, ID 950774-Watson, Martin, RA 11 033 539, Sergeant, 4th Ranger Company, TDY-G3-Eighth Army, in Evanhoe, *Dark Moon,* 62.

138. Evanhoe, *Dark Moon,* 61.

139. Ibid., 104.

140. The lieutenant's lack of special operations training was not known to McGee because Anderson presented Adams-Acton as a trained special forces officer. For his part, the enterprising Adams-Acton completed Baker Section's short parachute and demolitions training under the guise of his interest in "learning Yank techniques" (Evanhoe, *Dark Moon,* 106).

141. Ibid., 106.

142. Ibid., 108.

143. As described by Spitfire member Lieutenant Adams-Acton to Lt. David Sharp while the two were prisoners of war, Camp Two, Ch'ongsongjin, North Korea, 1952–53, in Evanhoe, *Dark Moon,* 112.

144. Malcom, *White Tigers,* 135.

145. Evanhoe, *Dark Moon,* 118.

146. Ibid., 133.

147. Cleaver et al., "UN Partisan Warfare in Korea," 91.

148. Ibid., 91, 94.

149. Malcom, *White Tigers,* 188.

150. Ed Evanhoe, e-mail interview with author, 13 November 1998.

151. Singlaub, *Hazardous Duty,* 181.

152. Black, *Rangers in Korea,* 219.

153. Johnston article, 2.

154. Ibid., 21.

155. Ibid., 10.

156. Manbahadur interview.

157. Malcom, *White Tigers,* 3.

158. Ibid., 137.

159. Cleaver et al., "UN Partisan Warfare in Korea," 73.

160. Ibid. See also Sandler, *Korean War,* 341.

161. To bolster the individual advisor's public authority and to save partisan "face" when taking orders from enlisted soldiers, all advisors below the rank of sergeant were still addressed as "sergeant." This was small enough ac-

knowledgment of their responsibilities, as many such young advisors were commanding entire battalions in all but name.

162. U.S. Army Forces, "UN Partisan Forces," 76.

163. Cleaver et al., "UN Partisan Warfare in Korea," 77.

164. This unique recruiting procedure was made possible with the "Lodge Bill" (Public Law 597), passed by Congress on 30 June 1950. The bill provided selected immigrants with the opportunity to earn American citizenship through their completion of an honorable duty tour in the U.S. Army.

165. From Headquarters, UN Partisan Infantry Korea, "Debriefing US Personnel," memorandum, 21 March 1954, in Cleaver et al., "UN Partisan Warfare in Korea," 203–6.

166. Lt. Col. Francis R. Purcell, G2 Section, Eighth Army, interview by Lt. Col. A. S. Daley and Maj. B. C. Mossman, 13 May 1953, in U.S. Army Forces, "UN Partisan Forces," 103–12.

167. WDGS, G-2, unsigned letter from individual with Headquarters, Western Task Forces, 26 November 1942, in Paddock, *U.S. Army Special Warfare,* 19.

168. Paddock, *U.S. Army Special Warfare,* 94.

169. Ibid., 10.

170. The phenomena of senior political officials demanding the activation of special operations forces over the objections of senior military officers has become the norm at least since President Roosevelt's directive in 1942 to establish the OSS. Beyond the OSS, examples include the establishment of the Office of the Chief, Psychological Warfare in 1951, President Kennedy's directives to form air force (Air Commando), army (Green Beret), and navy (SEAL) teams in the early 1960s, and the congressional Goldwater-Nichols Act, establishing the U.S. Special Operations Command in 1987.

171. Three years later the same FEC-G2, General Willoughby, would give the CIA fits as he stonewalled their attempts to operate in MacArthur's theater of operations. This stonewalling extended to his directing the use of Japanese undercover agents to tail CIA operatives as they moved about Japan.

172. Pease, *Psywar,* 15.

173. Ibid. See also Paddock, *U.S. Army Special Warfare,* 95.

174. Pease, *Psywar,* 16.

175. Paddock, *U.S. Army Special Warfare,* 95.

176. Pease, *Psywar,* 102.

177. Ibid., 96.

178. Ibid., 18.

179. Ibid., 96.

180. Ibid.

181. Ibid., 83.

182. Ibid., 17.

183. Paddock, *U.S. Army Special Warfare,* 95.

184. Kim and Johnson, "Evaluation of Effects," 6–7.

185. Kim, "Eyewitness," 8.

186. Pease, *Psywar,* 82.

187. A 105-mm howitzer shell, usually a converted smoke shell, carried four hundred four-by-five-inch leaflets. Delivery by artillery shell was an all-weather system, effective in conditions that grounded the PsyWar aircraft. Pease, *Psywar,* 39.

188. US, Department of Defense, Semiannual Report of the Secretary of Defense, 1 January–30 June 1951, 92, in Paddock, *U.S. Army Special Warfare,* 94. See also Pease, *Psywar,* 55.

189. Pease, *Psywar,* 115.

190. Ibid., 68–72.

191. Ibid., 72–73.

192. Ibid., 73.

193. Ibid., 74.

Chapter 2. U.S. Air Force Special Air Missions

1. The Fifth Air Force reported to Headquarters, Far East Air Forces, the senior air force component in General Headquarters, Far East Command.

2. For this mission Nichols received the Distinguished Service Cross, America's second highest decoration for valor.

3. "Negative Intelligence" was the practice of denying the enemy from acquiring intelligence on US forces, that is, the Counter-Intelligence Corps' primary mission.

4. Nichols, *How Many Times Can I Die?* 117.

5. Ibid., 126.

6. Ibid., 5.

7. Futrell, *United States Air Force in Korea,* 6.

8. This was not part of the Pusan jump school established by FEC's Liaison Group, as described in chapter 1.

9. Nichols, *How Many Times Can I Die?* 130.

10. Headquarters, Fifth Air Force, Office of Deputy for Intelligence, to Special Activities Unit Number One, 5 March 1951, subject: "Special Activities Unit Number One (Operating Instructions)," in U.S. Army Forces, "UN Partisan Forces," January 1954, 192.

11. Headquarters, Far East Command General Order No. 159, 22 June 1951.

12. Ibid.

13. March and McElfresh, *Submarine or Phantom Target?* 24–25.

14. Ibid., 26.

15. Ibid.

16. Nichols, *How Many Times Can I Die?* 148

17. Unit History, 6004th AISS, May–June 1952 (Maxwell Air Force Base, Ala.: U.S. Air Force Historical Research Agency), 31.

18. Diane Putney, "Air Force HUMINT 40th Anniversary," U.S. Air Force Special Activities Center (AFSAC) booklet (Fort Belvoir, Va.: N.d.), 5.

19. Schuetta, "Guerrilla Warfare and Airpower," 77.

20. Headquarters, Far East Air Forces General Order No. 336, Activation, Special Activities Unit No. One, 20 July 1951.

21. Semi-Annual History of 6004th AISS, 1 July 1952–31 December 1952 (Maxwell Air Force Base, Ala.: U.S. Air Force Historical Research Agency), 37–40.

22. Ibid., 79.

23. Unit History, 6004th AISS, May–June 1951, 28.

24. Semi-Annual History of 6004th AISS, 40.

25. Ibid.

26. Schuetta, "Guerrilla Warfare and Airpower," 99.

27. Virtually all the UN partisans were North Koreans who had chosen to flee south from the advancing Communists rather than live under their control. For the most sensitive intelligence missions CCRAK and Detachment 2 found the educated, Christian Koreans to be the most reliable agents.

28. Ibid., 100.

29. Nichols, *How Many Times Can I Die?* 132–33.

30. Unit History, 6004th AISS, 1 July 1952–31 December 1952, 42.

31. Semi-Annual History of 6004th AISS, 1 July 1952–31 December 1952, 45.

32. Ibid., 89.

33. Marion, "Air Force Special Operations Korean War Chronology," 17.

34. Schuetta, "Guerrilla Warfare and Airpower," 151–53.

35. Paschall, "Special Operations in Korea," 167.

36. Schuetta, "Guerrilla Warfare and Airpower," 186.

37. Budway memorandum, 9.

38. Report of Headquarters, Fifth Air Force, "Evasion & Escape Historical Synopsis," date obscured on original document, 3. Author's collection.

39. Ibid.

40. Director of Intelligence, Fifth Air Force, 12 September 1953, subject: "Reorganization of the 6004th Air Intelligence Service Squadron." Unclassified.

41. Ibid.

42. Sgt. Ray Dawson, telephone interview with author, 3 July 1995.

43. Stevens et al., "Intelligence Information by Partisans," vol. 2, app. 4, KLO letter, 23 January 1951, subject: "Study on Need for Special C-47; a research report."

44. Stevens et al., "Intelligence Information by Partisans," 2:212.

45. Unit History, 374th Troop Carrier Wing (H), 1–28 February 1951, Historical Data No. 1 (Maxwell Air Force Base, Ala.: U.S. Air Force Historical Research Agency).

46. Ibid., Historical Data No. 1.

47. Ibid., 3.

48. Ibid., Appendix 4, 213.

49. Stevens et al., "Intelligence Information by Partisans," 1:37.

50. Ibid., 10.

51. Ibid.

52. Aderholt oral history, 32.

53. Ibid., 39.

54. Pease, *Psywar,* 40.

55. Unit History, 21st TCS, October 1950, n.p.

56. Ibid., n.p.

57. Ibid.

58. Unit History, 21st TCS, March 1951, 7.

59. Unit History, 21st TCS, April 1951, 3–4.

60. Combat Doctrine, B Flight, 6167th Operations Squadron (hereafter cited as Combat Doctrine).

61. The glass-nosed B-26 housed the navigator's position, while the solid-nosed ground attack model held six .50-caliber heavy machine guns.

62. Unit History, 6167th ABG, 1 July–31 December 1952, 9.

63. Lt. Col. P. G. Moore, USAF (Ret.), interview with author, Shalimar, Fla., 14 March 1995.

64. Moore, interview with author, Shalimar, Fla., 11 July 1995.

65. Ibid. Note: A former USAF Special Operations boat crewman also described to me, without prompting, a mission in which his boat crew infiltrated a "blonde-haired, Chinese speaking" American into Manchuria later in the war.

66. Fifth Air Force General Order No. 637, award of the Distinguished Flying Cross, First Oak Leaf Cluster, to Maj. Paul G. Moore, 27 September 1953.

67. Unit History, 6167th ABG, 1 July–31 December 1952, n.p.

68. Evanhoe, *Dark Moon,* 42–43.

69. SFC William T. Miles of the U.S. Army and a Korean scout held off the attacking Communists long enough to allow the main partisan group to break contact. CIA agents in the area subsequently reported that a wounded American prisoner matching Miles's description was brought to a nearby town shortly after the fight, then shipped to a hospital elsewhere in North Korea. Unconfirmed CIA reports later indicated Miles was eventually moved by train to Siberia. Miles was not among the American prisoners repatriated to the United States at the close of the war, and his fate remains unknown.

70. Cleaver et al., "UN Partisan Warfare in Korea," 94.

71. Combat Doctrine, 3.

72. Kim and Johnson, "Evaluation of Effects," 8.

73. Ibid., 7.

74. Ibid.

75. Combat Doctrine, 2.

76. Unit History, 6167th ABG, 1 January–30 June 1953, n.p.

77. Unit History, 6167th ABG, 1 July–31 December 1952, n.p.

78. Robert Burns, "Report: China, N. Korea Kept U.S. POWS," Associated Press, 5 August 1997.

79. Ibid.

80. Aderholt oral history, 42.

81. Unit History, 6167th ABG, 1 July–31 December 1953, 5.

82. This stonewalling flared into a public spectacle with the infamous and ill-fated "Revolt of the Admirals" in 1949. The acrimonious fighting involved a classic roles and missions dispute between the navy's top aviators and their counterparts in the air force.

83. Lt. Col. Lester M. Adams Jr. (former commander 22 CRBS) to author, 5 May 1995, subject: "History of USAF Crash Rescue Boats."

84. Adams to author, 5 May 1995.

85. Unit History, Detachment 1, 6160th ABG, 25 June–31 October 1950 (Maxwell Air Force Base, Ala.: U.S. Air Force Historical Research Agency), Historical Data Section V.

86. Adams to author, 5 May 1995.

87. Ibid.

88. Far East Air Forces records report 1,041 aircraft lost to enemy action during the 1,107-day war (Futrell, *United States Air Force in Korea,* 692).

89. Futrell, *United States Air Force in Korea,* 692.

90. In the Korean language -*do* means "island," for example, Cho-Island.

91. Jim Jarvis (former CRBS crewman) to author, 9 December 1997. Author's collection.

92. Unit History, Detachment 1, 6160th ABG, January 1952.

93. Jarvis to author, 9 December 1997.

94. The U.S. Air Force authorized the use of naval ratings (e.g., "master" and "mate") on the crash rescue boats while maintaining standard air force rank for all other matters.

95. Donald Nichols, Commander, Detachment 2, 6004th AISS, to Commanding Officer, Headquarters Squadron, 6160th ABG, 11 January 1952, subject: "Letter of Appreciation." Filed in Unit History, Detachment 1, 6160th ABG.

96. Unit History, Detatchment 1, 6160th ABG, April 1952, 1.

97. Jarvis to author, 9 December 1997.

98. Ibid.

99. Robin Mansell Lloyd, graduate of the England's Royal Naval College and a Royal Navy officer during World War II, achieved American citizenship during his service in Korea (Jarvis to author, 9 December 1997).

100. Bud Tretter (CRBS crewman) to author, 19 December 1997. Author's collection.

101. Marion, "Air Force Special Operations Korean War Chronology," 13.

102. Adams to author, 5 May 1995.

103. Jarvis to author, 9 December 1997.

104. The crash rescue boats operating behind enemy lines were painted gray, in contrast to the high visibility white standard for all other CRBS detachments.

105. Headquarters, FEC Liaison Detachment—Korea to Commanders: Leopard, Wolfpack, Kirkland, Baker Section, 11 April 1952, subject: "Guerrilla Operations Outline, 1952."

106. Historical Data Pertaining to Crash Rescue Boats R-1-664 and R-1-676-DPU in the Korean Operation, December 1951–August 1953 (Maxwell Air Force Base, Ala.: U.S. Air Force Historical Division, December 1954).

107. History, Air Resupply & Communications Service, 1 July–31 December 1953, pt. 1, "The ARCS Mission and Program" (Maxwell Air Force Base, Ala.: U.S. Air Force Historical Research Agency), 2.

108. Paddock, *U.S. Army Special Warfare,* 52.

109. Ibid., 135.

110. Col. George Pittman, USAF (Ret.), to author, 13 December 1994.

111. Pittman, telephone interview with author, 10 September 1994.

112. Special Orders No. 5, issued by 581st ARCW, 8 January 1953. As quoted in *Arc Light* 11, no. 1 (January 1955): 9.

113. Bob Burns, "Secret Warriors," Associated Press, 29 August 1998.

114. Ibid.

115. Minutes of the meeting held 8 January 1955, between the Chinese, American, and UN negotiating team, Geneva, Switzerland, 31. Author's collection.

116. Ibid., 32.

117. Members of the 581st crew were actually interned for a period in the same cells holding the previously described CIA employees Fecteau and Downey.

118. Pittman interview.

119. *Arc Light* 1, no. 4 (October 1985): 3.

120. Pittman interview.

121. Burns, "Secret Warriors."

122. Pittman interview.

123. Ibid.

124. Prior to the activation of the 581st Helicopter Flight in December 1952, various elements of the 3d Air Rescue Squadron conducted a number of special air missions behind enemy lines (Marion, "Air Force Special Operations Korean War Chronology," 1, 4, 8–9).

125. Maj. Robert F. Sullivan, USAF (Ret.), telephone interviews (and memoirs) with author, April–May 1994. Corroboration provided by Helicopter Flight pilots Capt. Joseph Barrett and 1st. Lt. Frank Fabijan in subsequent interviews.

126. Citation to accompany the award of the Distinguished Flying Cross to Capt. Lawrence A. Barrett, First Oak Leaf Cluster, General Order No. 15, Headquarters, Far East Air Forces, 26 January 1954. Author's collection.

127. Lawrence A. Barrett to author, 25 April 1998.

128. No relationship to Lawrence Barrett.

129. Grateful naval authorities reportedly proposed to nominate the trio for the Navy Cross. The navy subsequently demurred after the air force responded that it would provide its own recognition to the airmen. On 21 May 1953 Capt. Joseph Barrett, 1st. Lt. Frank Fabijan, and A2C Thomas Thornton received Silver Stars for gallantry during the mission.

130. Robert Sullivan, copy of letter to Air Force Historical Research Agency, 25 April 1998. Author's collection.

131. *Arc Light* 11, no. 1 (January 1995): 1–3.

132. Col. Grover Ensley, USAF (Ret.), interview with author, Ft. Walton Beach, Fla., 8 May 1995.

133. Marion, "Air Force Special Operations Korean War Chronology," 19.

134. Pittman, telephone interview with author, 13 December 1994.

135. Pittman recalls the *low*-time CAT pilot had twelve thousand hours flight time.

Chapter 3. U.S. Navy Special Operations

1. To many of the navy's flag-rank aviators it appeared that Secretary of Defense Louis A. Johnson was giving priority to the air force's B-36 strategic bomber program at the expense of the navy's commitment to develop a number of "supercarriers." The admirals were right, though the subsequent growth of Cold War–era military budgets eventually allowed the navy to resume its aircraft carrier modernization plans.

2. Barlow, "Navy's View of the Revolt of the Admirals," 25.

3. Sandler, *Korean War,* 240.

4. Ibid.

5. In August 1950 nearly 30 percent of the close air support strikes attempted by NAVFE were canceled due to the lack of common radio systems between ground controllers and aircrews. And with tensions between the two services still raw from the navy "revolt" the previous fall, yet another nasty debate broke out between the naval aviators and their air force counterparts (Sandler, *Korean War,* 231–32).

6. Walter Karig, Malcom W. Cagle, and Frank A. Mason, *Battle Report: The War in Korea* (New York: Rinehart and Company, 1952), 59. See also Sandler, *Korean War,* 188–89, which claims all four torpedo boats were sunk.

7. Sandler, *Korean War,* 282.

8. Ibid., 152.

9. Andrade, "History of Naval Special Warfare," 13.

10. Clark, *Carrier Admiral,* 275–76.

11. Doyle was dual-hatted as both the operational commander of TF 90 (NAVFE's amphibious force) and administrative commander of Amphibious Group One. While conducting raids, the high-speed transports and their raiders operated as a component or task element of TF 90.

12. Karig, Cagle, and Mason, *Battle Report,* 152.

13. Capt. Alan Ray, USN (Ret.) (former commander of the *Horace A. Bass*), to author, 15 October 1998.

14. The boats were LCPR (landing craft, personnel-ramped) or LCVP (landing craft, vehicle-personnel).

15. The letters "AP" are used to identify transports, with the letter "D" added to denote transports built on destroyer-type hulls. The term "APD" is used informally to denote high-speed transports.

16. Lt. Hilary D. Mahin, former boat and gunnery officer aboard the *Horace A. Bass,* telephone interview with author, 15 August 1998.

17. The USS *Sea Lion* (SS-315) was destined for the Atlantic Fleet after its conversion to ASSP standard.

18. The removal of the torpedo tubes and main deck gun left the *Perch* with only two 40-mm cannon on the superstructure with which to defend itself.

19. Former *Perch* crewman M. E. Kebodeaux, interview with author, 11 August 1998.

20. War Patrol Report: Commanding Officer to CNO, series 0015, subject: "USS *Perch* (ASSP 313); Report of First War Patrol," September–October 1950, prologue, 3. Post-January 1946 Submarine War Patrol Reports File, Washington, D.C.: Naval Historical Center (hereafter cited as War Patrol Rep—*Perch*).

21. Dwyer, *Commandos from the Sea,* 110.

22. Hoyt, *Submarines at War,* endnotes, n.p.

23. Dwyer, *Commandos from the Sea,* 111.

24. War Patrol Rep—*Perch,* 1.

25. Kebodeaux interview.

26. War Patrol Rep—*Perch,* 4.

27. Hoyt, *Submarines at War,* 300.

28. War Patrol Rep—*Perch,* 2.

29. Ibid., 3.

30. Ibid.

31. War Diary, USS *Diachenko,* 1–31 August 1950.

32. The explosives necessary to destroy the target, a small railroad bridge, waited just offshore in an inflatable boat manned by sailors from the *Diachenko.* The mission was aborted, however, after a railway handcar carrying North Korean soldiers burst upon the scene, apparently by sheer accident. After Foley was wounded in the ensuing exchange of gunfire, Atcheson helped him back to the beach for the subsequent return to the *Diachenko* (Dockery, *SEALs in Action,* 72–74).

33. Dockery, *SEALs in Action,* 73.

34. George Atcheson to Dwyer, July 1985, in Dwyer, *Commandos from the Sea,* 237.

35. Capt. Ted Fielding, USN (Ret), to Dwyer, July 1985, in Dwyer, *Commandos from the Sea,* 239.

36. Pacific Fleet UDTs 1 and 3 were based at the Coronado Amphibious Base near San Diego, California, while Atlantic Fleet UDTs 2 and 4 were based at the Little Creek Amphibious base near Norfolk, Virginia.

37. Andrade, "History of Naval Special Warfare," 1–2.

38. Ibid., 5.

39. Hundevadt, "Spindrift: Recollections of a Naval Career," unpublished memoir, 153, in Andrade, "History of Naval Special Warfare," 6.

40. "Korean War, U.S. Pacific Fleet Operations, Interim Third Evaluation Report, 1 May 1951–31 December 1951," in Andrade, "History of Naval Special Warfare," 11.

41. Korean War–era UDT member Dr. James Short, interview with author, 13 April 1997.

42. Ibid.

43. Ibid.

44. Russ Eoff, ed., "UDT in Korea . . . 1950," undated paper, 3. Author's collection.

45. "Korean War, U.S. Pacific Fleet Operations, Interim Second Evaluation Report, 16 November 1950–30 April 1951," in Dwyer, *Commandos from the Sea,* 232–33.

46. Mahin interview, 25 September 1998.

47. Sandler, *Korean War,* 206.

48. Ibid, 207.

49. Ibid.

50. Karig, Cagle, and Mason, *Battle Report,* 152.

51. Andrade, "History of Naval Special Warfare," 17. See also Karig, Cagle, and Mason, *Battle Report,* 152.

52. Karig, Cagle, and Mason, *Battle Report,* 153.

53. Andrade, "History of Naval Special Warfare," 244.

54. Lt. Gen. George E. Stratemeyer, Commander, Far East Air Forces, to COMNAVFE, 12–16 August 1950, subject: "Operations of USS *Horace A. Bass.*" Alan Ray Collection.

55. Citation to accompany award of the Navy Unit Commendation to Special Operations Group, Amphibious Group One (USS *Horace A. Bass,* Underwater Demolition Team One, and Reconnaissance Company [Minus], First Marine Division, Fleet Marine Force), from the secretary of the navy (date not on citation). Author's copy from former *Bass* skipper, Alan Ray.

56. Hastings, *Korean War,* 94.

57. Dwyer, *Commandos from the Sea,* 246.

58. Hastings, *Korean War,* 94.

59. War Patrol Rep—*Perch,* 3.

60. Neillands, *In the Combat Zone,* 88–89.

61. Andrade, "History of Naval Special Warfare," 25–26.

62. COMNAVFE to CINCUNC, message, 19 September 1950, in Andrade, "History of Naval Special Warfare," 26.

63. CINCUNC to COMNAVFE, untitled message, 20 September 1950, in Andrade, "History of Naval Special Warfare," 25–26.

64. Goulden, *Korea,* 469.

65. Central Intelligence Agency, *Infiltration and Resupply of Agents in North Korea,* 1952–1953, vol. 1, December 1972, 37–38 (secret) (hereafter cited as *Infiltration,* followed by volume and page number). December 1972. Washington, D.C.: CIA. Information extracted is unclassified.

66. Goulden, *Korea,* 470.

67. *CIA in Korea* 1:123.

68. Dwyer, *Commandos from the Sea,* 251.

69. Hoyt, *Submarines at War,* 301.

70. War Patrol Rep—*Perch,* 1.

71. Ibid., 2.

72. Karig, Cagle, and Mason, *Battle Report,* 286.

73. Ibid., 3.

74. Hoyt, *Submarines at War,* 303.

75. Withdrawn from combat, the *Perch* participated in numerous amphibious training exercises throughout the Pacific during the following years. Returning to Mare Island for decommissioning in 1960, the boat emerged the following year absent its hallmark aft-deck storage hangar. For the following decade the *Perch* continued training U.S. and foreign special operations units in the Far East.

76. The *Bass* earned six battle stars and a Navy Unit Commendation for its Korean War Service.

77. By necessity the commandos had used the rubber raft technique aboard the *Perch.* Perhaps as a result of that experience, they did so again during their first combat raids from an APD in October 1950. This, however, appears to be their last such use of inflatable rafts before switching to "dry ramp landings."

78. Field, *History of United States Naval Operations in Korea,* 217.

79. Mahin interview, 25 September 1998.

80. Ibid.

81. Mahin interview, 14 October 1998.

82. War Diary, USS *Horace A. Bass,* October 1950, 2–3.

83. Tom Driberg, *Tom Driberg's Personal Diary: The Best of Both Worlds* (London: Phoenix House, 1953), 16–22.

84. Eoff, "UDT in Korea," 5.

85. Blair, *Forgotten War,* 545.

86. Eoff, "UDT in Korea," 6.

87. Action Report, UDT-3, 1 October 1950, Naval Historical Center, Washington, D.C., 7.

88. Ibid., 4.

89. After Action Report, UDT-1, 5 February 1951, Naval Historical Center, Washington, D.C., 3–4.

90. Lt. Col. F. N. Grant to Rear Adm. George C. Dyer, December 1951. Author's collection.

91. Report: Commander UN Blockading and Escort Force to Commander, Seventh Fleet, series 0031, subject: "Review of Operations and Comments on the United Nations Blockading Escort Force (TF95) from 28 March 1951 to 9 January 1952," 30 January 1952, 6, Post-January 1946 Action Rep Files, in Andrade, "History of Naval Special Warfare."

92. Sandler, *Korean War,* 46.

93. *CIA in Korea* 1:99–100. See also *Secret War in Korea,* 23.

94. At the war's end the UN General Assembly named a five-power commission to investigate the Communists' wartime claims of germ warfare, "but the communists were no longer interested in the question" (Sandler, *Korean War,* 47).

95. FEC General Order 94/51, for actions by Brig. Gen. Crawford F. Sams on night of 13–14 March 1951. See also *Secret War in Korea,* 23.

Chapter 4. CIA Covert Warfare

1. President Harry S. Truman had established the Central Intelligence Group (CIG) in January 1946, scarcely four months after he had disbanded its much larger predecessor, the Office of Strategic Services. The CIG's ineffectiveness stemmed in large part from the fact that its small staff and budget were drawn from multiple agencies throughout the Executive Branch.

2. Warner, *CIA Cold War Records,* xvii.

3. Ibid.

4. Ibid., xix.

5. Paddock, *U.S. Army Special Warfare,* 45.

6. William R. Corson, *The Armies of Ignorance: The Rise of the American Intelligence Empire* (New York: Dial Press, 1977), 304.

7. Fondacaro, "Strategic Analysis of U.S. Special Operations," 87.

8. TC-1 "graduate" Col. Edward B. Joseph, USAF (Ret.), interview with author, Arlington, Va., 18 September 1995.

9. Karalekas, "History of the Central Intelligence Agency," in Warner, *CIA Cold War Records,* xxv.

10. Warner, *CIA Cold War Records,* xxv. See also Sandler, *Korean War,* 67.

11. Factbook on Intelligence, Central Intelligence Agency Public Affairs Office, September 1991.

12. ORE 3-49 "Consequences of US Troop Withdrawal from Korea in the spring of 1949, in Warner, *CIA Cold War Records,* 268.

13. Warner, *CIA Cold War Records,* xxiv. See also Day, "Partisan Operations," 40.

14. Sandler, *Korean War,* 66.

15. Blair, *Forgotten War,* 58.

16. Goulden, *Korea,* 468–69.

17. Ibid., 471.

18. Ibid.

19. Ibid.

20. Sandler, *Korean War,* 66. See also Paddock, *U.S. Army Special Warfare,* 103.

21. Thomas Powers, *The Man Who Kept the Secrets: Richard Helms and the CIA* (New York: Alfred A. Knopf, 1979), 323–24.

22. Ibid.

23. *CIA in Korea* 3:98.

24. Ibid. 1:100.

25. Author, "CIA," working papers declassified by Central Intelligence Agency; Case No.: E96-0210, 24 (hereafter cited as CIA Case No.: E96-0210). Information extracted is unclassified. Author's collection.

26. *CIA in Korea* 1:103.

27. For security reasons, the OSO changed the name of its cover organization in Seoul from the Department of the Army Liaison Detachment to that of the Far East Command Department of the Army Research Unit in May 1952.

28. *Infiltration* 1:39.

29. *CIA in Korea* 3:96. See also Singlaub, *Hazardous Duty,* 181.

30. Blair, *Forgotten War,* 375.

31. *CIA in Korea* 3:97.

32. *Secret War in Korea,* 1, 20.

33. *CIA in Korea* 3:98.

34. *Infiltration* 1:34.

35. *CIA in Korea* 1:142.

36. *Secret War in Korea,* 3.

37. Ibid.

38. Ibid., 2.

39. Ibid., 4.

40. Ibid.

41. Ibid., 5.

42. Ibid., 1, 5.

43. Ibid., 5.

44. Ibid., 8–9.

45. Ibid., 9.

46. CCRAK followed the standard practice of separating its intelligence and operations staff functions, while taking the unusual step of combining its personnel and logistics activities into a single staff office.

47. Ibid., 11.

48. *Secret War in Korea,* 75.

49. Ibid., 78.

50. Ibid., 21.

51. Ibid., 78.

52. Ibid.

53. Ibid., 19.

54. *CIA in Korea* 3:96.

55. *Secret War in Korea,* 56.

56. *Infiltration* 1:33.

57. Ibid. 3:399.

58. North Asia Command, 23.

59. "Activities of U.S. Spy Enumerated," a broadcast from Peking Radio, 2 January 1955. U.S. government copy in author's collection.

60. North Asia Command, 24.

61. "Remarks of DCI George J. Tenet on Presentation of the Directors Medal to John T. 'Jack' Downey and Richard G. Fecteau," CIA press release 25 June 1998.

62. *Infiltration* 3:403.

63. Ibid. 3:405.

64. Ibid. 1:42.

65. Ibid. 3:405–6.

66. Ibid. 3:406.

67. Ibid. 3:404.

68. Budway memorandum, 3.

69. Unless otherwise specified, the E&E program described here refers to the agency's *covert* program, which operated exclusively behind enemy lines. Conventional military assets, primarily U.S. Air Force Air Rescue Service aircraft, fulfilled their separate roles throughout the war.

70. *Infiltration* 1:161.

71. Ibid. 1:37.

72. Dwyer, *Commandos from the Sea*, 247. See also *Infiltration* 1:161.

73. CIA Case No.: E96-0210, 20.

74. Clark, *Carrier Admiral*, 276–77.

75. CIA Case No.: E96-0210, 21.

76. Ibid.

77. Ibid., 22.

78. Ibid.

79. Ibid., 22–23.

80. *CIA in Korea* 1:192.

81. Ibid.

82. Ibid. 1:193.

Bibliography

Books and Periodicals

Barlow, Jeffrey G. "The Navy's View of the Revolt of the Admirals." *Occasional Papers*. Washington, D.C.: Society for History in the Federal Government, 1997.

Black, Robert W. *Rangers in Korea*. New York: Ivy Books, 1989.

Blair, Clay. *The Forgotten War: America in Korea, 1950–1953*. New York: Times Books, 1987.

Clark, J. J., with Clark G. Reynolds. *Carrier Admiral*. New York: David McKay, 1967.

Dockery, Kevin. *SEALs in Action*. New York: Avon Books, 1991.

Dwyer, John B. *Commandos from the Sea: The History of Amphibious Special Warfare in World War II and the Korean War*. Boulder, Colo.: Paladin Press, 1998.

Evanhoe, Ed. *Dark Moon: Eighth Army Special Operations in the Korean War*. Annapolis: Naval Institute Press, 1995.

———. "The Search for Gen. Dean: CIA/Eighth Army Plan Dramatic Rescue of American General." *Behind the Lines* (September/October 1994): 22.

Field, James A., Jr. *History of United States Naval Operations in Korea*. Washington, D.C.: Naval Historical Center, 1962.

Futrell, Robert F. *The United States Air Force in Korea: 1950–1953*. Rev. ed. Washington, D.C.: Office of Air Force History, 1983.

Goulden, Joseph C. *Korea: The Untold Story of the War*. New York: McGraw-Hill, 1982.

Hackworth, David H., and Julie Sherman. *About Face*. New York: Simon and Schuster, 1989.

Hastings, Max. *The Korean War*. London: Michael Joseph, 1987.

Hoyt, Edwin P. *Submarines at War: The History of the American Silent Service*. Briar Cliff Manor, N.Y.: Stein and Day, 1983.

Knox, Donald. *The Korean War: An Oral History, Pusan to Chosin*. New York: Harcourt Brace, 1987.

Leary, William M. "Robert Fulton's Skyhook and Operation Coldfeet." *Studies in Intelligence* 38, no. 5 (1995): 99–109.

Long, Gavin. *MacArthur as Military Commander*. Conshohocken, Pa.: Combined Publishing, 1969.

Malcom, Ben S., with Ron Martz. *White Tigers: My Secret War in North Korea*. Washington, D.C.: Brassey's, 1996.

March, Allison E., and Donald C. McElfresh. *Submarine or Phantom Target? A Search for the Truth*. Silver Springs, Md.: Edisto Press, 1998.

Neillands, Robin. *In the Combat Zone: Special Forces since 1945*. New York: New York University Press, 1998.

Nichols, Donald. *How Many Times Can I Die?* Brooksville, Fla.: Brooksville Printing, 1981.

Paddock, Alfred H., Jr. *U.S. Army Special Warfare: Its Origins*. Washington, D.C.: National Defense University Press, 1982.

Paschall, Col. Rod. "Special Operations in Korea." *Conflict* 7, no. 2 (November 1987): 155.

Pease, Stephen E. *Psywar: Psychological Warfare in Korea 1950–1953*. Harrisburg, Pa.: Stackpole Books, 1992.

Sandler, Stanley, ed. *The Korean War: An Encyclopedia*. New York: Garland Publishing, 1995.

Savada, Andrea Matles, ed. *North Korea: A Country Study*. Washington, D.C.: Federal Research Division, Library of Congress, 1993.

Singlaub, John K., with Malcolm McConnell. *Hazardous Duty: An American Soldier in the Twentieth Century*. New York: Summit Books, 1991.

Sutherland, Ian D. W. *Special Forces of the United States Army: 1952–1982*. San Jose, Calif.: R. James Bender Publishing, 1990.

Warner, Michael, ed. *The CIA under Harry Truman*. Washington, D.C.: History Staff, Center for the Study of Intelligence, Central Intelligence Agency, 1994.

Historical Studies

Central Intelligence Agency. *CIA in Korea: 1946–1965*. Vol. 1. Secret. Washington, D.C.: CIA, July 1973. Information extracted is unclassified.

———. *CIA in Korea: 1946–1965*. Vol. 3. Secret. Washington, D.C.: CIA, July 1973. Information extracted is unclassified.

———. *Infiltration and Resupply of Agents in North Korea, 1952–1953*. Vol. 1. Secret. Washington, D.C.: CIA, December 1972. Information extracted is unclassified.

———. *Infiltration and Resupply of Agents in North Korea, 1952–1953*. Vol. 3. Secret. Washington, D.C.: CIA, December 1972. Information extracted is unclassified.

———. *The Origins of CIA's Clandestine Organization in the Far East, 1945–1952*. Clandestine Services History. Secret. Washington, D.C.: CIA, June 1969. Information extracted is unclassified.

———. *The Origins of CIA's Clandestine Organization in the Far East, 1952–1956*. Clandestine Services History. Secret. Washington, D.C.: CIA, July 1969. Information extracted is unclassified.

———. *The Secret War in Korea, June 1950–June 1952*. Clandestine Services History. Secret. Washington, D.C.: CIA, July 1968. Information extracted is unclassified.

Unit/Ship Historical Reports

Command and Historical Report. November–December 1951, Commander, Naval Forces Far East. Washington, D.C.: Naval Historical Center.

McKinney, W. R., Commanding Officer. Action Report. 1 October 1950, Underwater Demolition Team Three. Washington, D.C.: Naval Historical Center.

Quinn, Robert D., Lt. Cdr., Commanding Officer. War Patrol Report: Commanding Officer to CNO, series 0015 subject: "USS *Perch* (ASSP-313); Report of First War Patrol," September–October 1950, Post–January 1946. Submarine War Patrol Reports File. Washington, D.C.: Naval Historical Center.

Unit History, 21st TCS, October 1950. Maxwell Air Force Base, Ala.: U.S. Air Force Historical Research Agency.

Unit History, 21st TCS, January–April 1951. Maxwell Air Force Base, Ala.: U.S. Air Force Historical Research Agency.

Unit History, 6167th ABG, 1 July–31 December 1952. Maxwell Air Force Base, Ala.: U.S. Air Force Historical Research Agency.

War Diary, USS *Diachenko,* August 1950. Washington, D.C.: Naval Historical Center.

War Diary, USS *Horace A. Bass,* October 1950. Washington, D.C.: Naval Historical Center.

Welch, D. F., Commanding Officer. Action Report. 19 January 1951, Underwater Demolition Team One. Washington, D.C.: Naval Historical Center.

———. Action Report. 5 February 1951, Underwater Demolition Team One. Washington, D.C.: Naval Historical Center.

Published Government Documents

Central Intelligence Agency. *Directors and Deputy Directors of Central Intelligence.* Washington, D.C.: CIA, 1994.

Department of the Navy. *U.S. Navy Active Force Levels: 1917–95.* Washington, D.C.: Naval Historical Center Fact Sheet, 1997.

Finley, James P. "The U.S. Military Experience in Korea: 1781–1982." Seoul: Command Historian's Office, Headquarters, USFK/EUSA, 1983.

Kim, Kilchoon, and E. A. Johnson. "Evaluation of Effects of Leaflets on Early North Korean Prisoners of War." Baltimore: Operations Research Office, Johns Hopkins University, February 1951.

U.S. Army Forces, Far East, 8086 Army Unit. "UN Partisan Forces in the Korean Conflict 1951–1952 (A Study of Their Characteristics and Operations)." MHD-3 Report, APO 301, 1954. USMHI Document Collection.

Unpublished Military Sources

Aderholt, Brig. Gen. Harry C., USAF (Ret.). U.S. Air Force Oral History Interview No. K239.0512-1716, 1986. Secret. U.S. Air Force Historical Research Agency, Maxwell Air Force Base, Alabama. Information extracted is unclassified.

Andrade, Dale. "History of Naval Special Warfare: World War II to Panama." Naval Historical Center, Washington, D.C., 1991.

Day, James Sanders. "Partisan Operations of the Korean War." Master's thesis, University of Georgia, 1989.

Fondacaro, Maj. Steve A. "A Strategic Analysis of U.S. Special Operations during the Korean Conflict 1950–1953." Master's thesis to U.S. Army Command and General Staff College, Fort Leavenworth, Kansas, 1988.

Haas, Col. Michael E., USAF. "CIA." Classified Working Papers. Author's collection. Case No.: E96-0210. Extracted information is unclassified.

Kim, Young Sik. "Eyewitness: A North Korean Remembers." Personal memoirs, 1995. Author's collection.

Marion, Maj. Forrest L. "Air Force Special Operations Korean War Chronology." Air Force Special Operations Command/History Office, Hurlburt Field, Florida, 1998.

Schuetta, Lt. Col. Lawrence V. "Guerrilla Warfare and Airpower in Korea, 1950–1953." U.S. Air Force Aerospace Studies Institute, Maxwell Air Force Base, Alabama, 1964.

Stevens, Lt. Col. Garth, Maj. Frank D. Bush, Capt. Robert B. Brewer, Capt. Jefferson DeR. Capps, and Capt. Charles J. Simmons. "Intelligence Information by Partisans for Armor." 2 vols. Student committee report to U.S. Army Armored Officer Advanced Course, Fort Knox, Kentucky, 1952.

Memorandums

Combat Doctrine, B Flight, 6167th Operations Squadron (U). Memorandum, Korean War–era date obliterated by declassification stamp. U.S. Air Force Historical Research Agency, Maxwell Air Force Base, Alabama.

Far East Command Liaison Detachment to Vice Adm. H. M. Martin, Commander Seventh Fleet. Memorandum, 28 September 1951. Subject: "Clandestine Activities, Korea." Author's collection.

ORO-T-4 (EUSAK). Technical memorandum. In "Evaluation of Effects of Leaflets on Early North Korean Prisoners of War," by Kilchoon Kim and E. A. Johnson. Baltimore: Operations Research Office, Johns Hopkins University, February 1951.

ORO-T-64 (AFFE). Technical memorandum. In "UN Partisan Warfare in Korea, 1951–1954," by Frederick W. Cleaver, George Fitzpatrick, John Ponturo, William Rossiter, and C. Darwin Stolzenbach. Baltimore: Operations Research Office, Johns Hopkins University, June 1956.

Index

About the Author

Michael E. Haas began his military career as a private in the U.S. Army infantry, subsequently serving in airborne, Ranger, Special Forces, and psychological operations units. He fought in the Republic of South Vietnam as an assault helicopter pilot and flight platoon commander.

Following an interservice transfer to the U.S. Air Force, Colonel Haas served in special operations and Special Tactics units, commanded the Pararescue Squadron, and completed Pentagon tours with the Joint Chiefs of Staff and Headquarters, U.S. Air Force. He holds U.S. Army Special Forces, Ranger, Expert Infantry, and aviator qualifications; U.S. Air Force command pilot, master parachutist, and military free-fall certifications; and U.S. Navy open- and closed-circuit scuba ratings.

Colonel Haas is the author of *Apollo's Warriors: United States Air Force Special Operations during the Cold War.* He currently lives in Incline Village, Nevada.

The Naval Institute Press is the book-publishing arm of the U.S. Naval Institute, a private, nonprofit, membership society for sea service professionals and others who share an interest in naval and maritime affairs. Established in 1873 at the U.S. Naval Academy in Annapolis, Maryland, where its offices remain today, the Naval Institute has members worldwide.

Members of the Naval Institute support the education programs of the society and receive the influential monthly magazine *Proceedings* and discounts on fine nautical prints and on ship and aircraft photos. They also have access to the transcripts of the Institute's Oral History Program and get discounted admission to any of the Institute-sponsored seminars offered around the country.

The Naval Institute also publishes *Naval History* magazine. This colorful bimonthly is filled with entertaining and thought-provoking articles, first-person reminiscences, and dramatic art and photography. Members receive a discount on *Naval History* subscriptions.

The Naval Institute's book-publishing program, begun in 1898 with basic guides to naval practices, has broadened its scope in recent years to include books of more general interest. Now the Naval Institute Press publishes about one hundred titles each year, ranging from how-to books on boating and navigation to battle histories, biographies, ship and aircraft guides, and novels. Institute members receive discounts of 20 to 50 percent on the Press's more than eight hundred books in print.

Full-time students are eligible for special half-price membership rates. Life memberships are also available.

For a free catalog describing Naval Institute Press books currently available, and for further information about subscribing to *Naval History* magazine or about joining the U.S. Naval Institute, please write to:

Membership Department
U.S. Naval Institute
291 Wood Road
Annapolis, MD 21402-5034
Telephone: (800) 233-8764
Fax: (410) 269-7940
Web address: www.usni.org